PENNSYLVANIA

GENEALOGICAL

RESEARCH

by
George K. Schweitzer, PhD, ScD
407 Ascot Court
Knoxville, TN 37923-5807

Word Processing by
Anne M. Smalley

TABLE OF CONTENTS

Chapter 1

PENNSYLVANIA BACKGROUND

1. Pennsylvania (PA) geography

The state of Pennsylvania (hereafter abbreviated PA), one of the thirteen original colonies, is located in the north central region of the eastern seaboard of the US. In shape, it resembles a rectangle with a jagged right end and a slight upward protrusion on the left end (see Figure 1). The state is about 300 miles from east to west, and it is about 150 miles wide. It is bounded on the south by DE, MD, and WV, on the west by WV and OH, on the north by Lake Erie and NY, and on the east by the DE River across which rest NJ and NY. Even though PA has no coastline, access to the Atlantic Ocean is provided through the deep-water port of Philadelphia (on the DE River which flows into DE Bay which connects with the Atlantic Ocean). The capital of the state is located at Harrisburg in the south central region, and the state is divided into 67 counties. The major cities of PA (with their approximate populations in thousands) are Philadelphia (1688K) in the southeast and Pittsburgh (424K) in the southwest. Other cities of PA with populations of 45K or over include Erie (119K) in the northwest, Penn Hills (58K) in the southwest, Altoona (57K), Harrisburg (53K), and York (45K) in the south central region, Lancaster (55K), Levittown (79K), and Reading (79K) in the southeast, Allentown (104K) and Bethlehem (70K) in the east central region, and Scranton (88K) and Wilkes-Barre (52K) in the northeast.

An understanding of the progressive settlement of the state and the genealogies of its early families is greatly enhanced by an examination of its major geographic regions and features. These are pictured in Figure 1. The first region consists of the Atlantic Coastal Plain (AC in a circle), a narrow strip of land along the southeastern corner. The terrain here is low and level, and the region can be readily reached by coming up into the Delaware Bay (D8) from the Atlantic Ocean. This region was the first part of PA to be settled (1643-66), with the seaports of Philadelphia (P) and Chester (C) being established very early. The second region, which is known as the Piedmont Region (PR in a circle), occupies most of southeastern PA. The area is one made up of gently rolling hills and broad shallow valleys. Early colonists moved readily from the Atlantic Coastal Plain (AC) into this territory which has much fertile land. Cities in the region include Reading (R), Lancaster (L), and York (Y). The

6

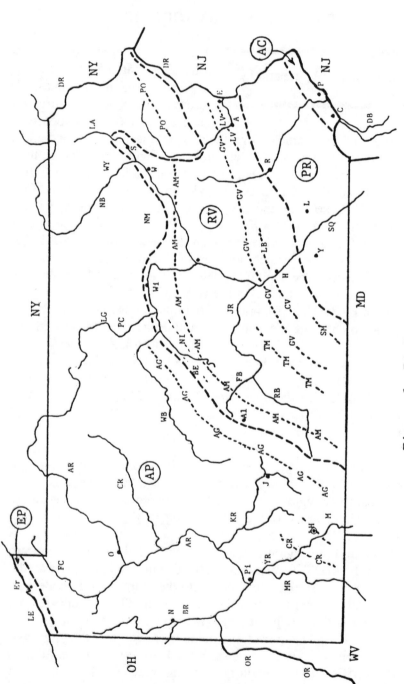

Figure 1. PA Geography

Key to Figure 1

A   Allentown
AC Atlantic Coastal Plain
AG Allegheny Mountains
Al Altoona
AM Appalachian Mountains
AP Allegheny Plateau Reg
AR Allegheny River
BE Bald Eagle Valley
BR Beaver River
C   Chester
CH Chestnut Ridge
CR Clarion River
CV Cumberland Valley
DB Delaware Bay
DR Delaware River
E   Easton
EP Erie Plain
Er Erie
FB Frankstown Branch
FC French Creek

GV Great Valley
H   Harrisburg
J   Johnstown
JR Juniata River
KR Kiskiminetas River
L   Lancaster
LA Lackawanna River
LB Lebanon Valley
LE Lake Erie
LG Little Grand Canyon
LH Laurel Hill
LR Lehigh River
LV Lehigh Valley
M   Mount Davis
MR Monongahela River
N   New Castle
NB North Branch
NM North Mountain
NV Nittany Valley
O   Oil City
OR Ohio River

P   Philadelphia
PC Pine Creek
Pi Pittsburgh
PM Pocono Mountains
PR Piedmont Region
R   Reading
RB Raystown Branch
RV Ridge & Valley Region
S   Scranton
SM South Mountain
SQ Susquehanna River
SR Schuylkill River
Su Sunbury
TM Tuscarora Mountains
W   Wilkes-Barre
WB West Branch
Wi Williamsport
WY Wyoming Valley
Y   York
YR Youghiogheny River

third region, which rests west and north of the Piedmont Region, is the Ridge and Valley Region (RV in a circle). The area contains a series of mountain ridges, known as the Appalachian Mountains (AM marks the tallest), which are separated by long narrow valleys. These mountain ridges and the valleys run in the northeasterly to southwesterly direction. The most notable of the valleys in the region is the Great Valley (GV), whose rich soil is very good for agriculture. About one-third of the state is within this area, which contains the cities of Scranton (S), Wilkes-Barre (W), Easton (E), Allentown (A), Sunbury (Su), Williamsport (Wi), Harrisburg (H), and Altoona (Al). The fourth and largest of the regions is the Allegheny Plateau Region (AP in a circle), which occupies over one-half of the state (approximately the western third and the northern half). This area is made up of numerous mountains, hills, valleys, and streams. Along the eastern border of the region are the high and rugged Allegheny Mountains (AG), but other regions are less mountainous with smaller mountains and gentler hills, especially in the northern section. Notable cities of this fourth region are Pittsburgh (Pi), Oil City (O), and New Castle (N). The fifth and final region is the Erie Plain (EP in a circle), a narrow strip along Lake Erie (LE) in the northwestern corner of the state. The land here is quite rich, and this along with the mild climate (moderated by the lake) makes it a very good farming area. The city of Erie (Er) is the major metropolitan area in the strip.

Figure 1 also depicts the major rivers of PA. It is important to have a good perception of them because they provided the main early transportation and communication routes of PA. The patterns of settlement therefore centered around them and the valleys which run along them. The state has three major river systems: the DE River system which drains the east, the Susquehanna River system which drains the center, and the OH River system which drains the west. The DE River (DR) which runs along the eastern border of PA begins in NY state and empties into the DE Bay (DB) just southwest of Chester (C) and Philadelphia (P). Its two major tributaries are the Lehigh River (LR) which joins it at Easton (E) and the Schuylkill River (SR) which joins it at Philadelphia (P). The Susquehanna River (SQ) flows southward from Sunbury (Su) where its North Branch (NB) and its West Branch (WB) combine to form the main stream. Major tributaries are the Lackawanna River (LA) which empties into the North Branch (NB) in northeastern PA, Pine Creek (PC) which joins the West Branch (WB) in north- central PA, and the Juniata River (JR) which comes into the Susquehanna (SQ) just north of Harrisburg (H). The Juniata River (JR) is made up of two branches, the Raystown Branch (RB) and the Frankstown Branch (FB).

Just southeast of York (Y) the Susquehanna River (SQ) moves into MD where it empties into Chesapeake Bay. In southwestern PA the OH River (OR) takes its beginning at Pittsburgh (Pi) where the confluence of the Allegheny River (AR) and the Monongahela River (MR) make it up. Note that French Creek (FC), the Clarion River (CR), and the Kiskiminetas River (KR) flow into the Allegheny (AR); the Youghiogheny River (YR) flows into the Monongahela (MR), and just northwest of Pittsburgh the Beaver River (BR) joins the OH River (OR). The OH River (OR) then moves out of PA to form the border between OH and WV. The three major port cities of PA (Philadelphia, Pittsburgh, Erie) are located on the three navigable waterways of the state (DE River, OH River, Lake Erie).

Now your attention needs to be called to the major valleys and mountain ranges of PA. In the eastern part of the state you will see the Wyoming Valley (WY) along the North Branch (NB) of the Susquehanna River, North Mountain (MN) just to the west, the Pocono Mountains (PM) along the upper reaches of the Lehigh River (LR), and the Lehigh Valley (LV) astraddle the lower Lehigh River (LR). In the central part of the state, starting in the north then moving south, take notice of the Little Grand Canyon (LG) along Pine Creek, Bald Eagle Valley (BE), Nittany Valley (NV), the Tuscarora Mountains (TM), Cumberland Valley (CV), Lebanon Valley (LB), and South Mountain (SM). In the southwestern section of PA, your attention should be directed to Chestnut Ridge (CH), Laurel Hill (LH), and Mount Davis (M).

2. Early colonial PA

Human settlement in what is now PA probably dates from about 9000 BC, when Indians entered the area. The white settlers who began coming into the region in the 1600s found over 15000 Indians making up a number of tribes, chief among them being the Delawares, the Conoys, the Nanticokes, the Shawnees, and the Susquehannocks. The first four tribes belonged to the Algonkian Confederacy, and the last tribe was loosely affiliated with the Iroquois, the major tribes of which lived in the territory that is now NY. Following the voyages of Columbus, the PA region was explored by several European nations. In 1609, Henry Hudson in the service of the Dutch explored Chesapeake Bay, DE Bay, and NY Bay, giving the Dutch a general claim to the middle Atlantic region. Soon they dispatched further explorers and traders to the area and before long the general region was called New Netherland. To protect the trade, several Dutch forts were built including Fort Beversrede at the mouth of the

Schuylkill River. This, however, did not stop the operation of Swedish traders who also were coming into the locality.

In 1637, Sweden established a colony near the site of present-day Wilmington, DE, which prospered after a very shaky start. This settlement which was named New Sweden was moved in 1643 up the DE River to Tinicum Island, which was located about 20 miles south of where Philadelphia now is. The colony thereby became the first permanent settlement in PA territory. It continued to prosper as the colonists built dwellings, set up farms, and traded with the Indians. When the Swedish governor in 1654 made the error of seizing a small Dutch fort across the river, the Dutch dispatched a sizable military force which took New Sweden in 1655 and made it a part of New Netherland, but permitted the settlers to remain. Then in 1664, England, operating out of its colonies in New England, MD, and VA, sent an armed force to New Amsterdam (the capital of New Netherland, now New York City) and forced the surrender of all of the Dutch territory. England now had control of the entire Atlantic coast, and the monarch Charles II granted all of the old Dutch lands to the Duke of York. During these changes in ownership, most of the original colonists stayed, and after 1664 a number of English settlers joined them.

In 1681, King Charles II granted the Quaker William Penn the lands that are now PA. This grant was in payment of a debt which the British Crown owed Penn's father who had willed his belongings to his son. Penn became Proprietor of the land and was designated to rule it in the King's name. The new colony became known as Pennsylvania, which means Penn's forest or Penn's woods. In 1682, Penn began the experiment of setting up a colony with a government founded on the Quaker beliefs in individual human dignity, freedom of conscience, and equality of all persons before God. He wrote a constitution which provided for government by the people through a Council and a General Assembly chosen by voters, freedom of religion, and provisions to prevent the wealthy from taking over the colony. Penn advertised his liberal government, religious freedom, and inexpensive land throughout Europe and this caused the colony to grow rapidly. Land was purchased (not just taken) from the Indians and sold to the new settlers so that the colony became a place of small, independent farmers. A capital was set up at Philadelphia, and three counties were established (Bucks, Chester, Philadelphia) in that beginning year of 1682. These counties were also given local governments in which the citizens played significant roles in the selection of the officials.

Penn returned to England in 1684 leaving a Deputy Governor in charge. In 1692, the British monarch withdrew Penn's authority to govern PA because he suspected Penn's loyalty, but in 1694 his powers were restored. In late 1699 William Penn returned to PA (now having 3000 people) drew up a new constitution which made PA the most democratic of the colonies, and in 1701, it was approved by the General Assembly. Under its provisions, the Assembly was to be elected by the voters to be the law-making body of the colony, some local officials were also to be elected, religious freedom was reaffirmed, and every individual had the right to be heard in court. When William Penn died in 1718, his wife took over the Proprietorship until her death in 1727, and then Penn's three sons took over until 1775, after which his grandson became Proprietor. The sons and grandsons ceased to be Quakers and became interested mainly in PA as a source of monetary profit.

When Penn came to PA in 1682, the Dutch, Swedes (and some Finns who came with them), and a few English were the only colonists. By 1684, the inexpensive land, religious freedom, and liberal government had begun to attract Europeans. They settled during the years to follow in various regions of PA which can be seen in Figure 2. Very soon after 1683 the Quakers became the largest group in PA and remained so for over 100 years. They settled mainly in the three original counties (Bucks, Chester, Philadelphia) where they worked as skilled artisans and traders, and contributed greatly to making Philadelphia a leading trading city. Germans started coming in during 1683 and settled the areas just west and north of the Quaker settlements where they set up small farms on the rich soil. These Germans were members of the Lutheran, German Reformed, Mennonite, Amish, Moravian, and German Baptist faiths. In addition to agriculture, the Germans made other important contributions to the growing colony: weaving, blacksmithing, wagonmaking, music, printing, art, and cooking. Much later, in the 1720s and afterward, the Scotch-Irish began to arrive in south central and later southwestern PA. These people made these regions into Presbyterian strongholds, established schools, and exercised a constant opposition to Quaker domination of the government. Other smaller groups of people who made contributions to the early growth of PA were the Roman Catholics (French, Irish, German), Jews, French Huguenots, and blacks.

The peoples who came to PA gradually pushed westward and northwestward from the only towns which were important up to 1730: Philadelphia, Chester, and Germantown (near Philadelphia). As colonists moved, more land was purchased from the Indians, the map in Figure 3 showing

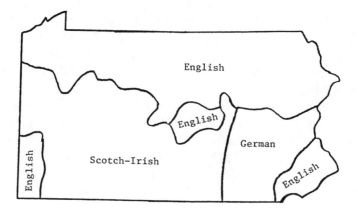

Figure 2. Early PA Settlement Pattern

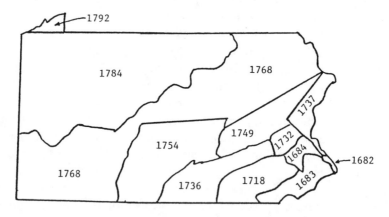

Figure 3. Indian Land Purchases and
US Purchase (1792)

the dates and boundaries. Just behind the ever-moving frontier, towns sprang up, roads were built, and the farms became more stable. In front of the frontier, hunters and traders moved, with many Indian trading posts later becoming town sites. The westward advance made a fourth county necessary, Lancaster County being taken out of Chester County in 1729. Then York County was established in 1749, then Cumberland County in 1750, then Bucks and Northampton Counties in 1752. As the frontier was settled, the older parts of PA prospered. Farmers produced abundant wheat, beef, pork, flaxseed, potash, and lumber, and in the winter hunted and trapped for furs and skins. These items were traded for manufactured goods which were shipped to the county seats from Philadelphia. All this activity made Philadelphia the trade center of the colony. From this center the colony's products were shipped to England, the West Indies, and the other colonies. Philadelphia grew rapidly in population, wealth, and culture, becoming America's largest and most important city. The wealth was used to encourage industry in PA, and soon many appeared and began to increase: gristmills, saw mills, iron production works (mines, furnaces, forges), clothing industries, shipbuilding, leathermaking, paper mills, potteries, glass factories, and handicrafts. This increase of trade and industry demanded improvements in water transportation (better boats), roads, and wagons.

Philadelphia became the cultural and educational center of the colonies, with Benjamin Franklin as its leading citizen and with him earning world renown as a scholar, diplomat, and scientist. The city became the site of the most important library, medical, and scientific activity in the colonies. Art, architecture, music, drama, and literary activity were well developed early in Philadelphia's history, as were newspaper, magazine, and book publishing and printing. Outside of Philadelphia, the churches functioned as the social and cultural centers of the colonists, most of which were farmers. These churches sponsored the earliest schools in the colony, but along about 1750 local groups slowly began starting community schools.

3. Later colonial PA

Even though the PA government bought land from the Indians for settlers, disagreements with regard to these purchases and shady practices by settlers and PA officials angered the Indians. By about 1750 they had been driven into western PA and OH. In addition, the French who had explored western PA as early as 1669, laid claim to the area, and had sent traders, hunters, and trappers into the region. Around 1753, they decided to enforce their occupation and claim, and began to build forts in western PA to stop the advance of PA colonists into the area. The mutual hostile attitude of the Indians and the French caused them to become allies against the westward-moving Pennsylvanians. The strongest of the four major French forts in western PA was Fort Duquesne which was built on the site of present-day Pittsburgh. In the spring of 1754, VA dispatched Colonel George Washington with a military force toward Fort Duquesne. They built a log stockade just southeast of the French fort, but were defeated by the French and Indians, who permitted them to return home. This engagement marked the beginning of the French and Indian War.

In 1755, the British dispatched troops under General Braddock to attempt to take Fort Duquesne. They were joined by colonial militia, mainly from VA and PA. As the combined force approached the fort, the French and Indians ambushed and disastrously defeated them. This opened the way for Indians to attack settlers all along the frontier which they did, many settlers being killed, many fleeing back east. Over the objection of Quakers, PA declared war on the Shawnees and Delawares, and in 1756 began to build forts on the frontier. The militiamen who manned these forts proceeded to make the frontier secure, and in July 1756, the main Indian base was attacked, many Indians killed, and their food supply destroyed. In 1758, a peace treaty was signed with these two Indian groups. Meanwhile, the British renewed the war against the French by dispatching soldiers to PA, and the colonies furnished supplies and raised militia to join them. This force of about 6000 moved west, and 2500 of them, in November 1758 took Fort Duquesne, which they renamed Fort Pitt (Pittsburgh). Shortly afterwards, news arrived that the main French fort in the colonies, Fort Niagara, had also fallen. Then, in a short time, the British defeated the French again at Quebec, which made all of Canada English. By August of 1759, the French had abandoned western PA, and early in 1763 a treaty was signed leaving Britain in possession of northeastern America. The Indians who had not made peace in 1758 and who had been fighting alongside the French decided to continue the war. In the summer of 1763, they attacked all along the PA frontier. Several British outpost forts were massacred, but the ones at Detroit and Fort Pitt survived. When the British sent troops to reinforce Fort Pitt, they were ambushed by the Indians, but defeated them in August 1763 in the Battle of Bushy Run. Thus the war ended, many of its campaigns having been fought in PA. The frontier was now almost entirely open, especially after further treaties with the Indians, and the people of PA moved quickly into southwestern PA. Only north central and northwestern PA remained unopened to settlers as of 1768.

As mentioned in the previous section, by 1752 there were 8 counties in PA: Philadelphia, Chester, Bucks, Lancaster, York, Cumberland, Berks, and Northampton. In 1771, Bedford County was established, in 1772 much of central PA became the large county of Northumberland, and in 1773 practically all of southwestern PA became Westmoreland County. Along with the counties, towns grew up: Lancaster (in 1730), York (1741), Bethlehem (1741), Reading (1748), Easton (1752), Bedford (1758), Pittsburgh (1758), Wilkes-Barre (1770), and Sunbury (1772). For many years, VA, MD, and CT claimed parts of PA, and as the frontier moved into these contested areas, clashes between the colonies occurred. The claimed regions are depicted in Figure 4. MD alleged that a southern strip of PA rightly belonged to them, but a British government survey of 1769 moved the border to where it now is. The claim of VA to a section of southwestern PA called for settlement when both VA and PA sent colonists there after the French and Indian War. The region was given to PA by a joint commission of VA and PA which met in 1786. CT and PA both had sent settlers into the eastern portion of the CT claim in the 1760s. During the period 1769-75, open war often broke out between the two groups of settlers, these conflicts being called the Pennamite Wars. By the outbreak of the Revolutionary War (1775), there were over 5000 New Englanders in the area. After the war, during which conflict among the settlers ceased, a court of commissioners in 1782 ruled in favor of PA. In all three cases (with MD, VA, and CT), the rights of all settlers were respected and they were afforded full citizenship. In 1792, PA bought the strip of land along Lake Erie in order to obtain a port on that important body of water.

4. The Revolution

Following the termination of the French and Indian War (1763), Britain found herself severely in debt, and began to tighten up her trade and taxation policies in the American colonies. Having become used to an independence fostered by previous British disinterest, the colonies strongly resented the new policies. In addition, the British forbid further settlement in western PA. Philadelphia merchants organized rallies and protest groups and became active in political affairs, rapidly taking over the leadership in eastern PA. They were joined by the people on the western frontier who had resented the political domination of the Legislature (which was controlled by easterners). Two hostilities thus began growing in PA: (1) against the British who were viewed as depriving the colonists of participation in their government, and (2) against the old provincial government which was viewed by the frontiersmen as doing the same.

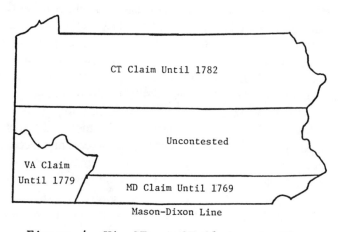

Figure 4. VA, MD, & CT Claims in PA

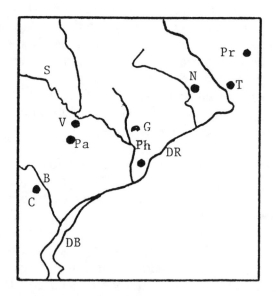

Figure 5. Revolutionary War Sites in PA. Key to
Abbreviations: B= Brandywine Creek, C= Chad's
Ford, DB= Delaware Bay, DR= Delaware River,
G= Germantown, N= Newton, Pa= Paoli, Ph= Phila-
delphia, Pr= Princeton, S= Schuylkill River,
T= Trenton, V= Valley Forge.

Soon a committee was organized to keep in touch with similar committees in the other colonies, which were also defying the British regulations. These committees were promoting unified action and cooperative support.

On 16 December 1773 some Bostonians broke into a British tea ship and destroyed its cargo as an act of defiance to the tea tax. Shortly thereafter, a large public meeting in Philadelphia sent the captain of another tea ship back to England with his unloaded tea. In 1774, the British blockaded Boston and sent in troops in reaction to MA's continued opposition and defiance. The other colonies sent the town supplies and pledged their support. All of this led to the calling of the First Continental Congress in Philadelphia on 05 September 1774. The Congress drew up an appeal to King George III to let them tax themselves and not be subject to unfair acts of Parliament, and they organized a boycott. The King rejected the plea and Parliament passed further oppressive laws. Relations between Britain and the 13 colonies continued to decay until finally open warfare broke out on 19 April 1775 at Lexington and Concord in MA. The colony of PA then intensified its recruitment of volunteer troops and its preparations for defense. By the time the Second Continental Congress met on 10 May 1775, the colonies were clearly in armed rebellion against the British.

Early in its proceedings the Congress appointed George Washington as commander of a new Continental Army, and then on 04 July 1776, declared the colonies independent. In this latter action, the PA delegates narrowly voted approval. This action reflected a three-fold split in the peoples of PA: (1) those who supported the revolution, called Patriots, (2) those who remained loyal to the King, called Tories or Loyalists, and (3) those who remained neutral, these being mainly Quaker, Mennonite, Amish, and Brethren pacifists. The government of the colony moved rapidly into the hands of the Patriots, and public meetings in the counties established new county governments which were in sympathy with the Revolution. PA then began to throw leaders, troops, money, supplies, and equipment into the long, bitter struggle which was just starting. Philadelphia became the capital of the new nation made up of thirteen loosely-united revolutionary states. Thirteen regiments were raised by PA for Washington's Continental Army, and other military groups (such as the Associators and the Rangers) were organized to function in defending the state against invaders. The latter group (Rangers) concerned itself particularly with the defense of the western frontier against Indians who were allied with the British. PA men fought in practically every battle of the Revolution.

Following the outbreak of war in MA in 1775, the British were forced to abandon Boston. They then attacked and captured New York City in 1776 and drove Washington's defeated and dwindling army across the DE River where he took up a position at Newtown, PA (see Figure 5). On 25 December 1776 Washington surprised the Hessians (British hired soldiers) at Trenton, NJ, and soundly defeated them. In less than two weeks, Washington defeated another Hessian army at Princeton, NJ. In the summer of 1777, the British launched two campaigns: two armies (under Burgoyne and St Leger) were dispatched from Canada to move into NY state, and the troops in New York City (under Howe) were to march to meet the westernmost army from Canada (Burgoyne). For some reason, Howe chose not to follow the plan, and instead headed for Philadelphia, PA. On 25 August 1777, Howe's forces landed south of Philadelphia on Chesapeake Bay. They then marched toward Philadelphia, defeated Washington at Brandywine on 08 September 1777, almost completely wiped out a 1500-man PA force at Paoli on 20 September 1777, and entered Philadelphia on 22 September 1777. Washington tried to free the city on 03 October 1777 but was overwhelmed at Germantown. In the face of all these depressing events, however, on 17 October 1777, Burgoyne's British army (coming south from Canada) was defeated at Saratoga and his entire army had to surrender. The other British force from Canada (St Leger) turned around and went back into Canada. This marked the failure of the British campaign in the middle states. They might have regained the advantage if they had attacked Washington in the winter of 1777-8 where he was camped at Valley Forge, PA with his troops suffering hunger, extreme cold, and illness.

Then in February 1778, France became America's ally against the British. And highly successful efforts at Valley Forge resulted in a new trained Continental Army. The British then carried the War to the southern states, but PA had to continue defending its frontier against Indians and Tory bands. In the spring of 1778, the Indians launched widespread attacks including a massacre in the Wyoming Valley on 03 July 1778. Three American armies were dispatched to deal with the Indian-Tory frontier threat. The Indian territories in southern NY and the Allegheny Valley in southwestern PA were invaded and Indian villages, food stores, and farmlands were destroyed. The frontier was thereby secured and Indian attacks essentially ended. On 18 June 1778, the British left Philadelphia, and the Continental Congress (which had escaped to Lancaster, then York) returned. The British, having left the north, launched a campaign in the southern states, taking Savannah, GA on 29 December 1778 and by February 1779 most of GA was theirs. After several months of siege, Charleston, SC was surrendered to the British on 12 May 1780.

In the fall of 1780, British General Cornwallis led an invasion of NC. This was stopped when a contingent of the British army was defeated on 07 October 1780 at Kings Mountain. In a second invasion of NC, Cornwallis met American forces at Guilford Court House, NC on 15 March 1781. The result of this engagement was that the British won the field, but were so weakened they had to fall back to Wilmington, NC, on the coast. From there Cornwallis moved north into VA finally ending up at Yorktown where he was bottled up by the French fleet and surrounded by American and French forces. After a short siege, the British surrendered on 19 October 1781, and the American Revolution was essentially over.

5. Early Statehood

In 1776, the colony of PA was given a new constitution, which, along with the events of the War, overthrew the proprietary government of the Penns, deprived the Quakers of control of the government, retained the unicameral legislature, abolished the office of governor and substituted a 12-member council, gave the western counties greater representation, confiscated the property of the Loyalists, and kept Philadelphia as the state capital. In 1780, the Legislature passed a slave emancipation law which did away with slavery in one generation. In early 1787, a Federal Constitutional Convention met in Philadelphia, and on 17 September 1787 completed a national Constitution. This document provided for a union of the thirteen states into a federation which had the powers to make and enforce laws, tax, regulate commerce, and raise military forces. After long debate, PA on 12 December 1787 became the second state to ratify the Constitution, the required ninth state ratified it on 21 June 1788, and on 30 April 1789 Washington was inaugurated as President. Except for a brief period in 1789-90, Philadelphia was to serve as the national capital until 1800, when it was moved to Washington City. In 1790, a new state constitution was approved, this revision conforming to the new Federal Constitution, restoring the office of governor, and providing for a bicameral legislature.

The decade of the 1790s was a testing time for the new national government in many matters. Of special importance in PA was the matter of taxation. In 1791, the US government passed a tax on whiskey. In 1794, the western PA farmers announced they would oppose all efforts to collect the tax. Washington dispatched militia from PA, NJ, VA, and MD to the region, and the rebellion collapsed. In 1798, another federal tax was placed on land, houses, and slaves, and a man named John Fries led a rebellion in 1799 in and around Bucks County. Again the US President dispatched troops, and this time the leaders were arrested. During these times, the westward and northwestward population expansion continued, pressure from the newly-settled areas bringing about the movement of the state capital to Lancaster in 1799. The expansion was strongly promoted by PA through the awarding of land to veterans of the Revolution and the sale of land at very low prices. Another asset to the expansion was the harbor on Lake Erie, which had been provided PA by the purchase of the area in 1792 from the US. Most settlers of the new land followed the river valleys and old Indian trails to the interior, but the trip beyond the Alleghenies was more difficult, since this required going across the mountains. The most used route was known as the Great PA Road, running from Philadelphia to Lancaster to York to Gettysburg to Chambersburg to Bedford to Somerset to Greensburg to Pittsburgh. The advancing frontiers of PA can be clearly seen in Figure 6. The rapid movement westward brought about another relocation of the capital of the state in 1812, this time to Harrisburg.

As the lands on the frontiers were occupied, new counties had to be organized. In the western part of the state, these were Washington (1781), Fayette (1783), Allegheny (1788), and Greene (1796). In central PA, they were Mifflin (1789) and Lycoming (1795), and Wayne County was organized in the northeast in 1798. In 1800, ten new counties were

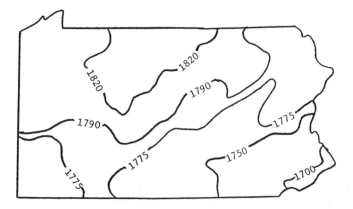

Figure 6. The Advancing PA Frontier

constituted (Armstrong, Adams, Butler, Beaver, Centre, Crawford, Erie, Mercer, Venango, Warren) and 1812-20 saw the establishment of six more (Lehigh, Lebanon, Columbia, Union, Pike, Perry). Along with these new counties, new county seats came into being, and so towns also grew rapidly, Pittsburgh expanding especially fast as a trading center and the gateway to the west. Pittsburgh also became an important industrial center, manufacturing tools, equipment, wagons, and boats for western settlers. Beginning in 1792, PA granted turnpike construction rights to private firms, and the endeavor was so successful that by 1832, over 200 such firms had built over 3000 miles of toll roads. These turnpikes enhanced both passenger and freight transport, which promoted the PA economy greatly. But PA transport was not only by road. The colony had made good use of the many PA rivers, and the state continued to do so. The usefulness of the waterways was markedly enhanced by the building of canals, the first canal (Schuylkill Canal) being completed in 1825. Then in 1827 the Susquehanna and Schuylkill Rivers were connected by the Union Canal. A canal fever hit PA because of the success of these canals, many more were rapidly built, and by 1834 a combined railroad-canal system connected Philadelphia and Pittsburgh. By 1835, PA was a literal beehive of travel with goods moving in rafts and keelboats in the shallow eastern rivers, in canal boats, in rail cars, and in large boats in the deep rivers of western PA which led into the OH and MS Rivers, connecting PA to markets to the west and the south. The first railroad in PA was built in 1832. By 1836, there were over 300 miles of track, and rapid increases in mileage were to be brought about in the next few decades, eventually causing railroads to overtake the canals as the main type of transportation. By the end of this period (1835-40), PA no longer had a frontier.

During this period of early statehood, the War of 1812 (1812-5) was fought with Britain. Actions of the English in the first decade of the 19th century to encourage Indians to attack the US, the searching of American ships and the impressment of US sailors, plus American greed for the land in Canada and FL led to the War. Most of the people of PA favored the War, but merchants and shippers opposed it because it would curtail the prosperous trade with England. PA supported the war effort as she contributed men, leadership, supplies, and money. The state dispatched troops to all battle fronts, but only two military encounters occurred on or near its territory: the British blockade of Philadelphia (only a temporary annoyance), and the Battle of Lake Erie on 10 September 1813. This naval engagement, in which Perry won a major naval battle over the British, was carried out with ships built in PA with PA lumber and with guns forged from PA iron. The war had involved much fighting around Detroit and Niagara, a failed US expedition into Canada, the burning of Washington, and the narrowly-won repulsion of the British takeover of Baltimore. After much negotiation, the War was ended in the Treaty of Ghent, which was signed on 24 December 1814. Before news of the peace reached America, US troops under Jackson cut an army of crack British soldiers to pieces in the Battle of New Orleans, leaving the country with a feeling of victory, even though the treaty left the boundaries as they were before the conflict.

6. The middle period

In the middle period of PA's history which extended from about 1835 to 1860, the most important occurrence was the transformation of the state by the development of industry. Even before 1835 there had been considerable industrial activity in PA, but this middle period experienced a remarkable increase. The development of mass production machinery which could be used by unskilled labor caused Philadelphia to become a leading textile center with textile manufacturing spreading to several other PA cities. Ironmaking, which had been important to PA from its very early days, expanded to become the largest industrial enterprise in the US. By the end of this period (1860), PA was the largest lumber-producing state, and the chief crop of the state, wheat, led PA to have a very large flour milling activity. The coming of all this industry required large amounts of coal, which PA had, and therefore coal mining was highly developed. Coal was also employed for heating, for producing gas for lighting, for making coal oil, and for the manufacture of coke to be used in ironmaking. The mining of the rich iron ore deposits was extensive, the mines of PA yielding more than half of the iron ore used in the US by 1860. In 1859, an oil field was discovered near Titusville, PA, and soon the fluid was being used for making kerosene and as a lubricant (its use for gasoline awaiting the 20th century).

As the industries developed, the population of PA moved from the farms to cities, many of these cities rising up in the area surrounding the factories. By 1840, there were 20 PA cities with over 2000 people, by 1860 there were 36. This population shift was especially evident in the sizable growths of Philadelphia and Pittsburgh. As the industries continued to expand, labor shortages developed, and many European immigrants (principally Irish and Welsh) came to PA to fill the job openings. A number of the industrial workers began to band together to obtain shorter workdays, improved conditions, and higher wages, and thus the

US labor union movement was born. All of the industrial activity also required turnpikes, canals, and railroads, so the building of these facilities accelerated. The laborers needed to be fed, and thus farm productivity had to rise to meet the demand. This was in turn assisted by industry, which provided new and improved farm machinery, including iron plows, the reaper, the mechanical planting drill, the cultivator, the hayrake, and the threshing machine. Agriculture was further enhanced by the rotation of crops and the use of fertilizers.

Not only did industry develop, but PA became much more democratic during this period, as industrial laborers and poorer farmers demanded that the vote be extended to all, not just to land owners. The revised constitution of 1838 placed more of the government in the hands of the people, ending all property requirements for voting, and making many more offices elective. The Free School Act of 1834 laid the foundations for a school system which eventually became open to all, and state institutions of higher education were established, joining the private colleges, some of which dated back to colonial times. This was a time also of reform movements, chief among the causes which were represented by strong organizations being women's rights, prison reform, humane treatment of the mentally ill, abolition of war, and the abolition of slavery. Further, there was rapid growth in democratically-oriented religious groups which appealed to the common people, the most important being the Methodists (100,000 by 1860) and the Baptists (40,000 in 1860). This middle period also saw an explosive increase in newspapers. As more persons learned to read, and as paper and printing became less costly, democracy came to be spread by the penny newspaper, which did much to broaden the interests and increase the knowledge of the people. By 1840, there were 187 newspapers in PA, the majority being published weekly.

Along about the middle of this middle period, the state of TX was annexed to the US. Mexican troops crossed into TX, bombarded Fort Taylor, and on 12 May 1846, the US declared war. The Mexican troops were driven back into Mexico, Santa Fe was captured, and CA switched over to American rule. In February 1847, the Mexican forces were defeated at Buena Vista, and the final campaign of the war began in March of that same year. US troops landed at Vera Cruz and a drive on Mexico City began. The city was taken on 14 September 1847, and the treaty of 02 February 1848 provided for Mexico's cession of two-fifths of its land to the US.

For several decades prior to 1860, the Northern and Southern states had been progressively becoming divided by a number of issues: sectional rivalry, industrial against agricultural interests, economic and trade regulation, federal centralization against states' rights, Congressional control, and slavery. Compromises had been worked numerous times, but they became increasingly unsatisfactory as the 1850s wore on, and conflict loomed large. PA had sizable interests in all of the issues, especially the industrial, economic, and slavery conflicts. PA people had been extremely active in anti-slavery movements since 1688, and in 1780 the state passed a law for the abolition of the practice. In the years just before the Civil War, PA had many stations on the Underground Railroad, which secretly moved slaves out of the south into Canada. The strong westward movement in the US was causing territories in the west to apply for statehood, and PA supported the view that slavery should be outlawed in the new states. The South feared that the growth of anti-slavery states would soon mean the North could outvote them in the Congress, and might even try to abolish slavery completely.

When Lincoln was elected president in 1860, the South clearly remembered his campaign statement that a government cannot endure permanently half slave and half free. Before the inauguration, SC seceded from the Union on 20 December, and by 01 February 1861 had been joined by AL, FL, GA, LA, MS, and TX. On 12 April 1861, US Fort Sumter in Charleston harbor fell to Confederate attackers, and Lincoln called for troops to defend the North. By the end of May, four other southern states had refused to answer Lincoln's call and had seceded (NC, VA, AR, TN) to join the Confederacy. The two sides, Union and Confederate, mobilized their men and resources, and four years of horrible conflict began. We will now summarize the War, and then we will look at PA's part in a bit of detail.

The intention of the Union came to be defeat of the Confederacy by invasion and subdual. Five strategies were to be pursued: (1) the blockading or capture of Southern ports to cut off supplies, (2) the taking of the Confederate capital Richmond by attack from the north, (3) the splitting of the Confederacy by driving down and up the MS River, (4) the further splitting of the Confederacy by driving from the northwest corner of TN down the TN and Cumberland Rivers to Nashville to Chattanooga to Atlanta to Savannah, and then (5) the driving north from Savannah into SC, then into NC, and finally into VA to assault Richmond from the south.

Strategy 1, the sea blockade, was accomplished early in the War with most Atlantic and Gulf ports blocked or captured by the end of 1862. Strategy 2, the drive toward Richmond from the north, failed again and again, the Confederacy even making two counter-invasions to threaten Washington, until success began to be had by Grant in 1864, Richmond falling on 02-03 April 1865. Strategy 3, the drives to take the MS River, had been completed with the collapse of Port Hudson on 09 July 1863. Strategy 4, the drive from northwest TN to Savannah, took 34 months, but ended in the capture of Savannah on 22 December 1864. Strategy 5, the drive north from Savannah, was accomplished by the taking of Charleston and Columbia in February 1865, then pushing into NC where one of the two remaining major Confederate Armies surrendered on 26 April 1865. The other had surrendered after the fall of Richmond at Appomattox on 09 April 1865.

The state of PA played an exceptionally important role in the Civil War. The state furnished 362,000 men for the Union Army and 14,000 men for the Union Navy plus a sizable number of armed state militia. Several of the high-ranking officers were Pennsylvanians, including McClellan, Hancock, Meade, Reynolds, Porter, and Dahlgren. PA's industry turned the state into the arsenal of the North, as it manufactured ships, rifles, cannons, munitions, textiles, and supplies in abundance. In October 1862, a Confederate raid on Chambersburg resulted in the looting of a large military storehouse.In the early summer of 1863, 75,000 Confederate troops under Lee invaded PA, hoping to capture Harrisburg and Philadelphia. Very quickly they attacked Chambersburg, York, Carlisle, Hanover, Greencastle, McConnellsburg, and Waynesboro. Then, on 01 July 1863 Union forces under Meade met the Confederate invaders at Gettysburg and heavy high-casualty fighting raged for three days. After the repulsion by the Union of a savage Confederate attack on 03 July 1863, Lee gave up the campaign and led his remaining forces back to VA. This battle was one of the major turning points of the War, marking the time after which the South could never again seriously threaten Northern territory. The final Civil War action on PA soil was a second Confederate attack on Chambersburg in July 1864, at which time the town was burned to the ground.

---

8. The post-war years

The Civil War left two major effects upon the life of PA, effects which were to have long-lasting consequences. These effects were the consolidation of the Republican Party in the state and the stimulation of PA's industry. And these two were to become inseparable mutually-beneficial partners for years to come. The Republican machine was to foster a program of taxation, tariffs, and labor policies which would promote the development of big business. And the businesses, growing rapidly under this support, were to make large contributions to the party, which it used to keep itself in power. The result was that very large industrial empires began to appear: steel (Carnegie), aluminum (Hall, Hunt, & Davis), and coal. To serve this expanding industry, PA's rail lines increased from 2000 miles (in 1865) to over 10,000 miles (in 1899). Telegraph and telephone lines also began to connect the state with over 15,000 miles of wire having been strung by 1895. After the Civil War, PA gradually declined as a grain-raising state, and its farmers turned to the production of fruit, vegetables, and dairy products. PA citizens during this period also made notable beginnings in food preservation, packing, and sales (Heinz), and in department, variety, and grocery store merchandising (Wanamaker, Woolworth, Robinson, Hunter).

During the period 1865-99, large numbers of immigrants entered PA to work in the mills and factories. For most of the time before 1865 the major immigrants to PA were English, German, and Scotch-Irish, but just before the Civil War, many Irish (factory workers, canal and railroad laborers) and Welsh (miners, ironworkers) came in. After the War, the chief groups came from Ireland and Germany, the Irish becoming city industrial laborers and the Germans establishing farms and small shops. Then from about 1890, settlers from southern and eastern Europe began to flow in (Italy, Russia, Poland, Austria-Hungary), as did Blacks from the Southern US.The many steel, coal, textile, and other industrial workers began to band together into unions to improve their conditions (pay, hours, working conditions, benefits), but found themselves opposed by most employers and numerous citizens. Considerable conflict ensued as union members called strikes and as employers made use of strike-breakers. There were riots in some instances, and several times troops had to be called in to terminate the violence. In spite of numerous repressions, the unions gradually gained strength and influence, and toward 1900 began to attain some of their goals.

In the years after the Civil War, a small group of political bosses came into control of both state and local government in PA. They tended to run things for their own advantage and for certain business groups who supported them. As time went on, citizens became increasingly aroused and began to act against these corrupt government officials, a new State

Constitution embodying laws against governmental abuses being enacted in 1873, and reform candidates being elected in 1882. These reform trends continued into the 20th century. In the Spanish-American War (1898), PA furnished over 17,000 men, with Pennsylvanians fighting at Manila and Puerto Rico.

The economy of PA continued to expand in the early years of the 20th century (1900s). Steel (Morgan) and aluminum (Alcoa) manufacturing increased greatly, as did coal mining, coke production, oil refining (Mellon, Pew), electrical generation and distribution, and automobile development. Immigrants continued to enter PA in large numbers, and the Union movement became stronger as better working conditions for PA's labor force were obtained. Education improved markedly with the coming of a compulsory school attendance law and the rapidly accelerating establishment of high schools. The Commonwealth of PA played a very important part in the winning of World War I, contributing more than 324,000 men to the armed forces, and devoting its full industrial capacity (mills, factories, shipyards) to support of the conflict. After World War I, PA's economy went into severe decline, its timber having been used up, the market for coal having dropped off (due to new fuels), and the rising out-of-state production of oil, steel, and textiles. This led directly into the Great Depression of the 1930s, during which hundreds of thousands of PA people were out of work. Even the industrial stimulus of World War II (1941-5) was insufficient to bring the state out of its economic difficulties. In this 4-year war, PA again supplied men (908,000 army, 307,000 navy) and industrial production. In the 1950s, PA's government began efforts to promote economic growth, and these efforts began to pay off in the early 1960s with many new plants being built and the unemployment rate falling considerably.

One of the major ways of seeing the development of PA, and a way of particular interest to genealogists, is to follow the increasing population of the state (given in parentheses in thousands [K] after the years: 1680 (0.7K), 1690 (11K), 1700 (18K), 1710 (24K), 1720 (31K), 1730 (52K), 1740 (86K), 1750 (120K), 1760 (184K), 1770 (240K), 1780 (327K), 1790 (434K), 1800 (602K), 1810 (810K), 1812 (862K), 1820 (1048K), 1830 (1348K), 1840 (1724K), 1850 (2312K), 1860 (2906K), 1870 (3522K), 1880 (4282K), 1890 (5258K), 1900 (6302K), 1910 (7665K), 1920 (8720K), 1930 (9631K), 1940 (9900K), 1950 (10498K), 1960 (11319K), 1970 (11794K), 1980 (11867K).

Among the major historic sites of genealogical interest are Amish Village (in Bird-in-Hand), Brandywine Battlefield Park (8 miles northeast of Kennett Square), Carlisle Barracks (1 mile north of Carlisle, US Army Military History Institute), Ephrata Cloister (in Ephrata, old 7th-Day Baptist settlement), Fort Necessity National Battlefield (11 miles southeast of Uniontown, site of opening battle of the French and Indian War), Gettysburg National Military Park (at Gettysburg, site of a major Civil War battle), Historic Allentown, Historic Bethlehem 18th Century Industrial Area, Historic Fallsington (in Bristol, Bucks County), Historic Schaeffertown (6 miles east of Cornwall), Historic York, Hopewell Village National Historic Site (15 miles southeast of Reading, restored village around early ironworks), Independence National Historical Park (in downtown Philadelphia, sites of Colonial and Revolutionary PA), Mennonite Information Center (5 miles north of Lancaster) and PA Dutch Visitors' Bureau (in Lancaster), Old Bedford Village (2 miles north of Bedford) and Fort Bedford Park (in Bedford), PA Dutch Folk Culture Center (5 miles east of Hamburg in Lenhartsville), Point State Park and Fort Pitt Museum (in Pittsburgh, site of old fort), Valley Forge National Historical Park (just west of King of Prussia, site of Rvolutionary War winter encampment), and Washington Crossing Historical Park (7 miles south of New Hope, site of Revolutionary War action against Trenton, NJ).

9. PA counties

The Commonwealth or State of PA is divided into 67 counties, each of which in turn is subdivided into townships. The township boundaries were generally laid out in patterns which followed natural land features such as creeks, streams, ridges, and demarcations between meadows, forests, and stony soil. The shapes of most townships are therefore quite varied as are their sizes. Within the counties and their townships are cities and boroughs, these having governments independent of the townships. [One important exception is Philadelphia in which the county and city governments have recently been combined.] The most important sources of genealogical records are the state and the county governments, although the other local governments (townships, cities, boroughs) have some records of value to family researchers. From the original three counties (Bucks, Chester, Philadelphia) which were set up in 1682, there came to be 4 counties as of 1729, 8 as of 1770, 11 as of 1773, 16 as of 1785, 21 as of 1790, 25 as of 1798, 35 as of 1800, 44 as of 1810, 51 as of 1820, 55 as of 1840, 64 as of 1850, and finally 67 counties as of 1878, which is the number there now are.

The 67 present counties of PA are shown in Figure 7. To locate a county, consult the following alphabetical list, and notice its abbreviations [in brackets] and its general region (in parentheses). NW stands for northwest, SW for southwest, NC for north central, SC for south central, NE for northeast, and SE for southeast. The small map in Figure 7 shows you the general region in which to look for the county. The counties are: Adams [A1] (SC), Allegheny [A2] (SW), Armstrong [A3] (SW), Beaver [B1] (SW), Bedford [B2] (SC), Berks [B3] (SE), Blair [B4] (SC), Bradford [B5] (NE), Bucks [B6] (SE), Butler [B7] (SW), Cambria [C1] (SC), Cameron [C2] (NC), Carbon [C3] (NE), Centre [C4] (NC), Chester [C5] (SE), Clarion [C6] (NW), Clearfield [C7] (NC), Clinton [C8] (NC), Columbia [C9] (NE), Crawford [CR] (NW), Cumberland [CU] (SC), Dauphin [D1] (SE), Delaware [D2] (SE), Elk [E1] (NC), Erie [E2] (NW), Fayette [F1] (SW), Forest [F2] (NW), Franklin [F3] (SC), Fulton [F4] (SC), Greene [G] (SW), Huntingdon [H] (SC), Indiana [I] (SW), Jefferson [J1] (NW), Juniata [J2] (SC), Lackawanna [L1] (NE), Lancaster. [L2] (SE), Lawrence [L3] (NW), Lebanon [L4] (SE), Lehigh [L5] (SE), Luzerne [L6] (NE), Lycoming [L7] (NC), Mercer [M1] (NW), Mifflin [M2] (SC), Monroe [M3] (NE), Montgomery [M4] (SE), Montour [M] (NC), McKean [M5] (NC), Northampton [N1] (SE), Northumberland [N2] (NC), Perry [P1] (SC), Philadelphia [P2] (SE), Pike [P3] (NE), Potter [P4] (NC), Schuylkill [S1] (SE), Snyder [S2] (SC), Somerset [S3] (SC), Sullivan [S4] (NE), Susquehanna [S5] (NE), Tioga [T] (NC), Union [U] (NC), Venango [V] (NW), Warren [W1] (NW), Washington [W2] (SW), Wayne [W3] (NE), Westmoreland [W4] (SW), Wyoming [W5] (NE), York [Y] (SC).

Figures 8 through 22 depict geographically the development of the 67 counties of PA. Each figure shows the counties existing as of a given date. The new counties which were created since the date of the previous figure are indicated by asterisks, and the dates of these county creations are given in parentheses in the label of the figure. The parent county or counties of each individual county are given in Chapter 4, where considerable detail about each county is given.

10. PA government

In order to do good genealogical research in PA, you need to understand several aspects of PA government. The most important are the PA judicial system, PA county government, and some agencies of the state government. The reason for this is that many very valuable records of genealogical importance are kept by these agencies. First, we will look at the PA judi-

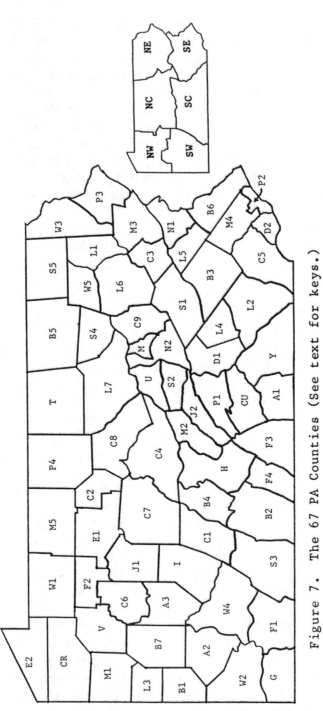

Figure 7. The 67 PA Counties (See text for keys.)

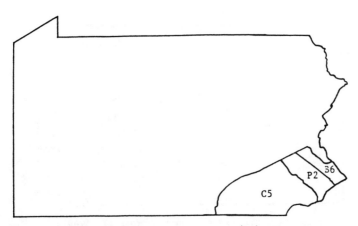

Figure 8. PA's Original Counties: Bucks (B6), Chester
(C5), Philadelphia (P2).

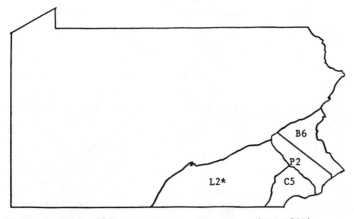

Figure 9. PA in 1729. New County: Lancaster (L2*-1729).

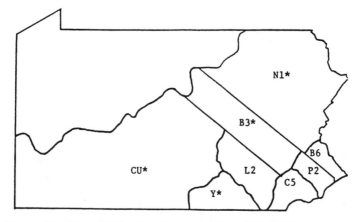

Figure 10. PA in 1770. New Counties: York (Y*-1749),
Cumberland (CU*-1750), Berks (B3*-1752), Northampton (N1*-1752).

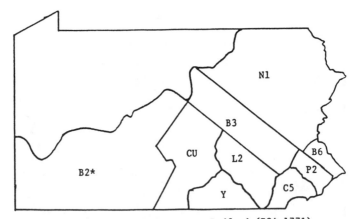

Figure 11. PA in 1771. New County: Bedford (B2*-1771).

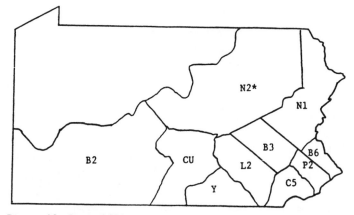

Figure 12. PA in 1772. New County: Northumberland (N2*-1772).

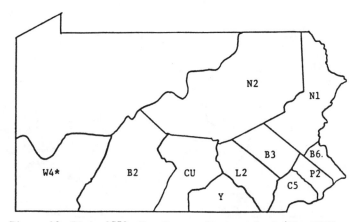

Figure 13. PA in 1773. New County: Westmoreland (W4*-1773).

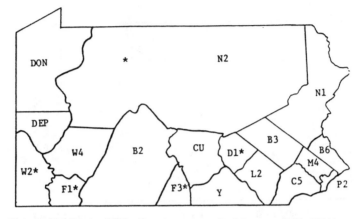

Figure 14. PA in 1785. New Counties: Washington (W2*-1781),
Fayette (F1*-1783), Montgomery (M4*-1784), Franklin
(F3*-1784), Dauphin (D1*-1785), Depreciation (DEP) and
Donation (DON) Lands in 1783, Northumberland Expanded
(*-1785).

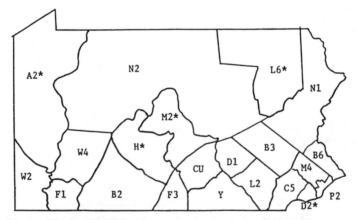

Figure 15. PA in 1790. New Counties: Luzerne (L6*-1786),
Huntingdon (H*-1787), Allegheny (A2*-1788), Delaware
(D2*-1789), Mifflin (M2*-1789).

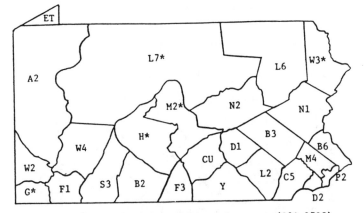

Figure 16. PA in 1798. New Counties: Somerset (S3*-1795), Lycoming (L7*--1795), Greene (G*-1796), Wayne (W3*-1798). Erie Triangle (ET) acquired 1792.

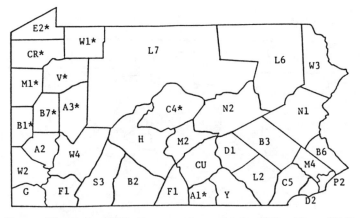

Figure 17. PA in 1800. New counties, all in 1800: Adams (A1*), Armstrong (A3*), Beaver (B1*), Butler (B7*), Centre (C4*), Crawford (CR*), Erie (E2*), Mercer (M1*), Venango (V*), Warren (W1*).

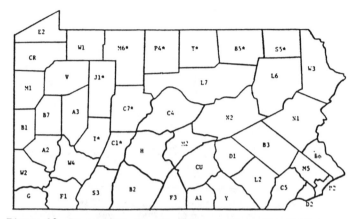

Figure 18. PA in 1810. New Counties: Indiana (I*-1803), Cambria (C1*-1804), Clearfield (C7*-1804), Jefferson (J1-1804), McKean (M6*-1804), Potter (P4*-1804), Tioga (T*-1804), Ontario (B5*-1810, became Bradford in 1812), Susquehanna (S5*-1810).

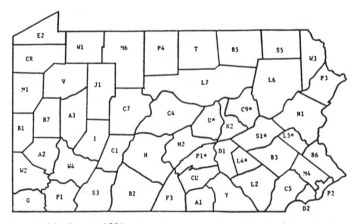

Figure 19. PA in 1820. New Counties: Schuylkill (S1*-1811), Lehigh (L5*-1812), Columbia (C9*-1813), Lebanon (L4*-1813), Union (U*-1813), Pike (P3*-1814), Perry (P1*-1820).

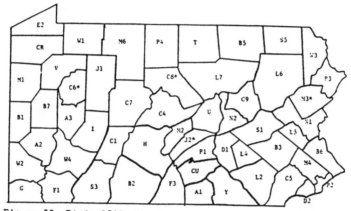

Figure 20. PA in 1840. New Counties: Juniata (J2*-1831), Monroe (M3*-1836), Clarion (C6*-1839), Clinton (C8*-1840).

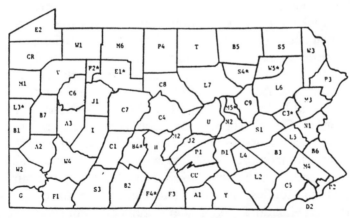

Figure 21. PA in 1850. New Counties: Wyoming (W5*-1842), Carbon (C3*-1843), Elk (E1*-1843), Blair (B4*-1846), Sulli-van (S4*-1847), Forest (F2*-1848), Lawrence (L3*-1849), Fulton (F4*-1850), Montour (M5*-1850).

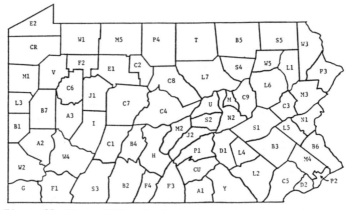

Figure 22. PA in 1787 and after. New Counties: Snyder
(S2*-1855), Cameron (C2*-1860), Lackawanna (L1*-1878).
Forest enlarged, Venango made smaller in 1866.

cial system. At the lowest level are the <u>Local</u> <u>Courts</u>. These courts are
presided over by justices of the peace in the townships and boroughs and
by magistrates or aldermen in the cities. They handle cases involving
minor violations of the law, minor disagreements among parties, and
disputes over small amounts of money. At the next level are the <u>District</u>
<u>Courts,</u> there being one in almost every county. There are a few
exceptions in which a low-population county makes use of the District
Court in a neighboring county. The judges of the District Courts act in
several different capacities since every district court is actually composed
of several sub-courts, each of them dealing with a certain type of cases.
These sub-courts are the Court of Common Pleas, the Court of Oyer and
Terminer and Jail Delivery, the Court of Quarter Sessions of the Peace,
and the Orphans' Court. The Court of Common Pleas handles civil suits
(cases in which one party sues another to seek damage or to stop some al-
legedly unfair action: divorce, libel, and contract cases, for example). The
Court of Oyer and Terminer and Jail Delivery hears major criminal cases.
The Court of Quarter Sessions of the Peace hears criminal cases involving
crimes, offenses, violations, and misdemeanors of lesser seriousness. The
Orphans' Court settles estates and thus handles wills, distribution of estates, and guardianship matters. To ease the case load in some high
population centers there are also a few other courts at this level, including
the Municipal Court of Philadelphia (juveniles, civil suits, minor criminal
cases), the Allegheny County Juvenile Court, and the County Court of
Allegheny County (civil cases). Above all of these many courts are the
<u>Superior</u> <u>Court</u> and the <u>State</u> <u>Supreme</u> <u>Court</u>, both of which hear appeals
from the actions of the lower courts.

Second, let us look at PA county government. Each county is governed by three elected county commissioners who conduct elections, maintain county institutions, pay county expenses, and levy and collect taxes. Records kept by them may include minutes, tax lists and assessments, veterans' burials, soldiers' discharges, military enrollment, and slave registers. There are a number of other elected county officials of particular pertinence to genealogists which will now be listed. The sheriff maintains law, runs the county jail, and carries out court orders. The coroner investigates unusual deaths. The district attorney investigates crimes and prosecutes persons accused of them. The prothonotary functions as the clerk of the Court of Common Pleas (making its arrangements and keeping its records), and also keeps records of the cases tried by justices of the peace. Among the records which this official maintains are the judgement dockets (chronological listing of cases with summaries) and case files of the court, naturalizations, sheriff's orders, and physicians' registers. The clerk of courts serves the Court of Oyer and Terminer and Jail Delivery and the Court of Quarter Sessions of the Peace. Among the duties of this office are the keeping of the records of these courts (minutes, dockets, trial summaries, case files, transcripts) as well as coroner's inquisitions and slave returns. The register of wills and clerk of the Orphans' Court makes arrangements for and keeps records of the proceedings of the Orphans' Court, records wills, births, deaths, marriages, guardianships, adoptions, and supervises the settlement of estates. In a few counties, the two functions of this office (register and clerk) are separated, but in most counties, they are combined. The recorder of deeds keeps records of property transactions including deeds, mortgages, surveys, mineral right leases, and warrants, as well as organization charters and military discharges. The surveyor measures property lines, boundaries, and roads. The treasurer receives and collects taxes and disburses funds as ordered by the commissioners, and the controller or auditors supervise all financial transactions and records.

Third, we will consider several agencies of the PA state government which have kept records of use to those investigating their family histories. In practically all of these agencies mentioned below, the pertinent records have been transferred to the PA State Archives. Researchers should not go to the agencies to examine the records, but to the Archives in Harrisburg. The Department of the Auditor General which was created in 1809, oversees receipts and expenditures of the state, and its records contain military service, military pension, and military claim accounts. The Office of Comptroller General, which existed only 1782-1809, oversaw financial matters for the state, and it left records on militia, Revolutionary War donation lands, service, and pensions, as well as some tax lists and warrants. The <u>Bureau</u> of <u>Land</u> <u>Records</u> is the modern successor to a series of colony and state agencies which kept records of original transfers of land from the colony or state to individuals or organizations. Their records include land lists, vouchers, warrants, ledgers, contracts, claims, and accounts. The <u>Department</u> of <u>Military</u> <u>Affairs</u> administers military matters in the state. Its records include military records of the militia, the Mexican War, the Civil War, the Spanish-American War, later wars, and of veterans' assistance. Among the records left by the <u>Proprietary</u> <u>Government</u> (1681-1775) are some naturalization lists and governor's accounts (including lists of marriage licenses). <u>PA's</u> <u>Revolutionary</u> <u>Governments</u> left many records, but those of forfeited estates (1777-90), marriage bonds (1784-6), and oaths of allegiance (1777-8) are the ones of greatest value to genealogists. The records of the <u>Supreme</u> <u>Court</u> and of the <u>Superior</u> <u>Court</u> consist of minutes, dockets, case files, claims papers, and naturalization papers. Please remember that practically all of the records mentioned in this paragraph are no longer in the custody of the agencies. They are in the PA State Archives in Harrisburg.

---

11. Recommended reading

A knowledge of the history of PA and of its local regions is of extreme importance for the tracing of the genealogies of its former inhabitants. This chapter has been a brief treatment of the history. Your next step should be the reading of one of the following, relatively brief one-volumed works:

___ S. K. Stevens, R. W. Cordier, and F. O. Benjamin, EXPLORING PA, Harcourt, Brace, and World, New York, NY, 1968.

___ T. C. Cochran, PA: A BICENTENNIAL HISTORY, Norton, New York, NY, 1978.

After this, it is recommended that you thoroughly read one of the following volumes. These are larger books which give much broader coverage of PA history.

___ W. F. Dunaway, A HISTORY OF PA, Prentice-Hall, Englewood Cliffs, NJ, 1948.

___ S. K. Stevens, PA: BIRTHPLACE OF A NATION, Random House, New York, NY, 1964.

___ P. A. Wallace, PA: SEEDS OF A NATION, Harper and Row, New York, NY, 1962.

___ P. S. Klein and A. Hoogenboom, A HISTORY OF PA, PA State University Press, University Park, PA, 1986.

If you care to go further, or if you wish to explore a special topic or a particular time span in greater detail, you may wish to employ one or more of the several multi-volumed histories of PA. Among the better ones are:

___S. K. Stevens, PA, THE KEYSTONE STATE, American Historical Publishing Co., New York, NY, 1956, 2 volumes.

___H. M. Jenkins, PA, COLONIAL AND FEDERAL, PA Historical Publ. Assn., Philadelphia, PA, 1903, 3 volumes.

___S. K. Stevens, PA, THE HERITAGE OF A COMMONWEALTH, American Historical Co., West Palm Beach, FL, 1968, 4 volumes.

___G. P. Donehoo, PA, A HISTORY, Lewis Historical Publishing Co., New York, NY, 1926, volumes 1-4.

In order to locate books dealing with certain time periods of PA history, certain regions or counties of PA, or certain trends, movements, or developments in PA history, consult the following historical bibliography and its supplements:

___N. B. Wilkinson, S. K. Stevens, and D. H. Kent, BIBLIOGRAPHY OF PA HISTORY, PA Historical and Museum Commission, Harrisburg, PA, 1957, with C. Wall, SUPPLEMENT TO BIBLIOG-RAPHY OF PA HISTORY, PA Historical and Museum Commission, Harrisburg, PA, 1977, and J. B. B. Trussell, PA BIBLIOGRAPHY, PA Historical and Museum Commission, Harrisburg, PA, 1980-5, 6 volumes, continued in PA HISTORY, 1989ff, volumes 56ff.

Individual county histories will be listed in Chapter 4 of this book, and other historical works dealing with regions, counties, cities, and towns of PA are listed in:

___M. J. Kaminkow, US LOCAL HISTORIES IN THE LIBRARY OF CONGRESS, Magna Carta Book Co., Baltimore, MD, 1975.

___P. W. Filby, BIBLIOGRAPHY OF AMERICAN COUNTY HISTORIES Genealogical Publishing Co., Baltimore, MD, 1985.

Three of the most important of the PA historical publications which you may want to look into are:

___THE PA MAGAZINE OF HISTORY AND BIOGRAPHY, Histori-cal Society of PA, Philadelphia, PA, 1877-. [Coverage chiefly for southeastern PA.]

___WESTERN PA HISTORICAL MAGAZINE, Historical Society of Western PA, Pittsburgh, PA, 1918-. [Coverage chiefly for western PA.]

___PA HISTORY, PA Historical Association, University Park, PA, 1933-. [Coverage for the entire state.]

12. The Internet

If you have computer access to the Internet, there are some materials which can be of help for PA genealogical research. These items can be brought up by using a search engine (Lycos, Yahoo, or similar) to ask for Pennsylvania Genealogy. Or you can enter http://libertynet.org/~gencap/pacounties.html#links. This will bring you to a menu which includes the following items (among others):

___US Gen Web Archives: PA Table of Contents
___PA Genealogical Resources
___Genealogical and Historical Organizations in PA
___PA Geneealogical Events
___Newspapers in PA
___Funeral Homes and Cemeteries in PA
___PA Maps

All of the above can be of assistance in locating records. Most of the items are self-explanatory, except the one entitled PA Genealogical Resources. This rich site leads to many items including these entries:

___PA Research Outline (from the Family History Library, FHL)
___Family History Centers (FHC) in PA
___PA Genealogy Books in the Library of Congress
___Fidonet Genealogical Bulletin Board Systems in PA
___PA-Dutch Research Site
___State Library of PA (SLP)
___PA State Archives (PSA)
___PA Commonwealth Land Office
___PA Vital Records Information
___Philadelphia City Archives
___National Archives, Mid Atlantic Region, Philadelphia Branch (NAPB)
___US Army Military Institute, Carlisle Barracks, PA
___Sons of Union Veterans of the Civil War

The SLP, PSA, Land Office, Vital Records, Philadelphia Archives, and US Army Military History Institute entries describe records available in the respective repositories, and some give historical background, open times, and contacts for further information.

Chapter 2

TYPES OF RECORDS

================ The state of Pennsylvania is relatively rich in ge-
1. Introduction   nealogical source materials, even though there
                   have been some sizable losses of records, especially
================ in the earlier years. A great deal of work has been
done by many people in accumulating, preserving, photocopying, microfilming, transcribing, abstracting, printing, and indexing records. Among the most important genealogical records of PA are the local county records (birth, court, death, divorce, land, marriage, plat, probate, tax, will). The originals of these records are largely in the court houses and/or local libraries and/or local historical society repositories in the 67 PA counties. Some original records (not a lot) are in the PA State Archives, but the Archives has microfilm copies of a fair number of county records for 55 of the counties and a few records for each of 106 municipalities.

The best overall centralized collections of genealogical materials for the commonwealth of PA are to be found in two buildings in the capital city Harrisburg. These are the buildings housing the State Library of PA (SLP) and the PA State Archives (PSA). The State Library of PA (SLP) has an exceptionally large collection of printed, microfilmed, and typescript copies of the following types of records and volumes: atlas, Bible, biography, birth, cemetery, census, church, city directory, colonial, county, court, DAR, death, divorce, ethnic, gazetteer, genealogical compilations, genealogical periodicals, histories (state, regional, county, city), immigration, land, military, naturalization, probate, published genealogies, tax, wills. They also have indexes to many of these, plus numerous other genealogical finding aids and alphabetical lists and files. In addition, there are excellent collections of manuscripts, maps, and newspapers. The PA State Archives (PSA) is the official state repository for original state records (birth, census, court, death, land, marriage, military, naturalization, passenger lists, prison, tax), has both state and private manuscripts (business, cemetery, church, diaries, family records, journals, letters, maps, military, organization, personal papers), has a very large collection of maps, and holds many microfilm copies of records (many of the above state records, plus numerous county records, and federal census, military, and tax lists). The PSA is custodian of the records of the PA State Land Office, which includes original land grants from the colony or state to the first landowner, these records dating from 1682.

In addition to the excellent record collections in Harrisburg, there are three other heavily-stocked library facilities in PA. One of these is in Philadelphia and two are in Pittsburgh. The library in Philadelphia is the Library of the Historical Society of PA (LHS). The collections tend to be heavy on southeastern PA and Philadelphia. The library holds published, typescript, and microfilmed city, county, state, and federal records of genealogical importance, as well as many private record materials (Bible, vital records, cemetery, church, DAR, ethnic, family, histories, maps, periodicals, newspapers). The manuscript collection, which is the largest in the US, contain many private, church, cemetery, and organization records as well as sizable numbers of family genealogies, and several very large genealogical collections.

The two heavily-stocked libraries in Pittsburgh, both of which have a strong western PA bias, are the Library of the Historical Society of Western PA and the Carnegie Library of Pittsburgh. The Library of the Historical Society of Western PA (LWP), has very much regional and a considerable amount of state historical material: books, pamphlets, periodicals, typescripts, microfilms, newspapers, maps, and manuscripts, along with indexes and finding aids. The Carnegie Library of Pittsburgh (CLP) has a sizable collection of genealogical books and microfilms, cemetery records, censuses, city directories, church histories, genealogical compilations, family genealogies, county histories, vital record data, manuscripts, and newspapers, plus several good indexes and alphabetical files.

There is a fairly sizable collection of books and microfilms of PA genealogical materials in the largest genealogical library in the world, namely, the Family History Library (FHL), which is located in Salt Lake City, UT. Not only are the materials available at the library in Salt Lake City, but the microfilms may be borrowed through the numerous Branch Family History Centers of the FHL (FHC), which are located all over the US. Among these branches in PA are: Doylestown, Lancaster, Philadelphia (Broomall), Pittsburgh, Reading, State College, Whitehall, York. Each Branch Library has microfilm copies of the major indexes which list the holdings of the main library in Salt Lake City, and from which microfilms may be ordered.

Many records pertaining to PA which were accumulated by the federal government are available in the National Archives (NA) in Washington, DC. These records include the following types: census, passenger arrival, naturalization, military service, pension, bounty land, Indian, Black, land, claims, court, maps. Many of the most useful of these materials have been microfilmed. Some of these microfilms are available in many of the PA libraries mentioned previously, and sizable numbers of them will be found in the eleven <u>National</u> <u>Archives</u> <u>Field</u> <u>Branches</u> (NAFB), one of which is in Philadelphia, PA, the National Archives Philadelphia Branch (NAPD).

In addition to the above collections, there are PA record collections in a number of <u>large</u> <u>genealogical</u> <u>libraries</u> (LGL) around the country, especially those in states near PA. Other collections, usually with an emphasis on a particular section of PA, are located in several good <u>regional</u> <u>libraries</u> (RL) in PA. Finally, <u>local</u> <u>libraries</u> (LL) in the county seats and some other towns often have good materials relating to their own areas. These local libraries may be city, county, or private (such as ones sponsored by local historical and genealogical societies). All of the archives, libraries, and repositories mentioned above will be discussed in detail in Chapter 3.

In this chapter, the many types of records which are available for PA genealogical research are discussed. Those records which are essentially <u>national</u> or <u>statewide</u> in scope will be treated in detail. Records which are basically <u>county</u> records will be mentioned and treated only generally, since detailed lists of them will be given in Chapter 4, where the major local county records available for each of the 67 PA counties will be presented.

---
2. Bible records

During the past 200 years it was customary for families with religious affiliations to keep vital statistics on their members in the family Bible. These records vary widely, but among the items that may be found are names, dates, and places of birth, christening, confirmation, baptism, marriage, death, and sometimes military service. Although most Bibles containing recorded information probably still remain in private hands, some of the information has been submitted for publication and some has been filed in libraries and archives. Bible records may be found in libraries and archives throughout PA. You should inquire about such records at every possible library and archives in and near your ancestor's county, especially the RL and LL. These repositories will be listed in Chapter 4 under the counties. You should also seek Bible records in the larger archives and libraries in PA: SLP, PSA, LHS, CLP. Also consult the indexes at FHC. In these repositories there may be a special Bible record index, or a special alphabetical

Bible record file, or as is more often the case, data from Bibles may be listed in indexes or alphabetical files labelled something other than Bible records. The most likely labels are family records, genealogies, manuscripts, names, surnames. Also do not fail to look in the major card index of each of these places for the names you are seeking. It is also important that you use the surname and locality indexes at the nearest FHC. Some of the better special indexes and alphabetical files of PA Bible records are:

___Card Index, Genealogical and Local History Room, SLP, Harrisburg, PA.

___Card Indexes, LHS, Philadelphia, PA.

___Card Indexes, CLP, Pittsburgh, PA.

Some PA Bible records have been compiled by various organizations and individuals and have been noted or indexed in published volumes. Among the volumes which you should examine are:

___E. K. Kirkham, AN INDEX TO SOME OF THE BIBLE AND FAMILY RECORDS OF THE US, Volume 2, Everton Publishers, Logan, UT, 1984.

___J. D. and E. D. Stemmons, THE VITAL RECORD COMPENDIUM, Everton Publishers, Logan, UT, 1979. [Many sources listed.]

Bible records also appear in genealogical periodical articles and in published family genealogies. These two record sources, as well as details on manuscript sources, will be discussed in sections 18, 21, and 30 of this chapter.

3. Biographies

There are several major national biographical works which contain sketches on nationally- prominent Pennsylvanians of the past. If you suspect or know that your ancestor was that well known, consult:

___NATIONAL CYCLOPEDIA OF AMERICAN BIOGRAPHY, White Co., New York, NY, 1893-present, over 54 volumes, cumulative index for volumes 1-51.

___DICTIONARY OF AMERICAN BIOGRAPHY, Scribners, New York, NY, 1928-37, 20 volumes, cumulative index.

___THE 20TH CENTURY BIOGRAPHICAL DICTIONARY OF NOTABLE AMERICANS, Gale Research, Detroit, MI, 1968, 10 volumes.

___AMERICAN BIOGRAPHY: A NEW CYCLOPEDIA, American Historical Society, New York, NY, 1916-33, 54 volumes, cumulative index for volumes 1-50.

__ENCYCLOPEDIA OF AMERICAN BIOGRAPHY, NEW SERIES, American Historical Co., West Palm Beach, FL, 1934-present, 4 volumes.

__WHO WAS WHO IN AMERICA, 1607-1896, Who's Who, Chicago, IL, 1967.

Most of these works and about 340 more have been indexed in a 3-volumed set which gives the sources of over 3 million biographies, all arranged in alphabetical order of the names:

__M. C. Herbert and B. McNeil, BIOGRAPHY AND GENEALOGY MASTER INDEX, Gale Research Co., Detroit, MI, latest edition.

Several good biographical compilations for the state of PA exist. These volumes list persons who have attained state-wide prominence in the fields of law, agriculture, business, politics, medicine, engineering, industry, science, military, manufacturing, teaching, public service, or philanthropy. Included among the better ones are:

__BIOGRAPHICAL ALBUM OF PROMINENT PENNSYLVANI-ANS, American Biographical Publishing Co., Philadelphia, PA, 1888-90, 3 volumes.

__C. Blanchard, THE PROGRESSIVE MEN OF THE COMMON-WEALTH OF PA, Bowen, Logansport, PA, 1900, 2 volumes.

__S. Day, HISTORICAL COLLECTIONS OF THE STATE OF PA, CONTAINING -----, BIOGRAPHICAL SKETCHES, -----, Philadelphia, PA, 1834, 2 volumes.

__G. P. Donehoo, PA, A HISTORY, Lewis Historical Publishing Co., New York, NY, 1926, 11 volumes, volumes 5-11 biographical.

__ENCYCLOPEDIA OF CONTEMPORARY BIOGRAPHY OF PA, Atlantic Publishing and Engineering Co., 1890.

__F. A. Godcharles, PA: POLITICAL, GOVERNMENTAL, MILI-TARY, CIVIL, AND BIOGRAPHICAL, American Historical Society, New York, NY, 1933, 5 volumes, volume 5 biographical.

__L. R. Hamersly, WHO'S WHO IN PA, Hamersly, New York, NY, 1904.

__J. W. Jordan, T. L. Montgomery, E. Spofford, F. A. Godcharles, and A. D. Keater, ENCYCLOPEDIA OF PA BIOGRAPHY, Lewis Historical Publishing Co., New York, NY, 1914-67, 32 volumes, with CUMULATIVE INDEX TO VOLUMES 1-20, and CUMULATIVE INDEX TO VOLUMES 21-32.

__THE PA MAGAZINE OF HISTORY AND BIOGRAPHY, Historical Society of PA, Philadelphia, PA, 1877-, Volumes 1-.

__S. W. Pennypacker, HISTORICAL AND BIOGRAPHICAL SKETC-HES, Philadelphia, PA, 1883.

__G. Reed, CENTURY CYCLOPEDIA OF HISTORY AND BIOG-
RAPHY OF PA, Century Publishing Co., Chicago, IL, 1904.

__C. Robson, THE BIOGRAPHICAL ENCYCLOPEDIA OF PA IN
THE 19TH CENTURY, Galaxy Publishing Co., Philadelphia, PA,
1874.

__H. H. Shenk, ENCYCLOPEDIA OF PA, National Historical Associa-
tion, Harrisburg, PA, 1932.

__S. K. Stevens, PA, THE HERITAGE OF A COMMONWEALTH,
American Historical Co., West Palm Beach, FL, 1968, 4 volumes,
volume 4 biographical.

__L. M. Williamson, PROMINENT AND PROGRESSIVE PENNSYL-
VANIANS OF THE 19TH CENTURY, Record Publishing Co.,
Philadelphia, PA, 1898, 3 volumes.

In addition to the state biographical works, there are also a number
of biographical collections for sections or regions of the state. Among the
more useful of these are:

__BOOK OF BIOGRAPHIES [17TH CONGRESSIONAL DISTRICT]
Biographical Publishing Co., Chicago, IL, 1899. [Montour, Columbia,
Northumberland, Sullivan Counties]

__COMMEMORATIVE BIOGRAPHICAL ENCYCLOPEDIA OF
CENTRAL PA, Beers, Chicago, IL, 1898.

__COMMEMORATIVE BIOGRAPHICAL ENCYCLOPEDIA OF
THE JUNIATA VALLEY, Runk and Co., 1897, 2 volumes.

__COMMEMORATIVE BIOGRAPHICAL RECORD OF NORTH-
EASTERN PA, Beers, Chicago, IL, 1900.

__HISTORY OF NORTHWESTERN PA, Lewis Historical Publishing
Co., New York, NY, 3 volumes, volume 3 biographical.

__A. Nevin, MEN OF MARK IN THE CUMBERLAND VALLEY,
1776-1876, Fulton, Philadelphia, PA, 1876.

__J. B. Nolan, A HISTORY OF THE COUNTIES OF SOUTHEAST-
ERN PA, Lewis Historical Publishing Co., New York, NY, 1943, 3
volumes, volume 3 biographical.

__J. Riesenmann, Jr., HISTORY OF NORTHWESTERN PA, New
York, NY, 1943, 3 volumes, volume 3 biographical.

__L. C. Walkinshaw, ANNALS OF SOUTHWESTERN PA, New York,
NY, 1939, 4 volumes, volume 4 biographical.

__S. T. Wiley, BIOGRAPHICAL CYCLOPEDIA OF THE 19TH
CONGRESSIONAL DISTRICT, Ruoff, Philadelphia, PA, 1897.

There are also some biographical volumes dedicated to particular professional groups of PA (physicians, dentists, ministers, military men, governmental officials, lawyers).

Not only are there national, state, regional, and professional biographical works for PA, there are also some local (county, township, borough, city) biographical compilations. If biographical volumes are available for a given PA county, this will be indicated under the county in Chapter 4. Practically all of the above biographical publications are available in SLP, LHS, and CLP, along with most of the local volumes. The local publications will also be found in the LL of the places of interest as well as in nearby RL. When you seek biographical compilations in a library, look under these headings in their card catalogs: US-Biography, PA-Biography, [County name]-Biography, [City name]--Biography. Large listings of biographical materials for PA will be found in the following volumes. These will be especially helpful for discovering what is available at the local level, where you are more likely to find reference to your ancestor.

___M. J. Kaminkow, US LOCAL HISTORIES IN THE LIBRARY OF CONGRESS, Magna Carta, Baltimore, MD, 1975, 5 volumes.

___F. G. Hoenstine, GUIDE TO GENEALOGICAL AND HISTORICAL RESEARCH IN PA, The Author, Hollidaysburg, PA, 1978, also SUPPLEMENTS.

Biographical information is also sometimes found in ethnic publications, genealogical compilations, genealogical periodicals, manuscripts, military records, newspapers, published genealogies, regional records, and historical works (state, regional, local). All of these sources except the histories will be discussed in sections 15, 17, 18, 22, 23-26, 29-31, with some regional histories being included in section 31. Important local histories will be mentioned in the county sections of Chapter 4. These and other histories are listed in the two books mentioned above (Kaminkow, Hoenstine), and may be located in library card catalogs under the headings: PA-History, [County name]-History, [City name]-History.

Finally, there are five very large compiled indexes to names from numerous PA records and publications. These often will refer you to biographies, and thus you definitely must not overlook them:

___GENEALOGICAL SURNAME CARD FILE, State and Local History (Genealogy Section), SLP, Harrisburg, PA.

___F. Rider, AMERICAN GENEALOGICAL [-BIOGRAPHICAL] INDEX, Godfrey Memorial Library, Middletown, CT, 1942-52, 48 volumes; 2nd series, 1952-, 180-volumes, continuing publication.

___F. G. Hoenstine, GUIDE TO GENEALOGICAL AND HISTORICAL RESEARCH IN PA, The Author, Hollidaysburg, PA, 1978, pp. 275-604, also SUPPLEMENT, 1985, pp. 77-214.

___CARD INDEX OF BIOGRAPHIES IN PA LOCAL HISTORIES, PA Room, CLP, Pittsburg, PA. Over 75,000 cards.

___PA ENCYCLOPEDIA OF BIOGRAPHY FIELD NOTES, WPA, Harrisburg, PA, 1939-40. At PSA, Harrisburg, PA.

4. Birth records

During the early formative years of the colony of PA (1676-82) a law was passed requiring birth registration but the regulation was largely ignored. Thus, for the long period 1682-1851 essentially no official state or county records of births were kept. During the few years 1852-4, the Register of Wills in each county was required to maintain birth records and to send duplicates to the state. However, reporting to the Register was often not done so the records are far from being complete, and some of them have since been lost. The registrations include name, place, date, and parents, including the mother's maiden name. The surviving originals of these birth reports are in CH, LL, or PSA. Microfilm copies of many of them are in PSA and FHL, the latter being available through FHC. The records in PSA have been gathered together and are available as:

___RECORD AND INDEXES OF BIRTHS, DEATHS, AND MAR-RIAGES, 1852-4, Record Group 26, PSA, Harrisburg, PA, originals and 6 microfilm rolls.

Not all counties are included in this collection and hence it is necessary for you to search the CH, LL, and FHL holdings in the cases of omitted counties. In Chapter 4, those counties whose 1852-4 records are in PSA, LHS, and/or FHL are indicated.

For the time span 1855-93, no official state or county birth records were kept, but some cities maintained registers. Chief among these are the following:

___PHILADELPHIA BIRTH RECORDS, 1860-1915, alphabetical by year, also indexes, Vital Statistics, Philadelphia Department of Public Health, City Hall Annex, Philadelphia, PA 19107.

___PITTSBURGH BIRTH RECORDS, 1870-1905, Office of Biostatistics, Pittsburgh Health Department, City-County Building, Pittsburgh, PA 15219; microfilms at CLP.

___ALLEGHENY CITY BIRTH RECORDS, 1882-1905, Office of Biostatistics, Pittsburgh Health Department, City-County Building, Pittsburgh, PA 15219.

___WILLIAMSPORT RECORD OF BIRTHS, 1869-1932, Record Group 48, PSA, Harrisburg, PA.

___HARRISBURG RECORD OF BIRTHS, 1875-9, 1883-6, Record
Group 48, PSA, Harrisburg, PA.
___EASTON RECORD OF BIRTHS, DEATHS, AND BURIALS,
1888-1907, Record Group 48, PSA, Harrisburg, PA.
In 1893, a new law required births to be reported to the County Clerk of
Orphans' Court who was to keep records. This situation continued
through 1905, and thus for births during 1893-1905, the records were filed
in the counties. The originals or copies of many of these records are in
PSA and/or FHL, but for a number of counties, they remain in the CH
(Clerk of Orphans' Court) or LL. Those counties for which the records
are in PSA and/or FHL are indicated in Chapter 4.

As of 01 January 1906, according to law, the state of PA began regis-
tering births. The counties gathered the data and then forwarded them to
the PA Division of Vital Statistics. It was not until about 1915 that 90%
completeness in the registration was being attained. Copies of birth
certificates may be obtained from PA Division of Vital Statistics, PO Box
1528, New Castle, PA 16103. You need to give them the name, the
approximate year of birth, any further information you can, your relationship to the person, the reason you want the data (genealogical
research), and the fee (check with them for the amount). Since PA is so
short on official birth records before 1893, other types of records have to
be consulted. Among the better ones (with the section of this chapter
where they are treated) are Bible (section 2), biography (3), cemetery (5),
census (6), church (7), manuscripts (21), military (23-26), mortuary (27),
naturalization (28), newspaper (29), and published genealogies (30).
There is a useful compilation of PA vital records which have been
published in two major PA genealogical periodicals. This compilation
contains many birth dates:
___PA Magazine of History and Biography and PA Genealogical Maga-
zine, PA VITAL RECORDS, Genealogical Publishing Co., Baltimore,
MD, 1983, 3 volumes. [Over100,000 names.]
Numerous non-official sources of PA births, both at the state and county
levels, are listed in:
___J. D. and E. D. Stemmons, THE VITAL RECORD COMPENDIUM,
Everton Publishers, Logan, UT, 1979.
When you are seeking birth date and place information in archives and
libraries, be certain to explore all the above mentioned sources, and don't
fail to look under the county listings and the following heading in library
card catalogs: Registers of births, etc.

5. Cemetery records

If you know or suspect that your ancestor was buried in a certain PA cemetery, the best thing to do is to write the caretaker of the cemetery, enclose an SASE and ask if the records or tombstone inscriptions show your forebear. Gravestones often show names, ages, dates of death and birth, and sometimes family names of wives. Tombstones of children often bear the names or initials of the parents. In order to locate the caretaker, try writing the local genealogical society, the local historical society, or the LL. If you do not find that your ancestor is buried there, then you should ask the above organizations and the LL about records for other cemeteries in the area. The addresses of these organizations will be given in Chapter 4. As you consider possible burial sites, please remember that most early cemeteries were in conjunction with churches. Therefore, if you know your ancestor's religious affiliation, this could be of help.

Another important cemetery record source is the numerous collections of cemetery records which have been made by the DAR, by the WPA, by state, regional, and local genealogical and historical societies, and by individuals. Some of these have been published, and some are in typescript or hand-written form. Many have been microfilmed. Sizable listings of many of these available cemetery records will be found in:

___J. D. and E. D. Stemmons, THE CEMETERY RECORD COMPEN-DIUM, Everton Publishers, Logan, UT, 1979.

___FHL and each FHC, FAMILY HISTORY LIBRARY CATALOG, LOCALITY SECTION, latest edition, look under county.

___A. S. McAllister, PA Gravestone Inscriptions, PUBLICATIONS OF THE GENEALOGICAL SOCIETY OF PA, Philadelphia, PA, Numbers 7-16, 1919-48.

___F. Clint, PA COUNTY AREA KEYS, Keyline Publishers, Elizabeth, CO, 1977-80, 67 volumes, one for each of the PA counties. Lists of cemeteries in each county and some listings of records.

___H. H. Woodroofe, GENALOGIST S GUIDE TO PA RECORDS [IN LHS], Genealogical Society of PA, Philadelphia, PA, 1994.

___H. Wilson, Genealogical Holdings of the LWP, WESTERN PA GENEALOGICAL SOCIETY QUARTERLY, Pittsburgh, PA, Volumes 2-4, 1977-9. Many listed items are now in CLP.

___Genealogical Society of UT, 1990, CEMETERY RECORDS OF PA, The Society, Salt Lake City, UT, 1946, 9 volumes. At FHL and available from FHC.

___Card and Computer Catalogs, SLP, LHG, LHS, CLP, FHC, RL, LL, check for microfilms and transcripts of epitaphs under surname, county, city, church, and cemetery name, also under the heading epitaphs.

The above references indicate that the main sources of PA cemetery records are SLP, LHS, CLP, FHC, RL, and LL. The LL usually have records of cemeteries of their own counties, and RL often have those in their regions. These libraries are listed under the counties in Chapter 4. In all the libraries the cemetery records may be located by looking under the surname, the county and/or the city, the church, the denomination, the ethnic group, and the cemetery name. Also look under the headings Epitaphs-PA and Cemeteries-PA. Further, you should not forget to inquire if there are special cemetery record indexes. Genealogical periodicals published in or near PA quite frequently carry cemetery listings (see section 18 of this chapter).

In Chapter 4, those counties for which local cemetery record compilations exist in printed, filmed, typed, or written form are indicated. Instructions for locating them will be presented in Chapter 3. Instructions for finding cemetery records in genealogical periodical articles are given in section 18 of this chapter.

6. Census records

Excellent ancestor information is available in seven types of census reports which have been accumulated for PA: some early lists of the period 1692-3, regular (R), agricultural (A), industrial (I), mortality (M), the special 1840 Revolutionary War pension census (P), and the special 1890 Union Civil War veteran census (C).

The early lists during 1692-3, even though incomplete, are valuable because they provide useful data during the colonial period. Among the most important of these are:
___PA PETITIONS OF 1692, PA Magazine of History and Biography, Volume 38, pp. 498-501.
___CENSUS ON THE DE RIVER, 1693, Genealogical Magazine of NJ, Volume 13, pp. 64-66.
During the early years of PA history, there were also numerous tax lists and taxpayer compilations which resemble censuses. These will be discussed in section 34. However, there is a very important one which will be listed here since it resembles a 1780 PA census. This long listing has been assembled from surviving tax lists of almost all counties in 1780.

___J. D. and E. D. Stemmons, PA IN 1780, A STATE-WIDE INDEX
OF TAX LISTS, The Compilers, Salt Lake City, UT, 1978. [28000
names from all counties except Westmoreland.]

There is also a CD-ROM which contains some colonial tax and census
records for PA:

___Tax and Census Index, Colonial America, 1634-1790, CD-ROM CD-
0310, available from AGLL, PO Box 329, Bountiful, UT 84011.

Regular census records (R) are available for practically all of PA in
1790, 1800, 1810, 1820, 1830, 1840, 1850, 1860, 1870, 1880, 1900, 1910
and 1920. A few segments are missing: for 1800 (part of Westmoreland
County), for 1810 (parts of Bedford, Cumberland, and Philadelphia
Counties), for 1820 (parts of Lancaster and Luzerne Counties), and for
1860 (all of Fayette County). The 1840 census and all before it listed the
head of household plus a breakdown of the number of persons in the
household according to age and sex brackets. Beginning in 1850, the
names of all persons were recorded along with age, sex, occupation, real
estate, marital, and other information, including the state or country of
birth. With the 1880 census and thereafter, the birthplaces of the mother
and father of each person are also shown. Chapter 4 lists the regular
census records (R) available for each of the 67 PA counties.

Census data for 1790 are available in both a published transcript and
two microfilms, the first and third items being indexed:

___US Bureau of the Census, HEADS OF FAMILIES AT THE FIRST
CENSUS OF THE US, 1790, PA, Genealogical Publishing Co., Baltimore, MD, 1970 (1908). [74000 names, indexed.]

___US Bureau of Census, FIRST CENSUS OF THE US, 1790, PA, The
National Archives, Washington, DC, Microfilm M637, Rolls 8-9.

___US Bureau of Census, FIRST CENSUS OF THE US, 1790, PA, The
National Archives, Washington, DC, Microfilm T498, Roll 2. [Micro-
film of the printed schedules, indexed.]

Microfilms of the remaining original census records (1800-1910) are available as:

___US Bureau of the Census, SECOND CENSUS OF THE US, 1800,
PA, The National Archives, Washington, DC, Microfilm M32, Rolls
35-44.

___US Bureau of the Census, THIRD CENSUS OF THE US, 1810, PA,
The National Archives, Washington, DC, Microfilm M252, Rolls
44-57.

___ US Bureau of the Census, FOURTH CENSUS OF THE US, 1820, PA, The National Archives, Washington, DC, Microfilm M33, Rolls 96-114.

___ US Bureau of the Census, FIFTH CENSUS OF THE US, 1830, PA, The National Archives, Washington, DC, Microfilm M19, Rolls 143-166.

___ US Bureau of the Census, SIXTH CENSUS OF THE US, 1840, PA, The National Archives, Washington, DC, Microfilm M704, Rolls 435-503.

___ US Bureau of the Census, SEVENTH CENSUS OF THE US, 1850, PA, The National Archives, Washington, DC, Microfilm M432, Rolls 743-840.

___ US Bureau of the Census, EIGHTH CENSUS OF THE US, 1860, PA, The National Archives, Washington, DC, Microfilm M653, Rolls 1057-1201.

___ US Bureau of the Census, NINTH CENSUS OF THE US, 1870, PA, The National Archives, Washington, DC, Microfilm M593, Rolls 1289-1470.

___ US Bureau of the Census, TENTH CENSUS OF THE US, 1880, PA, The National Archives, Washington, DC, Microfilm T9, Rolls 1085-1208.

___ US Bureau of the Census, TWELFTH CENSUS OF THE US, 1900, PA, The National Archives, Washington, DC, Microfilm T623, Rolls 1354-1503.

___ US Bureau of the Census, THIRTEENTH CENSUS OF THE US, 1910, PA, The National Archives, Washington, DC, Microfilm T624, Rolls 1292-1435.

___ US Bureau of the Census, FOURTEENTH CENSUS OF THE US, 1920, PA, The National Archives, Washington, DC, Microfilm T625, Rolls 1507-1669.

The 1790 census records are indexed in the published volume mentioned above, in the microfilm (T498) of the printed volume, and in the following CD-ROM:

___ US Census Index, 1790, CD-ROM CD-0311, available from AGLL, PO Box 329, Bountiful, UT 84011.

Indexes have been printed for the 1800, 1810, 1820, 1830, 1840, 1850, 1860 and 1870 census records, and there are also some CD-ROM indexes. Chief among these indexes are:

___ J. D. and E. D. Stemmons, PA IN 1800, AN INDEX TO THE FEDERAL POPULATION SCHEDULES, Institute of Family Research, Salt Lake City, UT, 1972. [96000 entries.]

___R. V. Jackson and G. R. Teeples, INDEX TO PA 1800 CENSUS, Accelerated Indexing Systems, Provo, UT, 1978. [96000 entries.]

___1800 PA CENSUS INDEX, Gendata Corporation, Salt Lake City, UT, 1971.

___US Census Index, 1800, CD-ROM CD-0312, available from AGLL, PO Box 329, Bountiful, UT 84011.

___OH Family Historians, INDEX TO THE 1810 CENSUS OF PA, OH Library Fund, Columbus, OH, 1966. [122000 names.]

___R. V. Jackson and G. R. Teeples, INDEX TO PA 1810 CENSUS, Accelerated Indexing Systems, Bountiful, UT, 1976. [130000 names.]

___US Census Index, 1810, CD-ROM CD-0313, available from AGLL, PO Box 329, Bountiful, UT 84011.

___R. V. Jackson, G. R. Teeples, and D. Schaefermeyer, INDEX TO PA 1820 CENSUS, Accelerated Indexing Systems, Bountiful, UT, 1978. [164000 names.]

___US Census Index, 1820, CD-ROM CD-0314, available from AGLL, PO Box 329, Bountiful, UT 84011.

___R. V. Jackson, G. R. Teeples, and D. Schaefermeyer, INDEX TO PA 1830 CENSUS, Accelerated Indexing Systems, Bountiful, UT, 1976. [220000 names.]

___US Census Index, 1830, CD-ROM CD-0315, available from AGLL, PO Box 329, Bountiful, UT 84011.

___R. V. Jackson and G. R. Teeples, INDEX TO PA 1840 CENSUS, Accelerated Indexing Systems, Bountiful, UT, 1978. [295000 names.]

___US Census Index, 1840, CD-ROM CD-0316, available from AGLL, PO Box 329, Bountiful, UT 84011.

___R. V. Jackson and G. R. Teeples, INDEX TO PA 1850 CENSUS, Accelerated Indexing Systems, Bountiful, UT, 1976. [687000 names.]

___M. B. Penrose, HEADS OF FAMILIES INDEX, 1850 FEDERAL CENSUS, CITY OF PHILADELPHIA, Liberty Bell Associates, Franklin Park, NJ, 1974. [26000 names.]

___E. P. Bentley, INDEXES TO THE 1850 CENSUS OF PA, Genealogical Publishing Co., Baltimore, MD, 1974-. [County by county indexes.]

___US Census Index, 1850, CD-ROM CD-0317, available from AGLL, PO Box 329, Bountiful, UT 84011.

___R. V. Jackson and others, INDEX TO 1860 PA CENSUS, Accelerated Indexing Systems, Salt Lake City, UT, 1985, 5 volumes.

___US Census Index, 1860, CD-ROM CD-0318, available from AGLL, PO Box 329, Bountiful, UT 84011.

___R. V. Jackson and others, INDEX TO 1870 PA CENSUS, AIS, Salt Lake City, UT, 1991-3, 9 volumes.

___B. Steuart, INDEX TO THE PA CENSUS OF 1870, Precision
Indexing, Bountiful, UT, 1991-3. Also available on CD-ROMs ACD-
0003 and ACD-0007, available from AGLL, PO Box 329, Bountiful,
UT 84011.

In addition to the above bound and CD-ROM indexes, there is a
microfilm index which contains only those families with a child under 10
in the 1880 census. There are also complete microfilm indexes to the
1900, 1910 and 1920 censuses. The 1880, 1900, and 1920 censuses are
indexed by a code called Soundex and the 1910 census is indexed by a
code called Miracode. Librarians and archivists can show you how to use
these codes. The indexes are:
___US Bureau of the Census, INDEX (SOUNDEX) TO THE 1880
POPULATION SCHEDULES: PA, National Archives, Washington,
DC, Microfilm T769, Rolls 1-168.
___US Bureau of the Census, INDEX (SOUNDEX) TO THE 1900
POPULATION SCHEDULES: PA, National Archives, Washington,
DC, Microfilm T1068, Rolls 1-590.
___US Bureau of the Census, INDEX (MIRACODE) TO THE 1910
POPULATION SCHEDULES: PA, National Archives, Washington,
DC, Microfilm T1274, Rolls 1-688.
___US Bureau of the Census, INDEX (SOUNDEX) TO THE 1920
POPULATION SCHEDULES: PA, National Archives, Washington,
DC, Microfilm M1584, Rolls 1-716.

The indexes listed in the two previous paragraphs are exceptionally
valuable as time-saving devices. However, few indexes of any sort are
perfect, and therefore you need to exercise a little caution in using them.
If you do not find your ancestor in them, do not conclude that he or she
is not in the state; this may mean only that your forebear has been
accidentally omitted or that the name has been misread, misspelled, or
misprinted. Once you have located a name in the indexes, you can go directly to the reference in the census microfilms and read the entry. When
indexes are not available (partially for 1880), it is necessary for you to go
through the census listings entry-by-entry. This can be essentially
prohibitive for the entire state, so it is necessary for you to know the
county in order to limit your search. Both the census records and the
indexes are available in SLP, PSA, and FHL (through FHC) and many
are in LHS, CLP, LGL, and RL. Ones pertaining to specific counties are
often in LL. Both the NA and the NAFB (including NAPB) also have
the microfilms and printed indexes. They are located in or near Boston
(Waltham), New York (Manhattan), Philadelphia, Atlanta (East Point),

Chicago, Kansas City, Fort Worth, Denver, San Francisco (San Bruno), Los Angeles (Laguna Niguel), and Seattle. Their exact addresses and telephone numbers can be obtained from the telephone directories in these cities or from the pamphlet:

___National Archives, REGIONAL BRANCHES OF THE NATIONAL ARCHIVES, The Archives, Washington, DC, latest edition.

Also, the microfilmed census records and the microfilmed indexes may be borrowed for you by your local library through interlibrary loan [from AGLL, PO Box 244, Bountiful, UT 84010]. There is a charge of a few dollars per roll.

Agricultural census records (A), also known as farm and ranch census records, are available for 1850, 1860, 1870, and 1880 for PA. These records list the name of the owner, size of farm or ranch, value of the property, crops, livestock, and other details. If your ancestor was a farmer (quite likely), it will be worthwhile to seek him in these records. No indexes are available, but you will probably know the county, so your entry-by-entry search should be fairly easy. Microfilm copies of the records are available in the SLP, Hillman Library in Pittsburgh, and the NA.

___US Bureau of the Census, AGRICULTURAL CENSUS SCHED-ULES, PA FEDERAL DECENNIAL CENSUSES, 1850/60/70/80, National Archives, Washington, DC, Microfilm T1138, Rolls 1-62.

Industrial census records (I) are available for 1820, 1850, 1860, 1870, and 1880. There were fragmentary records of this sort in 1810, which were added to the regular census. The records list manufacturing firms which produced articles having an annual value of $500 or more (for the 1850-80 periods). Given in the later records are the name of the firm, the owner, the product(s), the machinery, number of employees, and other details. Indexes accompany the 1820 microfilmed records, but the others are unindexed. The microfilmed records are available at SLP, Hillman Library in Pittsburgh, and in the NA:

___US Bureau of the Census, RECORDS OF THE 1820 CENSUS OF MANUFACTURES, The National Archives, Washington, DC, Microfilm M279, Rolls 1-27.

___US Bureau of the Census, NON-POPULATION CENSUS SCHED-ULES, 1850-80, PA, MANUFACTURERS, The National Archives, Washington, DC, Microfilm Rolls 1-14.

Mortality census records (M) are available for the one-year periods 01 June (1849, 1859, 1869, 1879) to 31 July (1850, 1860, 1870, 1880). The records give information on persons who died in the year preceding the 1st of June of each of the census years 1850, 1860, 1870, and 1880. The data contained in the compilations include name, age, sex, occupation, place of birth, and other information. The originals or microfilm copies of them are available at the SLP, the FHL (through FHC), and the NA. These microfilms are:

___US Bureau of the Census, MORTALITY CENSUS SCHEDULES MICROFILM, 1850, 1860, 1870, 1880: PA, The National Archives, Washington, DC, Microfilm T956, Rolls 1-12.

Indexes to these records are available in published form:

___R. V. Jackson, D. W. Samuelson, and S. Rosenkilde, INDEXES TO PA MORTALITY SCHEDULES, 1850, 1860, 1870, 1880, Accelerated Indexing Systems, Salt Lake City, UT, 1979-91.

___US Mortality Schedules Index, 1850/60/70/80, CD-ROM CD-0164, available from AGLL, PO Box 329, Bountiful, UT 84011.

Revolutionary War pensioners (P) were included in a special census taken in 1840. This compilation was an attempt to list all pension holders, however, there are some omissions and some false entries. The list and an index have been published:

___1840 CENSUS OF PA PENSIONERS FOR REVOLUTIONARY MILITARY SERVICE, Genealogical Publishing Co., Baltimore, MD, 1965 (1841).

This volume is available in SLP, LHS, CLP, FHL (FHC), in most LGL, in many RL, and in some LL.

Civil War Union veterans (C) were included in a special census taken in 1890, as were widows of the veterans. These records are arranged by county, so it is well if you know your ancestor's county. Microfilm copies of the records are available at SLP, PSA, CLP, NA, FHL (FHC), most LGL, and some RL. These records show the veteran's name, widow's name (if applicable), rank, company, regiment or ship, and other pertinent military data. The microfilms are:

___Veteran's Administration, SPECIAL SCHEDULES OF THE ELEVENTH CENSUS (1890) ENUMERATING UNION VETERANS AND WIDOWS OF UNION VETERANS OF THE CIVIL WAR, The National Archives, Washington, DC, Microfilm M123, Rolls 78-91.

There is an excellent set of maps which clearly show the counties and enumeration subdivisions for each of the Federal censuses 1790-1920. These maps can be exceptionally useful aids to following your ancestor as the county boundaries of PA shifted from decade to decade.

___W. Thorndale and W. Dollarhide, MAP GUIDE TO THE FEDERAL CENSUSES, PA, 1790-1920, Dollarhide Systems, Bellingham, WA, 1984.

7. Church records

Many PA families were affiliated with a church, and so for these families, there is the possibility of valuable records. The major denomination of the early years of PA was the Quakers or Friends. But their policy of religious freedom encouraged the coming of many immigrant religious groups. The result was that very rapidly a large number of religious denominations became established in the colony. As of 1776-90, the main religious groups in PA (in the order of their size) were Presbyterian, Lutheran, German Reformed, Quaker, Roman Catholic, Baptist, Mennonite, Episcopal, Moravian, and Methodist. Seven decades later, in 1850, the largest churches (in the order of number of members) were Presbyterian, Methodist, Lutheran, Baptist, German Reformed, Roman Catholic, Episcopal, Quaker, Moravian, and Mennonite. The major denominations at the present are Roman Catholic, Lutheran, United Methodist (including the former United Brethren in Christ), Presbyterian, United Church of Christ (including the former German Reformed), and Baptist. However, you need to remember that many denominations and sects (including numerous very small ones) settled PA. Some of these early groups had a profound influence upon the early history of the colony, even though they are now no longer large in numbers.

The records of PA churches often prove very useful since they frequently contain information on one or more of the following items: births, christenings, baptisms, confirmations, marriages, deaths, burials, admissions, dismissals, reprimands, contributions, communion attendance, officers, and ministers. The church data are particularly important because PA counties did not keep many vital records until quite late (1885, 1893). Some of the church records of PA have been inventoried, some have been copied into books, periodicals, and manuscripts, some have been microfilmed, some have been deposited in denominational, state, local, or private archives (or libraries), and many remain with the individual churches. The major places where they may be found are in the individual churches, in denominational archives (listed later), in LL,

RL, SLP, LHS, CLP, and FHL (FHC), and in some PA college and university archives.

Some major listings of PA church records and some finding aids to assist you in locating them are:
___F. Clint, PA COUNTY AREA KEYS, Keyline Publishers, Elizabeth, CO, 1977-80, 67 volumes, one for each PA county. Detailed lists of church records plus location information.
___J. D. and E. D. Stemmons, VITAL RECORD COMPENDIUM, Everton Publishers, Logan, UT, 1979.
___J. D. and E. D. Stemmons, CEMETERY RECORD COMPEN-DIUM, Everton Publishers, Logan, UT, 1979.
___E. K. Kirkham, SURVEY OF AMERICAN CHURCH RECORDS, Everton Publishers, Logan, UT, 1978.
___A. R. Suelflow, PRELIMINARY GUIDE TO CHURCH RECORD REPOSITORIES, Society of American Archivists, St. Louis, MO, 1969.
___PA Historical Records Survey, PA COUNTY CHURCH RECORDS INVENTORIES, 1934-41, unpublished typescripts, PSA, Harrisburg, PA.
___Card indexes in SLP, LHS, CLP, FHL (FHC), RL, LL in your ancestor's county, and in denominational archives. Look under county, church name, and denominational name. Also ask about special indexes, listings, finding aids, and inventories.
___H. H. Woodroofe, GENEALOGISTS GUIDE TO PA RECORDS [IN LHS], Genealogical Society of PA, Philadelphia, PA, 1994,
___H. Wilson, Genealogical Holdings of the LWP, WESTERN PA GENEALOGICAL SOCIETY QUARTERLY, Volumes 2-4, 1977-9. Many listed items are now in CLP.
These volumes, articles, and indexes list many published and microfilmed church records, church record manuscripts, original church records, and church record surveys, inventories, and sources. Especially valuable are the volumes by Clint, even though they are somewhat out of date. This deficiency can be made up by consulting the card indexes mentioned above.

Should you have the good fortune to know or strongly suspect your ancestor's church, you can write directly. Send an SASE, a check for $5, your ancestor's name, and the pertinent dates. Request a search of the records or information on the location of the records if the church no longer has them. If they neither have them nor know where the records are, dispatch an inquiry to the PA or national denominational depository (listed later), enclose an SASE, and ask them if they know where the records are. Also consult the materials listed in the previous paragraph to try to locate the records.

If, as is often the case, you do not know your ancestor's church, you will need to dig deeper. Knowing your ancestor's nationality, his PA county, where in the county he lived, and perhaps other pertinent details, you should be able to make a good guess about his denomination. Early Germans were most likely Lutheran, German Reformed, Brethren, Mennonite, or Moravian. Early English were Quaker, Episcopalian, Methodist, or Baptist. Early Scotch-Irish were generally Presbyterian. Irish, French, Italian, Polish, and people from southern Germany were usually Roman Catholic. The Methodists were very active on the frontier and therefore many people switched to them as the westward PA expansion occurred. Having guessed the denomination, examine the indexes of the indexed church records of the pertinent county. Many of these can be located by using the aids listed in the third paragraph. Should this not yield success, try indexed records of other denominations. Should you still not find what you are seeking, examine maps of your ancestor's county which show churches, and observe those churches near your forebear's property. Suitable maps for this purpose are listed in section 17 of this chapter, especially those maps available from the US Geological Survey. Now investigate these nearby churches, seeking their records by using the items listed in the third paragraph of this section. Letters to LL (listed later), to local genealogical or historical societies (listed later), and to denominational repositories (listed later) concerning churches in your ancestor's part of the county and the records of these churches should be dispatched.

The names and addresses of the PA denominational depositories for the major denominations of early PA will now be given, along with a bit of pertinent historical information. These early denominations will be treated alphabetically, but you need to look at the listings carefully since some mergers have recently occurred. This means that the early denominational names may no longer be in use, and therefore you may need to seek records under the new merged name.

The earliest <u>Baptist</u> Church in PA was formed at Cold Spring in 1684. The archives for the PA churches of the American Baptist Churches in the USA are:
___Eastern Baptist Theological Seminary, City Line and Lancaster Ave., Philadelphia, PA 19151.

___American Baptist Historical Society, 1100 South Goodman St., Rochester, NY 14620.

Useful histories of Baptists in PA include:

___R. G. Torbet, A SOCIAL HISTORY OF THE PHILADELPHIA BAPTIST ASSOCIATION, Westbrook, Philadelphia, PA, 1944.

___CENTENARY OF ORGANIZED BAPTIST WORK IN AND AROUND PITTSBURGH, Pittsburgh, PA, 1913.

___H. C. Vedder, A HISTORY OF THE BAPTISTS IN THE MIDDLE STATES, American Baptist Publication Society, Philadelphia, PA, 1898.

Several Brethren groups (Dunkards, Seventh Day Baptist, German Baptist) arose in PA from the many German Protestants who settled there or from their descendants. Included were the Brethren in Christ (1778), the Church of the Brethren (1719), and the Church of the United Brethren in Christ (1800). By virtue of several mergers, the last mentioned group is now part of the United Methodist Church (see later). Important archives are:

___Archives of the Brethren in Christ Church, Messiah College, Grantham, PA 17027.

___Brethren Historical Library and Archives, 1451 Dundee Ave., Elgin, IL 60120.

___Library, Juniata College, Huntingdon, PA 16652.

___Seventh Day Baptist Library, Seventh Day Baptist Bldg., Plainfield, NJ 07060.

Among the standard historical works treating the Brethren are:

___M. G. Brumbaugh, HISTORY OF THE GERMAN BAPTIST BRETHREN IN EUROPE AND AMERICA, AMS Press, New York, NY, 1971 (1899), with H. Chance, INDEX TO HISTORY OF THE BRETHREN, Bookmark, Knightstown, IN, 1977 (1969).

___G. M. Falkenstein, GERMAN BAPTIST BRETHREN OR DUNKERS, PA German Society Proceedings, Volume 10 (1899), pp. 5-148.

___EASTERN PA CHURCH OF THE BRETHREN HISTORY, Bookmark, Knightstown, IN, 1915 (1977).

___W. J. Hamilton, TWO CENTURIES OF THE CHURCH OF THE BRETHREN IN WESTERN PA, 1751-1950, Brethren Publishing House, Elgin, IL, 1953.

___H. R. Holsinger, HISTORY OF THE TUNKERS AND THE BRETHREN CHURCH, Bookmark, Knightstown, IN, 1977 (1901).

___THE BRETHREN ENCYCLOPEDIA, Brethren Encyclopedia, Philadelphia, PA, 1983, 3 volumes.

Congregational churches were established in PA by CT settlers who came into the Wyoming Valley during 1761-9. In 1931, the Congregational Church and the Christian Church united to form the Congregational Churches, which in 1957 became part of the United Church of Christ. Archival repositories for Congregational records are:

___Archives of the United Church of Christ, 555 West James St., Lancaster, PA 17603.

___Congregational Library 14 Beacon St., Boston, MA 02108.

___Divinity School Library, Harvard University, Cambridge, MA 02138.

___University and Divinity School Libraries, Yale University, New Haven, CT 06520.

___Library, Hartford Theological Seminary, Hartford, CT 06105.

Among the better works chronicling the history of the Congregational faith are:

___W. Walker, THE HISTORY OF THE CONGREGATIONAL CHURCHES IN THE US, American Church Historical Society, New York, NY, 1894.

___G. G. Atkins and F. L. Fagley, HISTORY OF AMERICAN CONGREGATIONALISM, Pilgrim Press, Boston, MA, 1942.

Episcopalian or Church of England services were first held in PA in 1695 and their primary church in the state, Christ Church in Philadelphia, was established soon thereafter. Records of Episcopal Churches are to be found in the individual parishes, in LHS, and in:

___The History Committee, The Episcopal Diocese of PA, 202 West Rittenhouse Square, Philadelphia, PA 19103.

___The Church Historical Society, Protestant Episcopal Church, 606 Rathervue Place, Austin, TX 78705.

Useful volumes relating to PA Episcopal history include:

___S. M. J. Anderson, HISTORY OF THE CHURCH OF ENGLAND IN THE COLONIES, 3 Volumes, 1845.

___W. S. Perry, HISTORICAL COLLECTIONS RELATING TO THE AMERICAN COLONIAL CHURCH, The Subscribers, Hartford, CT, Volume 2, 1885.

German Reformed church members began coming into PA beginning early in the 1700s. Gradually churches were organized, one of the earliest being at Falkner's Swamp in 1725. In 1934, the German Reformed Church united with the German Evangelical Synod to constitute the Evangelical and Reformed Church. This church then in 1957 joined the Congregational Christian Churches to make up the United Church of

Christ. The major repository for records of the German Reformed churches is:

___Evangelical and Reformed Historical Society, Schaff Library, Franklin and Marshall College, 555 West James St., Lancaster, PA 17603.

Chief among books which treat the early history of the German Reformed congregations are:

___H. S. Dotterer, HISTORICAL NOTES RELATING TO THE PA REFORMED CHURCH, Perkiomen, Philadelphia, PA, 1900.

___J. H. Dubbs, THE REFORMED CHURCH IN PA, PA German Society, Lancaster, PA, 1902.

___C. H. Glatfelter, PASTORS AND PEOPLE: GERMAN LUTHER-AN AND REFORMED CHURCHES IN THE PA FIELD, 1717-93, PA German Society, Philadelphia, PA, 1980.

___W. J. Hinke, MINISTERS OF THE GERMAN REFORMED CONGREGATIONS, Historical Commission of the Evangelical and Reformed Church, Lancaster, PA, 1951.

___PA GERMAN CHURCH RECORDS, Genealogical Publishing Co., Baltimore, MD, 1983, 3 volumes.

Jewish religious activity in the state of PA brought about the dedication of the first PA synagogue in 1782 at Philadelphia. Records of Jewish congregations may be sought in the following places (in addition to the individual synagogues):

___Philadelphia Jewish Archives Center, Balch Institute, 18 South 7th St., Philadelphia, PA, 19106.

___American Jewish Archives, 3101 Clifton Ave., Cincinnati, OH 45220.

___American Jewish Historical Society, 2 Thornton Rd., Waltham, MA 02154.

Historical works which are of value for tracing PA Jewish religious groups include:

___H. P. Rosenbach, HISTORY OF THE JEWS OF PHILADELPHIA, Stern, Philadelphia, PA, 1883.

___E. Wolf and M. Whiteman, THE HISTORY OF THE JEWS OF PHILADELPHIA FROM COLONIAL TIMES TO THE AGE OF JACKSON, Jewish Publication Society, Philadelphia, PA, 1957.

___J. R. Marcus, EARLY AMERICAN JEWRY, 1655-1790, Jewish Publication Society, Philadelphia, PA, 1951-3, 2 Volumes.

Lutherans from Sweden and Holland settled early on the DE River, and English Lutherans were meeting in Philadelphia in 1694. The major Lutheran history of PA, however, centers on the Germans, who organized their first congregation at New Hanover in 1703. Archives having good record collections for PA churches are:

___Central PA Lutheran Synod, 2600 North Third St., Harrisburg, PA 17110.

___Wentz Library, Lutheran Theological Seminary, Gettysburg College, Gettysburg, PA 17325.

___Lutheran Archives Center, 7301 Germantown Ave., Mt. Airy, Philadelphia, PA 19119.

___Library and Archives, Thiel College, Greenville, PA 16125.

The repository at Gettysburg has translations of most colonial Lutheran church registers plus many records for the period after the Revolutionary War. There are also some very useful guidebooks to Lutheran records in the counties of central PA:

___F. S. Weiser, GUIDES TO CENTRAL PA LUTHERAN CHURCH RECORDS, The Author, New Oxford, PA, 1980-2. [One for each county.]

There are also many Lutheran records in LHS. Basic for PA Lutheran history are:

___T. E. Schmunk, THE LUTHERAN CHURCH IN PA, 1638-1820, General Council, Philadelphia, PA, 1903.

___C. H. Glatfelter, PASTORS AND PEOPLE: GERMAN LUTHERAN AND REFORMED CHURCHES IN THE PA FIELD, 1717-93, PA German Society, Breinigsville, PA, 1980-1, 2 volumes.

The Mennonites, Germans who were basically Anabaptist in faith, settled at Germantown in 1682-3. There were also quite a number of later Mennonites who were Swiss and a conservative branch which was known as the Amish. Good sources of records are:

___Lancaster Mennonite Conference Historical Society, 2215 Mill Stream Rd., Lancaster, PA 17602.

___Menno Simons Historical Library and Archives, Eastern Mennonite College, Harrisonburg, VA 22801.

___The Archives of the Mennonite Church, 1700 South Main St., Goshen, IN 46526.

Among the useful historical and reference works for these groups are the following:

___C. H. Smith and H. S. Bender, THE MENNONITE ENCYCLOPEDIA: A COMPREHENSIVE REFERENCE WORK ON THE BAPTIST-MENNONITE MOVEMENT, Mennonite Brethren Publishing House, Hillsboro, KS, 4 Volumes, 1955-9.

___C. H. Smith, MENNONITE IMMIGRATION TO PA IN THE 18TH CENTURY, PA German Society Proceedings, Volume 35, PA German Society, Philadelphia, PA, 1929.

___C. G. Bachman, THE OLD ORDER AMISH OF LANCASTER COUNTY, PA German Society, Lancaster, PA, 1942.

___H. E. Cross and B. Hostetler, INDEX TO SELECT AMISH GENE-ALOGIES, John Hopkins University, Baltimore, MD, 1970.

___C. J. Dyck, AN INTRODUCTION TO MENNONITE HISTORY, Lancaster Mennonite Historical Society, Lancaster, PA, 1993.

___S. M. Nolt, A HISTORY OF THE AMISH, Lancaster Mennonite Historical Society, Lancaster, PA, 1992.

The Methodist denomination began in 1768 when services were first held in Philadelphia. The church expanded very rapidly as its circuit-riding ministers accompanied settlers who pressed westward in the state. The present day United Methodist Church rose in 1968 from the unification of the Methodist Church and the Evangelical United Brethren Church. The Evangelical United Brethren Church was formed in 1946 with the merger of the Evangelical Church and the United Brethren in Christ, both of which had originated in PA among German settlers in the early 1800s. The major repositories for PA include:

___Historical Society of the Philadelphia Annual Methodist Conference, 326 New St., Philadelphia, PA 19106.

___Archives Room, Academic Bldg., Lycoming College, 1400 West Fourth St., Williamsport, PA 17701. [Records for central PA.]

___Historical Society, Western PA Methodist Conference, R. D. 1, Box 316A, Apollo, PA 15613.

___United Methodist Archives Center, General Commission on Archives and History, Drew University, Madison, NJ 07940.

Among the more useful historical works dealing with the Methodists and their copartners in the United Methodist Church are:

___A. Stevens, HISTORY OF THE METHODIST EPISCOPAL CHURCH IN THE US, Carlton & Porter, New York, NY, 1864-7, 4 Volumes.

___W. C. Barclay, EARLY AMERICAN METHODISM 1769-1844, Board of Missions, Methodist Church, New York, NY, 1949.

___S. M. Stiles, METHODISM IN PA, The Author, Philadelphia, PA, 1871.

___R. W. Albright, HISTORY OF THE EVANGELICAL CHURCH, Evangelical Press, New Berlin, PA, 1942.

___J. W. Owen, A SHORT HISTORY OF THE CHURCH OF THE

UNITED BRETHREN IN CHRIST, United Brethren General Board of Education, Dayton, OH, 1944.

Moravian church members founded Bethlehem, Nazareth, and Lititz, PA in 1740. The record depository for this religious group is:
___The Archives of the Moravian Church, 66 West Church St., Bethlehem, PA 18018.
Histories of the denomination include:
___E. A. DeSchweinitz, HISTORY OF THE CHURCH KNOWN AS UNITAS FRATRUM OR THE UNITY OF THE BRETHREN, Moravian Publ. Concern, Bethlehem, PA, 1901.
___J. M. Levering, HISTORY OF BETHLEHEM, PA, 1741-1872, Times, Bethlehem, PA, 1903.

Presbyterian history in PA goes back to 1692 when services were held in Philadelphia. Records for this large denomination may be found in the local churches, in various libraries and archives in PA, and in:
___History Department, Presbyterian Church, 520 Witherspoon Bldg., 425 Lombard St., Philadelphia, PA 19147. [See the special Biographical Index to books, newspapers, and periodicals.]
For the history of the Presbyterian movement in PA, consult:
___G. S. Klett, PRESBYTERIANS IN COLONIAL PA, University of PA Press, Philadelphia, PA, 1937.
___M. W. Armstrong, A. L. Lefferts, and C. A. Anderson, THE PRESBYTERIAN ENTERPRISE: SOURCES OF AMERICAN PRESBYTERIAN HISTORY, Westminster Press, Philadelphia, PA, 1956.

The Quakers (Society of Friends) were the strongest religious denomination in the very early years of the colony of PA and their influence dominated many aspects of the culture up until the American Revolution. The origin of PA was co-extensive with the coming of William Penn and the Quakers in 1682. Even before this time, a few Quakers had held the first PA Quaker meeting in 1675 near Chester. Important repositories for the records of this religious society are:
___Friends Historical Library, Swarthmore College, Swarthmore, PA 19081. [Many records, also a large card index of thousands of names.]
___Magill Historical Library, Haverford College, Haverford, PA 19041.
___Department of Records, Quaker Philadelphia Yearly Meeting, 302 Arch St., Philadelphia, PA 19106.
Important historical works, some of which contain many names and indexes, include:

___W. W. Hinshaw, ENCYCLOPEDIA OF AMERICAN QUAKER GENEALOGY, Genealogical Publishing Co., Baltimore, MD, 1969/91 (1938/46), Volume 2. [Many names.]

___W. Heiss, QUAKER BIOGRAPHICAL SKETCHES OF THE YEARLY MEETING OF PHILADELPHIA, 1682-1800, Indianapolis, IN, 1972.

___W. W. Hinshaw, INDEX TO QUAKER MEETING RECORDS IN THE FRIENDS' LIBRARY IN SWARTHMORE COLLEGE, Swarthmore, PA 19081.

___PA Historical Survey of the WPA, INVENTORY OF [PA QUAKER] CHURCH ARCHIVES, Society of Friends, Philadelphia, PA, 1941.

___A. C. Myers, QUAKER ARRIVALS AT PHILADELPHIA, 1682-1750, Genealogical Publishing Co., Baltimore, MD, 1978 (1902).

___Elbert Russell, HISTORY OF QUAKERISM, MacMillan, New York, NY, 1942.

___R. M. Jones, THE LATER PERIODS OF QUAKERISM, MacMillan, New York, NY, 1921, 2 Volumes.

___W. W. Comfort, THE QUAKERS, PA Historical Assn., University Park, PA, 1948.

The Roman Catholic denomination in PA traces its origin to St. Joseph's parish which was established in Philadelphia in 1732. In searching for Catholic records, inquiries should be made first at the parish level, then if that is not successful, try the diocese. Addresses for both will be found in:

___THE OFFICIAL CATHOLIC DIRECTORY, Kenedy and Sons, Skokie, IL, latest edition.

Further inquiries may be made at:

___Archives of the American Catholic Historical Society of Philadelphia, St. Charles Boromeo Seminary, Overbrook, Philadelphia, PA 19151.

For reading on the history of the Roman Catholics in PA, consult:

___E. Adams and B. B. O'Keefe, CATHOLIC TRAILS WEST, THE FOUNDING CATHOLIC FAMILIES OF PA, Genealogical Publishing Co., Baltimore, MD, 1988.

___J. T. Ellis, CATHOLICS IN COLONIAL AMERICA, Helicon Press, Baltimore, MD, 1963.

___L. G. Fink, OLD JESUIT TRAILS IN PENN'S FOREST, Paulist Press, New York, NY, 1933.

Among the small German sects which came to PA were the Schwenkfelders who arrived in Philadelphia in 1733-4. Many of their records are to be found in:

___Schwenkfelder Library, Seminary Ave., Pennsburg, PA 18073.

Genealogical records of numerous of their families are printed in:
___ S. K. Brecht, THE GENEALOGICAL RECORD OF THE
SCHWENKFELDER FAMILIES, Rand McNally, New York, NY,
1923.
___ R. Kriebel, GENEALOGICAL RECORDS OF THE DESCEN-
DANTS OF THE SCHWENKFELDERS WHO ARRIVED IN PA,
1733-7, Yeakel, Manayunk, PA, 1879.
And their history is chronicled in
___ H. W. Kriebel, SCHWENKFELDERS IN PA, New Era, Lancaster,
PA, 1904.

As you search for your ancestor's church records, you need to carefully bear in mind the wide variety of places where the records may be.
The original, transcribed, microfilmed, and/or published records may be
located in the local church, in local libraries or archives (city, county,
college, university, society), in regional libraries or archives (university,
church, society), in state-wide libraries or archives (state government,
church, society), or even in national libraries or archives (federal government, church, society).   Helpful places to inquire as to the
whereabouts of the records include the local church, local societies, local
libraries, denominational headquarters and archives (as listed above), and
SLP, LHS, CLP, and FHL (FHC). When seeking church records in a
library or archives card catalog, you should look under the county name,
the church name, and the denomination name. In addition, the reference
works mentioned in the third paragraph of this section should be consulted.   Church records are also often found in several other sources
which are discussed in different sections of this chapter: cemetery (section
5), city and county histories (section 9), colonial (10), DAR, ethnic (15),
genealogical indexes and compilations (17), genealogical periodicals (18),
manuscripts (21), mortuary (27), newspaper (29), published genealogies
(30), regional records (31), and WPA records. Denominational histories,
in addition to those listed above, along with some volumes containing
names will be listed in:
___ N. B. Wilkinson, BIBLIOGRAPHY OF PA HISTORY, PA Historical
and Museum Commission, Harrisburg, PA, 1957, with C. Wall,
SUPPLEMENT TO BIBLIOGRAPHY OF PA HISTORY, PA
Historical and Museum Commission, Harrisburg, PA, 1977, and J. B.
B. Trussell, PA BIBLIOGRAPHY, PA Historical and Museum
Commission, Harrisburg, PA, 1980; and J. B. B. Trussell, PA HIS-
TORICAL BIBLIOGRAPHY IV, PA Historical and Museum Com-
mission, Harrisburg, PA, 1983.

___D. E. Washburn, THE PEOPLES OF PA, University of Pittsburgh, Pittsburgh, PA, 1981.

Several volumes of church records have been published, some of the earlier and/or more extensive ones being:

___J. Cuthbertson, REGISTER OF MARRIAGES AND BAPTISMS PERFORMED BY REV. JOHN CUTHBERTSON, 1754-91, Genealogical Publishing Co., Baltimore, MD, 1934 (1983).

___C. A. Fisher, CENTRAL PA MARRIAGES, 1700-1896, Genealogical Publishing Co., Baltimore, MD, 1946 (1982).

___C. R. Hildeburn, BAPTISMS AND BURIALS FROM THE RECORDS OF CHRIST CHURCH, PHILADELPHIA, 1709-60, Genealogical Publishing Co., Baltimore, MD, 1877-93 (1982).

___D. R. Irish, PA GERMAN MARRIAGES, Genealogical Publishing Co., Baltimore, MD, 1984.

___PA German Society, PA GERMAN CHURCH RECORDS OF BIRTHS, BAPTISMS, MARRIAGES, BURIALS, Genealogical Publishing Co., Baltimore, MD, 1983, 3 volumes.

___J. C. Stoever, EARLY LUTHERAN BAPTISMS AND MARRIAGES IN SOUTHEASTERN PA, Genealogical Publishing Co., Baltimore, MD, 1896 (1984).

___T. C. Tappert and J. W. Doberstein, THE JOURNALS OF HENRY M. MUHLENBERG, Muhlenberg Press, Philadelphia, PA, 1942-58, 3 volumes.

___F. Weis, COLONIAL CLERGY OF THE MIDDLE COLONIES: NY, NJ, PA, 1628-1776, American Antiquarian Society, Worcester, MA, 1957.

8. City directories

During the late 18th century and throughout the 19th many larger cities in PA began publishing city directories. These volumes usually appeared erratically at first, but then began to come out regularly (annually or biennially) later on. They usually list heads of households and workers plus their home addresses and their occupations, and sometimes the names and addresses of their places of employment. Businesses, professions, institutions, churches, and organizations are also usually listed.

Notable among the PA city directories are those of the following cities. For each of these cities, the earliest and a few of the succeeding directories are listed, then afterwards a date from which publication became fairly regular (annually or biennially): Erie (1853/4/7/9, 1861-),

Harrisburg (1839/42/3/5, 1860-), Lancaster (1843/53/7/9, 1861-), Philadelphia (1785/91/3, 1794-), Pittsburgh (1813/5/9/26/37, 1839-), Reading (1806/56, 1860-). For each of the following cities, the earliest directory is listed: Allentown (1864), Altoona (1873), Bethlehem (1864), Chester (1859), New Castle (1841), Norristown (1860), Scranton (1861), West Chester (1857), Wilkes-Barre (1871), Williamsport (1866), York (1877). There were also some early county or regional directories, some of them being business listings only. Among them were those for Bucks (1884), Crawford (1874), Erie (1859), Lancaster (1859), Lebanon (1880), Lehigh (1885), Mercer (1898), Monongahela Valley (1859), PA Regional (1860). There was also a PA Law Directory (in 1844) and a PA Business Directory (for 1854).

Many of the directories mentioned in the previous paragraph have been microfilmed, quite a few of them through the 1901 volume. The microfilms and/or the original directories should be sought in the Library of Congress, SLP, LHS, CLP, Hillman Library of Pittsburgh, RL, and LL. Other cities also issued directories, usually at dates later than the above ones started, but you should not fail to look for them, especially in RL and LL in the pertinent places.

The telephone was invented in 1876-7, underwent rapid development, and became widespread fairly rapidly. By the late years of the century telephone directories were coming into existence. Older issues can often be found in LL, and as the years have gone on, they have proved to be ever more valuable genealogical sources.

----

9. City and county histories

Histories for many PA counties and numerous PA cities have been published. These volumes usually contain biographical data on leading citizens, details about early settlers, histories, organizations, businesses, trades, and churches, and often list clergymen, lawyers, physicians, teachers, governmental officials, farmers, military men, and other groups. Several works which list many of these histories are:

___M. J. Kaminkow, US LOCAL HISTORIES IN THE LIBRARY OF CONGRESS, Magna Carta, Baltimore, MD, 1975, 4 volumes.
___P. W. Filby, BIBLIOGRAPHY OF COUNTY HISTORIES IN AMERICA, Genealogical Publishing Co., Baltimore, MD, 1985.
___New York Public Library, US LOCAL HISTORY CATALOG, Hall, Boston, MA, 1974.

___N. B. Wilkinson, BIBLIOGRAPHY OF PA HISTORY, PA Historical and Museum Commission, Harrisburg, PA, 1957, with C. Wall, SUPPLEMENT TO BIBLIOGRAPHY OF PA HISTORY, PA Historical and Museum Commission, Harrisburg, PA, 1977, and J. B. B. Trussell, PA BIBLIOGRAPHY, PA Historical and Museum Commission, Harrisburg, PA, 1980, and J. B. B. Trussell, PA HISTORICAL BIBLIOGRAPHY IV, PA Historical and Museum Commission, Harrisburg, PA, 1983.

Most of the PA volumes in these bibliographies can be found in SLP, LHS, CLP, and the Library of Congress in Washington, DC, and some are usually in LGL. RL and LL are likely to have those relating to their particular areas. A sizable number of the earlier PA county histories have been microfilmed, and this has made them more broadly available. In Chapter 4, you will find listed under the counties the dates on which county histories are available. There will also be an indication under each county which has city and/or town and/or township histories available. In libraries, the easiest way to find local histories is to look under the names of the county, the city, and the town.

In the Carnegie Library in Pittsburgh (CLP) there is an exceptionally useful card index. This finding aid includes names of biographees from the county histories which CLP has in its collection. Since their collection is an exceptionally large one, this index has a very broad coverage and should not be overlooked.

___INDEX TO PA COUNTY HISTORY BIOGRAPHIES, CLP, Pittsburgh, PA.

---

10. Colonial record compilations

The colonial period for PA extended from 1682 until 1775, during which time the area was a colony of Great Britain. Many other sections in this chapter describe specific types of records relating to colonial PA, particularly sections 3, 5, 7, 9, 11, 15, 16, 17, 18, 22, 23, 25, 31, 32, 33, 34, and 35. This section, therefore, will be made up of two sub-sections, one dealing with general reference materials to all the colonies (including PA), a second dealing with general reference materials to colonial PA.

Among the most important genealogical materials relating to all the colonies are the following. They should be consulted for your colonial PA ancestor. However, some of the volumes must be used with care since some of the information in them is not from original sources, and is therefore often inaccurate.

___F. A. Virkus, THE ABRIDGED COMPENDIUM OF AMERICAN GENEALOGY, Genealogical Publishing Co., Baltimore, MD, 1968 (1925-42), 7 volumes. [425,000 names of colonial people]

___G. M. MacKenzie and N. O. Rhoades, COLONIAL FAMILIES OF THE USA, Genealogical Publishing Co., Baltimore, MD, 1966 (1907-20), 7 volumes. [125,000 names]

___H. Whittemore, GENEALOGICAL GUIDE TO THE EARLY SETTLERS OF AMERICA, Genealogical Publishing Co., Baltimore, MD, 1967 (1898-1906).

___T. P. Hughes and others, AMERICAN ANCESTRY, Genealogical Publishing Co., Baltimore, MD, 1968 (1887-9), 12 volumes.

___BURKE'S DISTINGUISHED FAMILIES OF AMERICA, Burke's Peerage, London, England, 1948.

___W. M. Clemens, AMERICAN MARRIAGE RECORDS BEFORE 1699, Genealogical Publishing Co., Baltimore, MD, 1867 (1926-30). [10,000 entries]

___C. E. Banks, PLANTERS OF THE COMMONWEALTH, Genealogical Publishing Co., Baltimore, MD, 1972.

___G. R. Crowther, III, SURNAME INDEX TO 65 VOLUMES OF COLONIAL AND REVOLUTIONARY PEDIGREES, National Genealogical Society, Washington, DC, 1975.

___M. B. Colket, Jr., FOUNDERS OF EARLY AMERICAN FAMILIES, Order of Founders and Patriots of America, Cleveland, OH, 1975.

___H. K. Eilers, NSDAC BICENTENNIAL ANCESTOR INDEX, National Society Daughters of American Colonists, Ft. Worth, TX, 1976.

___National Society of Daughters of Founders and Patriots of America, FOUNDERS AND PATRIOTS OF AMERICA INDEX, The Society, Washington, DC, 1975.

___National Society of the Colonial Dames of America, REGISTER OF ANCESTORS, The Society, Richmond, VA, 1979.

___N. Currer-Briggs, COLONIAL SETTLERS AND ENGLISH ADVENTURERS, Genealogical Publishing Co., Baltimore, MD, 1971.

___P. W. Filby and M. K. Meyer, PASSENGER AND IMMIGRATION LIST INDEX, Gale Research, Detroit, MI, 1981, 3 volumes, plus annual SUPPLEMENTS. [500 sources, 1,000,000 names]

___G. F. T. Sherwood, AMERICAN COLONISTS IN ENGLISH RECORDS, Sherwood, London, England, 1932, 2 Volumes.

___P. W. Coldham, ENGLISH ESTATES OF AMERICAN COLO-
NISTS, Genealogical Publishing Co., Baltimore, MD, 1980-1, 3
volumes.

___J. C. Hotten, THE ORIGINAL LISTS OF PERSONS OF QUAL-
ITY, Genealogical Publishing Co., Baltimore, MD, 1980 (1874).

___National Society Colonial Daughters of the 17th Century, LINEAGE
BOOK, The Society, Rotan, TX, 1982 (1979). [2000 names]

___Daughters of the American Revolution, DAR PATRIOT INDEX,
The Daughters, Washington, DC, latest edition.

___National Genealogical Society, INDEX OF REVOLUTIONARY
WAR PENSION APPLICATIONS IN THE NATIONAL AR-
CHIVES, The Society, Washington, DC, 1976.

___F. Rider, THE AMERICAN GENEALOGICAL BIOGRAPHICAL
INDEX, Godfrey Memorial Library, Middletown, CT, 1942-52, 48
volumes; also F. Rider, AMERICAN GENEALOGICAL BIO-
GRAPHICAL INDEX, Godfrey Memorial Library, Middletown, CT,
new series, 1952-, in process, over 180 volumes published.

There are also important genealogical and historical compendia and
indexes relating specifically to colonial PA which you should search. The
most important of these is:

___[PUBLISHED] PA ARCHIVES, AMS Press, New York, NY,
1838-1935 (1971-6), 128 volumes arranged in ten series: Colonial
records (16 volumes), Series 1 (12 volumes), Series 2 (19 volumes),
Series 3 (31 volumes), Series 4 (12 volumes), Series 5 (8 volumes),
Series 6 (15 volumes), Series 7 (5 volumes), Series 8 (8 volumes),
Series 9 (10 volumes).

These 128 volumes resulted from the publication of large amounts of the
archival records of PA during the years 1838 through 1935. Notice that
there are ten series of volumes: a so-called Colonial Records series plus
nine further series (numbered 1 through 9), making a total of ten series.
They contain a vast amount of information relating to the Colonial period
of PA (and after). The volumes which contain sizable Colonial materials
are as follows [the series is listed first as a C for Colonial or a number,
then the volume is given in parentheses): C(1-16), 1(1-12), 2(2, 5-9,
16-19), 3(1-4, 8-12, 14, 17-19, 22, 24-26), 4(1-3), 5(1), 6(6, 11), 8(1-8).
The easiest way to examine these records for your ancestor is to make
use of the indexes in the records [the series is listed first, then the volume
in parentheses, then the pages]. For example, the listing 4(12)643-963
means 4th Series, Volume 12, pages 643 through 963.

___INDEXES IN THE [PUBLISHED] PA ARCHIVES AMS Press, New York, NY, 1838-1935 (1971-6): C(Volume entitled GENERAL INDEX TO THE COLONIAL RECORDS AND PA ARCHIVES)1-433, 1(Volume entitled GENERAL INDEX TO THE COLONIAL RECORDS AND PA ARCHIVES)437-653, 2(Indexes at end of each volume except 8-11 and 13), 3(27)i-331, 3(27)337-790, 3(28), 3(29), 3(30), 4(Indexes at end of each volume), 4(12)643-963, 6(15), 7(1-5), 8(No published index, manuscript index at PSA), 9(No published index, incomplete card file index at PSA).
___M. Dunn, INDEX TO PA'S COLONIAL RECORD SERIES, Genealogical Publishing Co., Baltimore, MD, 1992.

When you have examined these indexes, you will have searched a very large volume of records applying both to colonial and post-colonial times. However, you need to be aware that some of the indexes are only partial (particularly some of those in Series 3), and also that a few volumes are unindexed (tables of contents only for volume 3 and 10 of Series 3, for example). Many sorts of records are gathered in the [PUBLISHED] PA ARCHIVES including colonial government, military, church, land, immigrant, and tax.

In addition to the [PUBLISHED] PA ARCHIVES (PPA), there are also a number of other useful published works dealing with colonial records which may not be mentioned in other sections. Among them are:
___J. G. B. Bullock, ORDER OF WASHINGTON, 1914. [A society of people with colonial ancestors.]
___M. Gubi, Mrs. R. C. Clarke, and Mrs. H. A. Best, HISTORY OF THE PA STATE SOCIETY OF THE DAUGHTERS OF THE AMERICAN COLONISTS, The Daughters, Pittsburgh, PA, 1969.
___J. W. Jordan, W. Jordan, and T. H. Bateman, COLONIAL AND REVOLUTIONARY FAMILIES OF PA, GENEALOGICAL AND PERSONAL MEMOIRS, Genealogical Publishing Co., Baltimore, MD, 1911-65 (1978), 17 volumes.
___D. H. Kent, M. L. Simonetti, G. Dailey, and G. R. Beyer, GUIDE TO THE MICROFILM OF THE RECORDS OF THE PROVINCIAL COUNCIL, 1682-1776, PA Historical and Museum Commission, Harrisburg, PA, 1966.
___National Society of Colonial Dames of America in the Commonwealth of PA, REGISTER OF MEMBERS AND ANCESTORS, The Society, Philadelphia, PA, editions of 1898, 1902, 1907, 1928, 1951, 1976.

━━━━━━━━━━━━━━

11. Court records

━━━━━━━━━━━━━━

As was discussed in section 10 of Chapter 1, which dealt with PA government, PA has three levels of courts. These are the Local Courts at the township, borough, and city level (Justice of Peace, Magistrate, Alderman), the District Courts at the county level (Court of Common Pleas, Court of Oyer and Terminer and Jail Delivery, Court of Quarter Sessions of the Peace, Orphans' Court), and the State Courts at the state level (Superior Court, Supreme Court). The Local Courts handle minor cases. The District (County) Courts and the matters they handle are: Court of Common Pleas (civil suits), Court of Oyer and Terminer and Jail Delivery (major criminal cases), Court of Quarter Sessions of the Peace (lesser criminal cases), Orphans' Court (estates, guardianships). In 1681/2 when PA was being established, County Courts were set up, and appeals could be put before the Provincial Council. In 1684, a Provincial Court was authorized to hear appeals and to conduct trials. Until 1701, both the Provincial Council and the Provincial Court exercised judicial functions, but after that date only the Provincial Court did so. In 1706, the Provincial Court was first designated as the Supreme Court, and actions in 1710 and 1722 made this designation official. The justices of this court held court in several places (called Supreme Court districts) to accommodate the people. The court acted as both a trial court and as an appeals court until 1874, when it became only an appeals court. To relieve the Supreme Court of its heavy load, an intermediate appeals court, the Superior Court, was set up in 1895. Many of the records of the Local and District Courts and some of those of the Supreme and Superior Courts have definite genealogical value, and must not be overlooked by any researcher hoping to do a thorough job.

Some of the valuable records of the Local and District Courts or of officials associated with them are treated in other sections of this chapter (birth, death, divorce, land, marriage, naturalization, tax, will, estate, guardian). Therefore, the other major category of Local and District Court records will be discussed here: the records of the cases (both civil and criminal) brought before the trial courts (Court of Common Pleas, Court of Oyer and Terminer and Jail Delivery, Court of Quarter Sessions of the Peace). Sometimes you will find indexes to these case records, but often there will be none, or they will be selective, partial, or incomplete. Practically every court maintained one or more dockets, which were simply chronological listings of the cases the court heard. When indexes do not exist, the docket can be scanned to see if you can pick up your ancestor's name. Be careful to examine all dockets, since courts frequently kept several kinds dealing with different sorts of cases. The next kind of record kept by courts is called the <u>minutes</u>, these being brief notes describing the actions and decisions of the court in chronological order. The records are usually not indexed, but they can generally be searched through fairly rapidly because of their brevity. Another sort of record which you may expect to find consists of <u>orders</u> and <u>judgments</u>, these being more detailed records of orders, decisions, proceedings, actions, and awards made by the court. They are likely to be found under numerous headings such as journals, writs, presentments, executions, decrees, verdicts, decisions, and reports. Finally, there are the <u>case</u> <u>files</u> or packets. These files are made up of the original papers which the court considered and recorded as it acted upon the case: affidavits, writs, evidence, testimonies, subpoenas. These files are usually of exceptional genealogical value because they often have a great deal of detailed family information in them. They consist of copies of evidence, testimony, documentation, court proceedings and other information too voluminous to record in the minutes, orders, or judgments, Information provided in the dockets, minutes, orders, and judgments, especially the dates of the cases, will lead you to the case files. All of the above-mentioned case records need to be sought in the court houses of the PA counties.

Records of the PA Supreme Court (1740-1971) and the PA Superior Court (1895-1967) are largely to be found in Record Groups 33 and 38, respectively, in the PSA in Harrisburg. Among the records of genealogical importance are:

___NATURALIZATION LISTS OF THE SUPREME COURT AND COURTS OF NISI PRIUS, 1740-73, Record Group 21, PSA, Harrisburg, PA. [Printed as PPA 2(2) and M. S. Giuseppi, NATURALIZATION OF FOREIGN PROTESTANTS IN THE AMERICAN AND WEST INDIAN COLONIES, Huguenot Society of London, London, England, 1921.]

___NATURALIZATION PAPERS, SUPREME COURT, Eastern District, 1794-1868, Record Group 33, PSA, Harrisburg, PA. [Arranged chronologically.]

___INDEX TO NATURALIZATION PAPERS, SUPREME COURT, Eastern District, 1794-1824, 1842-68, Record Group 33, PSA, Harrisburg, PA.

___NATURALIZATION PAPERS, SUPREME COURT, Southern District, 1815-29, Record Group 33, PSA, Harrisburg, PA. [Arranged chronologically.]

__NATURALIZATION PAPERS, SUPREME COURT, Western District, 1831, 1840-1, 1844-56, Record Group 33, PSA, Harrisburg, PA. [Arranged by years, then alphabetically.]

__NATURALIZATION DOCKET, SUPREME COURT, Western District, 1812-67, Record Group 33, PSA, Harrisburg, PA. [Alphabetical.]

__DECLARATIONS OF INTENTION, SUPREME COURT, Eastern District, 1832-70, 1873-5, 1881-1906, Record Group 33, PSA, Harrisburg, PA. [Partial indexes, but somewhat unreliable.]

__DIVORCE PAPERS, SUPREME COURT, Eastern District, 1786-1815, Record Group 33, PSA, Harrisburg, PA. [Alphabetical.]

__GENERAL MOTIONS (1750-1837) AND DIVORCE DOCKET (1800-5), SUPREME COURT, Group 33, PSA, Harrisburg, PA. [Arranged by date.]

__CORONER'S INQUISITIONS, SUPREME COURT, 1751, 1768-90, 1792-6, Record Group 33, PSA, Harrisburg, PA. [Investigations of out of the ordinary deaths.]

__ESCHEATS, SUPREME COURT, 1796-1822, Record Group 33, PSA, Harrisburg, PA. [Persons dying without heirs.]

__REVOLUTIONARY WAR PENSION FILE, SUPREME COURT AND ORPHANS' COURT, 1785-1809, Record Group 4, PSA, Harrisburg, PA. [Alphabetical.]

__REVOLUTIONARY WAR SOLDIERS' CLAIMS, SUPREME COURT, Eastern District, PSA, Harrisburg, PA. [Alphabetical.]

__COURTS OF OYER AND TERMINER AND GENERAL GAOL DELIVERY DOCKETS, SUPREME COURT, 1778-1828, PSA, Harrisburg, PA. [Criminal cases arranged chronologically.]

Many other documents of the Supreme and Superior Courts are listed in:

__R. M. Dructor, GUIDE TO GENEALOGICAL SOURCES AT THE PSA, PA Museum and Historical Commission, Harrisburg, PA, 1980. [See index.]

__F. M. Suran, GUIDE TO RECORD GROUPS IN THE PSA, PA Museum and Historical Commission, Harrisburg, PA, 1980. [See index.]

Included among the other records listed in these two guides are dockets, minutes, case files, papers, executions, jury lists, petitions, registrations of attorneys, and other documents.

Numerous actions of the lower courts were appealed to the Supreme and Superior Courts of PA. PA cases were also tried and decided in the US Supreme Court, Court of Appeals, Federal Court, and Federal District Courts. Many of these cases are listed in the following volumes:

__1906 DECENNIAL EDITION OF THE AMERICAN DIGEST: A COMPLETE TABLE OF AMERICAN CASES FROM 1658 TO 1906, West Publishing Co., St. Paul, MN, 1911, volumes 21-25. [Alphabetical by surname.]

__VALE PA DIGEST, TABLE OF CASES, 1682-1950, West Publishing Co., St. Paul, MN, 1950, volumes 44-44A. [Alphabetical by surname.] Do not fail to look your PA ancestor up in these volumes. They will be found in most law libraries in PA and in larger law libraries outside the state. The references in the books will lead you to printed detailed descriptions of the cases.

Many cases were not heard by the courts mentioned above, but by PA legislative or administrative agencies. Quite a number of these and numerous other legal matters may have involved your ancestors. Many references to PA laws and statutes may be found in:

__C. C. Livengood, GENEALOGICAL ABSTRACTS OF THE LAWS OF PA AND THE STATUTES AT LARGE, Family Line Publications, Westminster, MD, 1990.

12. Death records

During the early formative years of the colony of PA (1647-82) a law was passed requiring death registration, but the regulation was largely ignored. Thus for a long period 1682-1851 almost no official state or county records of deaths were kept. Two exceptions are the following records which are found in PSA:

__PA CORONER'S INQUISITIONS, 1751, 1768-90, 1792-6, Record Group 33, PSA, Harrisburg, PA. [Inquiries into questionable deaths.]

__PA ESCHEATS, 1796-1822, Record Group 33, PSA, Harrisburg, PA. [People who died without a will and without heirs.]

Both of the types of documents give approximate dates of death. During the few years 1852-4, the Register of Wills in each county was required to maintain death records and to send duplicates to the state. However, reporting to the Register was often not done, so the records are far from being complete and some of them have since been lost. The registrations include name, age, place, date, cause, burial place, and sometimes names of parents, spouse, and/or children. The surviving originals of these death reports are in CH, LL, or PSA. Microfilm copies of many of them are in PSA and FHL, the latter being available through FHC. The records in PSA have been gathered together and are available as:

___RECORD AND INDEXES OF BIRTHS, DEATHS, AND
MARRIAGES, 1852-4, Record Group 26, PSA, Harrisburg, PA,
originals and 6 microfilm rolls.

Not all counties are included in this collection and hence it is necessary
for you to search the CH, LL, and FHL holdings in the cases of omitted
counties. In Chapter 4, those counties whose 1852-4 records are in PSA
and/or FHL are indicated.

For the time span 1855-93, no official state or county death records
were kept, but some cities maintained registers. Chief among these are
the following:

___PHILADELPHIA DEATH RECORDS, 1803-1915, alphabetically by
year, also indexes, Vital Statistics, Philadelphia Department of Public
Health, City Hall Annex, Philadelphia, PA 19107.

___PITTSBURGH DEATH RECORDS, 1851-7, 1870-1905, Office of
Bio-statistics, Pittsburgh Health Department, City-County Bldg., Pittsburgh, PA 15219; microfilms at CLP.

___ALLEGHENY CITY DEATH RECORDS, 1882-1905, Office of Bio-
statistics, Pittsburgh Health Department, City-County Bldg., Pittsburgh, PA 15219.

___HARRISBURG REGISTER OF DEATHS, 1883-6, 1892, Record
Group 48, PSA, Harrisburg, PA.

___POTTSVILLE BOARD OF HEALTH MINUTE BOOKS, 1872-4,
Record Group 48, PSA, Harrisburg, PA.

___EASTON RECORD OF BIRTHS, DEATHS, AND BURIALS,
1888-1907, Record Group 48, PSA, Harrisburg, PA.

In 1893, a new law required deaths to be reported to the County Clerk of
Orphans Court who was to keep records. This situation continued
through 1905, and thus for deaths during 1893-1905, the records were
filed in the counties. The originals or copies of many of these records are
in PSA and/or FHL, but for a number of counties, they remain in the CH
(Clerk of Orphans' Court) or LL. Those counties for which the records
are in PSA and/or FHL are indicated in Chapter 4.

As of 01 January 1906, according to law, the state of PA began regis-
tering deaths. The counties gathered the data and then forwarded them
to the PA Division of Vital Statistics. In the short time of about a year
(by 1907) 90% completeness in the registration was being attained. The
certificates contain name, place, date, marital status, cause, burial place,
and parents, including the mother's maiden name. Copies of death
certificates may be obtained from PA Division of Vital Statistics, PO Box
1528, New Castle, PA 16103. You need to give them the name, the

approximate year of birth, any further information you can, your relationship to the person, the reason you want the data (genealogical research), and the fee (check with them for the amount). Since PA is so short on official death records before 1893, other types of records have to be consulted. Among the better ones (with the section of this chapter where they are treated) are Bible (section 2), biography (3), cemetery (5), mortality census (6), church (7), manuscripts (22), military pension (25-27), mortuary (28), newspaper (30), published genealogies (31), tax lists (33), and will-probate records (34). There is a useful compilation of PA vital records which have been published in two major PA genealogical periodicals. This compilation contains many death dates.

___PA Magazine of History and Biography and PA Genealogical Magazine, PA VITAL RECORDS, Genealogical Publishing Co., Baltimore, MD, 1983, 3 volumes. [Over 100,000 names.]

Numerous non-official sources of PA deaths, both at the state and county levels, are listed in:

___J. D. and E. D. Stemmons, THE VITAL RECORD COMPENDIUM, Everton Publishers, Logan, UT, 1979.

When you are seeking death date and place information in archives and libraries, be certain to explore all the above mentioned sources, and don't fail to look under the county listings and the following heading in library card catalogs: Registers of births, etc.

13. Divorce records

In the early years of PA's history (1682-1773), divorce could be granted by the Governor/Council or the Legislature (Assembly). During the time 1773-85, the Legislature was the governing body to which pleas for divorce action could be submitted. Then beginning in 1785 and continuing through 1804, either the Supreme Court or the Legislature could act on divorce matters. From 1804 through 1847, the Legislature and the Courts of Common Pleas were the governmental institutions overseeing divorce proceedings. And finally, in 1847, the Court of Common Pleas became the sole body which handled divorces, this practice continuing until the present. Since the Prothonotary is the Clerk of the Court of Common Pleas, the records are kept in that office in the pertinent county seat. In 1946, a law requiring all divorces to be reported to the State Health Department was passed, but records are not generally available through them.

Divorces were quite rare in colonial PA, during the Revolutionary War, and for some years of early statehood. A number of PA divorces as recorded by the Legislative Assembly and the Supreme Court may be found in:

__STATUTES AT LARGE OF PA, Volumes 7ff.

__C. C. Livengood, GENEALOGICAL ABSTRACTS OF PA AND THE STATUTES AT LARGE, Family Line Publications, Westminster, MD, 1990.

__PUBLICATIONS OF THE GENEALOGICAL SOCIETY OF PA, Volume 1, Number 4, December 1898, pp. 185-192.

__SUPREME COURT DIVORCE PAPERS, Eastern District, 1786-1815, arranged alphabetically, and SUPREME COURT GENERAL MOTIONS (1750-1837) AND DIVORCE DOCKET (1800-5), arranged by date, PSA, Record Group 33, originals and 7 microfilms, Harrisburg, PA.

Another useful source of divorces is in local newspapers, which often published notices of these actions. For divorce records from 1804 forward, write the Prothonotary in the county of interest. In some instances, the earlier records may have been transferred to a local library or archives, so you may need to make your search in the CH and in LL, including libraries of historical and genealogical societies.

14. Emigration and immigration

Since PA was one of the thirteen original colonies, many early settlers came in (immigrated) and many of them or their descendants moved out (emigrated) chiefly to the west and south. There are a number of good volumes available which list immigrants to the areas that became the US. You should consult these volumes because they include both people who came directly to PA and people who came to some other colony or state and then to PA. The first set of volumes is an index to hundreds of ship passenger lists and contains over a million listings. These references have been abstracted from many published lists. Each listing gives the full name of the immigrant, the names of accompanying relatives, ages, the date and port of arrival, and the source of the information. The volumes in the set are:

__P. W. Filby and M. K. Meyer, PASSENGER AND IMMIGRATION LISTS INDEX, Gale Research Co., Detroit, MI, 1981-5, 6 volumes, supplemental volumes each year since.

Do not fail to look for every possible immigrant ancestor of yours in this very large index. Also of importance for locating passengers or passenger lists are:

___H. Lancour, R. J. Wolfe, and P. W. Filby, BIBLIOGRAPHY OF SHIP PASSENGER LISTS, 1538-1900, Gale Research Co., Detroit, MI, 1981.

___US National Archives and Records Service, GUIDE TO GENEALOGICAL RESEARCH IN THE NATIONAL ARCHIVES, The Service, Washington, DC, 1982, pp. 41-57.

___A. Eakle and J. Cerny, THE SOURCE, Ancestry Publishing Co., Salt Lake City, UT, 1984, pp. 453-516.

___P. W. Coldham, BONDED PASSENGERS TO AMERICA, 1615-1775, Genealogical Publishing Co., Baltimore, MD, 1981-3, 9 volumes.

___P. W. Coldham, CHILD APPRENTICES IN AMERICA FROM CHRIST'S HOSPITAL, LONDON, 1617-1778, Genealogical Publishing Co., Baltimore, MD, 1990.

___P. W. Coldham, ENGLISH ADVENTURERS AND EMIGRANTS, 1609-1773, Genealogical Publishing Co., Baltimore, MD, 1984-5.

___P. W. Coldham, ENGLISH CONVICTS IN COLONIAL AMERICA, Genealogical Publishing Co., Baltimore, MD, 1982, 3 volumes.

___P. W. Coldham, ENGLISH ESTATES OF AMERICAN COLONISTS, 1610-1858, Genealogical Publishing Co., Baltimore, MD, 1980-1.

___P. W. Coldham, THE BRISTOL REGISTERS OF SERVANTS SENT TO FOREIGN PLANTATIONS, 1654-86, Genealogical Publishing Co., Baltimore, MD, 1983.

___P. W. Coldham, THE COMPLETE BOOK OF EMIGRANTS IN BONDAGE, 1614-1775, Genealogical Publishing Co., Baltimore, MD, 1988.

___P. W. Coldham, THE COMPLETE BOOK OF IMMIGRANTS, 1607-60, Genealogical Publishing Co., Baltimore, MD, 1987.

___R. J. Dickson, ULSTER EMIGRATION TO COLONIAL AMERICA 1718-75, Ulster-Scot Historical Foundation, Belfast, Ireland, 1976.

___D. Dobson, DIRECTORY OF SCOTTISH SETTLERS IN NORTH AMERICA, Genealogical Publishing Co., Baltimore, MD, 1984-6, 6 volumes.

___I. A. Glazier and P. W. Filby, GERMANS TO AMERICA, LISTS OF PASSENGERS ARRIVING AT US PORTS, 1850-93, Scholarly Resources, Wilmington, DE, 1993.

___B. Mitchell, IRISH PASSENGER LISTS, 1847-71, LISTS OF PASSENGERS SAILING FROM LONDONDERRY TO AMERICA ON SHIPS OF THE J. AND J. COOKE LINE AND

THE McCORKELL LINE, Genealogical Publishing Co., Baltimore, MD, 1988.

___T. Schenk, R. Froelke, and I. Bork, THE WUERTTEMBERG EMIGRATION INDEX, Ancestry, Salt Lake City, UT, 1986-, in progress, 10 volumes so far.

___J. Wareing, EMIGRANTS TO AMERICA, INDENTURED SERVANTS RECRUITED IN LONDON, 1718-33, Genealogical Publishing Co., Baltimore, MD, 1985.

Then you can look into some works (microfilms and books) dealing especially with immigration to PA. Among these are:

___PASSENGER LISTS OF VESSELS ARRIVING IN PHILADELPHIA, 1800-82, Microfilm M425, 108 rolls, National Archives, Washington, DC.

___INDEX TO PASSENGER LISTS OF VESSELS ARRIVING AT PHILADELPHIA, 1800-1906, Microfilm M360, 151 rolls, National Archives, Washington, DC.

___SUPPLEMENTAL INDEX TO PASSENGER LISTS OF VESSELS ARRIVING AT ATLANTIC AND GULF COAST PORTS, 1820-74, Microfilm M334, 188 rolls, National Archives, Washington, DC.

___INDEX TO PASSENGER LISTS OF VESSELS ARRIVING AT PHILADELPHIA, 1883-1948, Microfilm T526, 60 rolls, National Archives, Washington, DC.

___BOOK INDEXES, PHILADELPHIA PASSENGER LISTS, 1906-26, Microfilm T791, 23 rolls, National Archives, Washington, DC.

___E. P. Bentley and M. Tepper, PASSENGER ARRIVALS AT THE PORT OF PHILADELPHIA, 1800-1819, Genealogical Publishing Co., Baltimore, MD, 1986.

___C. Boyer, SHIP PASSENGER LISTS, VOLUME 3, PA AND DE, 1641-1825, The Author, Newhall, CA, 1981.

___S. H. Cobb, THE PALATINE OR GERMAN IMMIGRATION TO NY AND PA, Wyoming Historical and Geological Society, Wilkes-Barre, PA, 1897.

___A. K. Burgert, EIGHTEENTH CENTURY IMMIGRANTS FROM GERMAN SPEAKING LANDS TO NORTH AMERICA, PA German Society, Birdsboro, PA, 1983-1986, 2 volumes.

___A. K. Burgert and H. Z. Jones, Jr., WESTERWARD TO AMERICA: SOME 18th CENTURY GERMAN IMMIGRANTS, 1989.

___C. N. Smith, GERMAN-AMERICAN GENEALOGICAL RESEARCH SERIES, Westland Publications, McNeal, AZ, 1973-81, 14 volumes.

___M. H. Tepper, EMIGRANTS TO PA, 1641-1819, Genealogical Publishing Co., Baltimore, MD, 1975 (1979). [6000 names.]

___W. Hacker, AUSWANDER SERIES, Various German Publishers, Stuttgart, Munich, Singen, and Detmold, West Germany, 1969-80, 8 volumes.

___F. R. Diffenderffer, THE GERMAN IMMIGRATION INTO PA THROUGH THE PORT OF PHILADELPHIA, 1700-75, Genealogical Publishing Co., Baltimore, MD, 1900 (1979).

___K. F. Geiser, REDEMPTIONERS AND INDENTURED SERVANTS IN THE COLONY AND COMMONWEALTH OF PA, Yale Review, New Haven, CT, 1901.

___M. K. Graeff, 1723-1973: TWO HUNDRED FIFTY YEARS TULPEHOCKEN, Tulpehocken Settlement Historical Society, Womelsdorf, PA, 1973. [Palatine emigration to America, 1709-10.]

___O. J. Harvey, HISTORY OF WILKES-BARRE, Wilkes-Barre, PA, 190930, 5 volumes. [Includes people coming into northeastern PA from CT.]

___Historical Records Survey, MARITIME RECORDS, PORT OF PHILADELPHIA, The Survey, Harrisburg, PA, 1942. [Includes Port Warden's Minutes (1776-1880) 11 volumes, Index of Naturalization (1794-1880) 11 volumes, Arrivals of Ships (1783-1880) 5 volumes, Lists of Ship Crews (1789-1880) 37 volumes, Alphabetical Ship Crew List (1798-1880) 108 volumes, Index of Names and Ships 42 volumes, Record of Wrecks (1874-1937) 12 volumes, Slave Manifests (1800-41) 1 volume, Letters of Marque (1804-15) 1 volume.]

___W. A. Knittle, EARLY 18TH CENTURY PALATINE EMIGRATION, Genealogical Publishing Co., Baltimore, MD, 1937 (1979).

___F. Krebs and M. Rubineau, EMIGRANTS FROM THE PALATINATE TO THE AMERICAN COLONIES IN THE 18TH CENTURY, PA German Society, Norristown, PA, 1953.

___O. Langguth, PA GERMAN PIONEERS FROM THE COUNTY OF WERTHEIM, PA German Society, Breinigsville, PA, 1948. [272 families.]

___H. F. Macco, PALATINE CHURCH VISITATIONS, 1609, Genealogical Society of PA, Philadelphia, PA, 1930.

___Mayor of Philadelphia, RECORD OF INDENTURES OF INDIVIDUALS BOUND OUT AS APPRENTICES, SERVANTS, ETC., AND OF GERMAN AND OTHER REDEMPTIONERS, 1771-3, PA German Society, Philadelphia, PA, 1907. [Over 5000 names.]

___A. C. Myers, IMMIGRATION OF THE IRISH QUAKERS INTO PA, 1682-1750, Genealogical Publishing Co., Baltimore, MD, 1902 (1978).

___G. E. McCracken, THE WELCOME CLAIMANTS, Welcome Society of PA, Genealogical Publishing Co., Baltimore, MD, 1970. [Over 2000 families.]

___PA German Folklore Society, PUBLICATIONS, The Society, Allentown, PA, 1936-62, Volume 1 (ZWEIBRUCKEN IMMIGRANT LIST, 1728-49), Volume 9 (GERMANS FROM NY TO PA IN THE COLONIAL PERIOD), Volume 10 (EMIGRANTS FROM WURTTEMBERG), Volume 11 (PA GERMAN PIONEERS FROM WERTHEIM), Volume 16 (GERMAN IMMIGRANTS FROM ZWEIBRUCKEN AND SCHAFFHAUSEN, 1734-71).

___I. D. Rupp, A COLLECTION OF UPWARDS OF 30,000 NAMES OF GERMAN, SWISS, DUTCH, FRENCH, AND OTHER IMMIGRANTS TO PA, 1727-76, Genealogical Publishing Co., Baltimore, MD, 1876 (1980).

___W. L. Sheppard, Jr., PASSENGERS AND SHIPS PRIOR TO 1684, Heritage Books, Bowie, MD, 1985.

___A. Stapleton, MEMORIALS OF THE HUGUENOTS IN AMERICA, WITH SPECIAL REFERENCE TO THEIR EMIGRATION TO PA, Genealogical Publishing Co., Baltimore, MD, 1901 (1964).

___R. B. Strassburger and W. J. Hinke, PA GERMAN PIONEERS, ARRIVALS IN THE PORT OF PHILADELPHIA, 1728-1808, Genealogical Publishing Co., Baltimore, MD, 1934 (1980). Also see supplemental list in PA Genealogical Magazine 21 (1960) 235.

___J. Tribbeko, LISTS OF GERMANS FROM THE PALATINATE WHO CAME TO ENGLAND IN 1709, Genealogical Publishing Co., Baltimore, MD, 1909-10 (1965). [Families which later came to PA.]

___D. Yoder, PA GERMAN IMMIGRANTS, 1709-86, Genealogical Publishing Co., Baltimore, MD, 1984.

___D. Yoder, RHINELAND IMMIGRANTS: LISTS OF GERMAN SETTLERS IN COLONIAL AMERICA, Genealogical Publishing Co., Baltimore, MD, 1981.

___SHIPS REGISTERS, 1762-76, AND FOREIGNERS ARRIVING IN PA, 1786-1808, PPA 2(1) 384-413, 2(2) 631-71, 2(17) 521-667.

___Historical Records Survey, SHIP REGISTERS OF THE PORT OF PHILADELPHIA, The Survey, Philadelphia, PA, 1942, Volume 1, A-D.

___S. Urlspenger, DETAILED REPORTS ON THE SALZBURGER EMIGRANTS WHO SETTLED IN AMERICA, University of GA Press, Athens, GA, 1968, 2 volumes.

___PALATINES ARRIVING IN PA, 1718-42, PPA C(3), C(4).
___SHIP REGISTERS FOR THE PORT OF PHILADELPHIA, 1726-75, PA Genealogical Magazine, Volumes 23-26.

Many additional source materials will be found in the books by Miller, Bodnar, and Meynen, which will be listed at the end of this section. In addition to works on immigration, there are also several volumes on emigration, that is, movements out of PA to settle areas to the west and south. Among those which might help you in your search for a migratory PA progenitor are:

___EARLY GERMAN SETTLERS OF WESTERN NY WHO CAME FROM PA, in W. H. Egle, NOTES AND QUERIES, Genealogical Publishing Co., Baltimore, MD, 1898 (1970).

___C. Hammer, RHINELANDERS ON THE YADKIN, Rowan Publishing Co., Salisbury, NC, 1943. [PA Germans in NC.]

___J. U. Kellogg, TULPEHOCKEN-VA NOTES, The Author, No place, 1945. [PA German families who went to VA.]

___C. E. Kemper, EARLY SETTLERS IN THE VALLEY OF VA PRIOR TO 1775. William and Mary Quarterly, 2nd Series, Volume 5 (No. 4) p. 259, Volume 6 (No. 1) p. 55.

___N. E. Kyger and others, THE PA GERMANS OF THE SHENANDOAH VALLEY, Schlecters, Allentown, PA, 1964.

___D. W. Nead, THE PA GERMAN IN THE SETTLEMENT OF MD, Genealogical Publishing Co., Baltimore, MD, 1914 (1980).

___N. Parkin, PENNSYLVANIANS IN NV, PA Genealogical Magazine, Volume 24, p. 188.

___PA German Folklore Society, PUBLICATIONS, The Society, Allentown, PA, 1936-62, Volume 11 (PA GERMANS IN ONTARIO), Volume 19 (PA GERMANS IN WI), Volume 26 (PA GERMANS OF THE SHENANDOAH VALLEY, VA).

___PENNSYLVANIANS IN CLERMONT AND ADAMS COUNTIES, OH, Your Family Tree, Volume 15 (No. 1) p.12, Volume 15 (No. 2) p. 40.

___G. E. Reaman, THE TRAIL OF THE BLACK WALNUT, McClelland and Stewart, Toronto, Canada, 1965. [PA Germans who emigrated to Ontario].

___A. B. Sherk, THE PA GERMANS IN CANADA, PA German, Volume 8, pp. 101-4.

Numerous other immigration and emigration listings, especially ones published in periodicals, are referenced in the following works:

___O. K. Miller, MIGRATION, EMIGRATION, IMMIGRATION, Everton Publishers, Logan, UT, 1974, 1981, 2 volumes.

___J. E. Bodnar, ETHNIC HISTORY OF PA: A SELECTED BIBLIOGRAPHY, PA Historical and Museum Commission, Harrisburg, PA, 1974.

___E. Meynen, BIBLIOGRAPHY OF GERMAN SETTLEMENTS IN COLONIAL NORTH AMERICA ESPECIALLY ON THE PA GERMANS AND THEIR DESCENDANTS, 1683-1933, Gale Research Co., Detroit, MI, 1966. [1700 family histories listed.]

If you do not locate your ancestor in the major references listed in the previous paragraphs, use these three reference works to locate many smaller sources. Finally, do not forget to look in the main card catalogs of SLP, LHS, CLP, and other LGL under the heading PA-EMIGRATION AND IMMIGRATION.

15. Ethnic records

The ethnic background of PA settlement is exceptionally rich, the earliest major groups being English, German, and Scotch-Irish. Later on these peoples were followed by Irish, Africans, Slavs, Italians, Jews, and others. Smaller groups which came include Welsh, Swiss, Swedish, Dutch, and French. Since most of these groups adhered to particular religious affiliations, many publications relating to them need to be sought among church records and histories. Instructions for locating these were given in section 7 of this chapter. Careful attention should also be paid to immigration and naturalization records, these being treated in sections 14 and 29 of the present chapter. There are several very helpful bibliographic volumes which will lead you to ethnically-oriented histories and records. Those which you should use include:

___D. E. Washburn, THE PEOPLES OF PA, University of Pittsburgh Press, Pittsburgh, PA, 1981.

___O. K. Miller, MIGRATION, EMIGRATION, IMMIGRATION, Everton Publishers, Logan, UT, 1974, 1981, 2 volumes.

___J. E. Bodnar, ETHNIC HISTORY OF PA, PA Historical and Museum Commission, Harrisburg, PA, 1974.

___J. E. Bodnar, THE ETHNIC EXPERIENCE IN PA, Bucknell University Press, Lewisburg, PA, 1973. [See bibliographies at ends of articles.]

___E. Meynen, BIBLIOGRAPHY OF GERMAN SETTLEMENTS IN COLONIAL NORTH AMERICA, ESPECIALLY ON THE PA GERMANS AND THEIR DESCENDANTS, 1683-1933, Gale Research Co., Detroit, MI, 1966.

___N. B. Wilkinson, BIBLIOGRAPHY OF PA HISTORY, PA Historical and Museum Commission, Harrisburg, PA, 1957, with C. Wall, SUPPLEMENT TO BIBLIOGRAPHY OF PA HISTORY, PA Historical and Museum Commission, Harrisburg, PA, 1977, and J. B. B. Trussell, PA Historical and Museum Commission, Harrisburg, PA, 1980, and J. B. B. Trussell, PA HISTORICAL BIBLIOGRAPHY IV, PA Historical and Museum Commission, Harrisburg, PA, 1983.

To get you started, we will now list some of the most important ethnic volumes relating chiefly to the earlier and larger groups which came into PA. The early English settlement of PA is well covered in
___W. L. Sheppard, Jr., and G. E. McCracken, PENN'S COLONY, Welcome Society of PA, Genealogical Publishing Co., Baltimore, MD, 1970, 2 volumes.
For the German groups, a great deal of work has been done as evidenced by the many volumes which have appeared. Notable among them are these:
___W. H. Egle, PA GENEALOGIES, CHIEFLY SCOTCH-IRISH AND GERMAN, Genealogical Publishing Co., Baltimore, MD, 1896 (1969). [2500 surnames]
___H. F. Eshleman, HISTORIC BACKGROUND AND ANNALS OF THE SWISS AND GERMAN PIONEER SETTLERS OF SOUTHEASTERN PA, Genealogical Publishing Co., Baltimore, MD, 1917 (1969). [2200 names]
___Free Library of Philadelphia, THE PA GERMAN FRAKTUR COLLECTION OF THE FREE LIBRARY, The Library, Philadelphia, PA, 1916, 2 volumes. [Over 2000 names]
___J. E. Fryer, TWENTY-FIVE YEAR INDEX TO PA FOLKLIFE, 1949-76, PA Folklife Society, Collegeville, PA, 1980.
___A. H. Gerberich, PA GERMAN FAMILIES, Carlyle, PA, no date, 12 volumes.
___E. W. Hocker, GENEALOGICAL DATA RELATING TO THE GERMAN SETTLERS OF PA FROM ADS IN GERMAN NEWSPAPERS, 1743-1800, Genealogical Publishing Co., Baltimore, MD, 1981.
___W. I. Hull, WILLIAM PENN AND THE DUTCH QUAKER (ALSO GERMAN) IMMIGRATION TO PA, Genealogical Publishing Co., Baltimore, MD, 1935 (1970).
___D. R. Irish, PA GERMAN MARRIAGES, MARRIAGES AND MARRIAGE EVIDENCES IN PA GERMAN CHURCHES, Genealogical Publishing Co., Baltimore, MD, 1984.

___L. O. Kuhns, THE GERMAN AND SWISS SETTLEMENTS OF COLONIAL PA, AMS Press, New York, NY, 1901 (1971).

___PA German Society, PA GERMAN CHURCH RECORDS OF BIRTHS, BAPTISMS, MARRIAGES, BURIALS, Genealogical Publishing Co., Baltimore, MD, 1983, 3 volumes.

___PA German Society, PROCEEDINGS, ADDRESSES, AND PUBLI-CATIONS, The Society, Philadelphia, PA, 1891-1966, 63 volumes; New Series, 1968-, Vol. 1-.

___S. W. Pennypacker, THE SETTLEMENT OF GERMANTOWN AND THE BEGINNING OF GERMAN EMIGRATION TO NORTH AMERICA, Campbell, Philadelphia, PA, 1899.

___J. F. Sachse, THE GERMAN PIETISTS OF PROVINCIAL PA, 1694-1708 AMS Press, New York, NY, 1895 (1970).

___J. F. Sachse, THE GERMAN SECTARIANS OF PA, 1708-1800, AMS Press, New York, NY, 1899 (1970-1), 2 volumes.

___O. H. Stroh, PA GERMAN TOMBSTONE INSCRIPTIONS, The Author, Harrisburg, PA, 1980.

___F. S. Weiser, SOURCES AND DOCUMENTS OF THE PA GER-MANS, PA German Society, Breinigsville, PA, 1975-, Vols. 1-.

Volumes which give historical detail on the many Irish people who settled in PA and which will lead you to further information are:

___A. C. Myers, IMMIGRATION OF IRISH QUAKERS INTO PA, 1682-1750, Genealogical Publishing Co., Baltimore, MD, 1902 (1978).

___W. V. Shannon, THE AMERICAN-IRISH, MacMillan, New York, NY, 1963.

___D. Clark, THE IRISH IN PHILADELPHIA, Temple University Press, Philadelphia, PA, 1973.

An excellent volume describing the pioneer settlements of the Polish people in PA is:

___M. Harman, POLISH PIONEERS OF PA, Polish Roman Catholic Union of America, Chicago, IL, 1941.

Among the numerous works describing in detail the Scots-Irish or Ulster Scot ethnic character and contributions are to be found in the following useful volumes:

___C. K. Bolton, SCOTCH-IRISH PIONEERS IN ULSTER AND AMERICA, Genealogical Publishing Co., Baltimore, MD, 1910.

___J. W. Dinsmore, THE SCOTCH-IRISH IN AMERICA, Winona Publishing Co., Chicago, IL, 1906.

___W. F. Dunaway, THE SCOTCH-IRISH OF COLONIAL PA, Univer-sity of NC Press, Chapel Hill, NC, 1944.

___W. H. Egle, PA GENEALOGIES, CHIEFLY SCOTCH-IRISH AND GERMAN, Genealogical Publishing Co., Baltimore, MD, 1896 (1969). [2500 surnames]

The Slovak ethnic group is treated in the following valuable works:

___E. Balch, OUR SLAVIC FELLOW CITIZEN, Arno Press, New York, NY, 1910 (1969).

___J. Stasko, SLOVAKS IN THE USA, Dobra kniha, Cambridge, Ontario, Canada, 1974.

When doing research on Swiss peoples who came to PA, these books can be consulted with profit:

___H. F. Eshleman, HISTORIC BACKGROUND AND ANNALS OF THE SWISS AND GERMAN PIONEER SETTLERS OF SOUTH-EASTERN PA, Genealogical Publishing Co., Baltimore, MD, 1917 (1969).

___A. B. Faust and G. Brumbaugh, LIST OF SWISS EMIGRANTS IN THE 18TH CENTURY TO THE AMERICAN COLONIES, Genealogical Publishing Co., Baltimore, MD, 1976. [Do not use earlier editions.]

Notable reference volumes dealing with the Welsh are:

___C. H. Browning, WELSH SETTLEMENT OF PA, Genealogical Publishing Co., Baltimore, MD, 1912 (1967).

___T. A. Glenn, MERION IN THE WELSH TRACT, Genealogical Publishing Co., Baltimore, MD, 1896 (1970).

___T. A. Glenn, WELSH FOUNDERS OF PA, Genealogical Publishing Co., Baltimore, MD, 1911/3 (1970).

Other books relating to some of the other ethnic groups include:

___(Dutch) W. I. Hull, WILLIAM PENN AND THE DUTCH QUAKER MIGRATION TO PA, Genealogical Publishing Co., Baltimore, MD, 1935 (1970).

___(Finns) J. H. Wuorinen, THE FINNS ON THE DELAWARE, 1638-55, AMS Press, New York, NY, 1938 (1966).

___(French) W. F. Dunaway, THE FRENCH RACIAL STRAIN IN COLONIAL PA, Huguenot Society of PA, Philadelphia, PA, 1930.

___(Italians) E. L. Biagi, THE ITALIANS OF PHILADELPHIA, Carleton Press, New York, NY, 1967.

___(Jews) H. S. Morais, THE JEWS OF PHILADELPHIA, Levytype Co., Philadelphia, PA, 1894.

___(Swedes) A. Johnson, THE SWEDES IN AMERICA, Swedish Colonial Foundation, Philadelphia, PA, 1953.

___(Swedes) A. Johnson, THE SWEDISH SETTLEMENTS ON THE DELAWARE, 1638-64, Genealogical Publishing Co., Baltimore, MD, 1911 (1969).

The blacks of PA constitute an important ethnic group. There are sizable federal, state, county, and private records which are especially pertinent to blacks. Details and/or listings of many of these records are given in the following:

___National Archives and Records Service, GUIDE TO GENEALOGI-CAL RESEARCH IN THE NATIONAL ARCHIVES, The Service, Washington, DC, 1982, Chapter 12, pp. 173-185.

___The six references listed in the first paragraph of this section.

Among the best of the descriptions of the ethnic character and history of blacks in PA is the following:

___C. L. Blockson, PA'S BLACK HISTORY, Portfolio Associates, Phila-delphia, PA, 1975.

Most of the above volumes will be found in SLP, LHS, and CLP, many in FHL (available through FHC) LGL, and RL, and some in LL. You should not fail also to look in library card catalogs under English in ---, Scotch-Irish in ---, Germans in ---, and so forth.

16. Gazetteers, atlases, and maps

Detailed information regarding PA geography is exceptionally useful to the genealogical searcher, especially with regard to land records. They usually mention locations in terms requiring an understanding of local geographical features. Several sorts of geographical aids are valuable in this regard: gazetteers, atlases, and maps. Gazetteers are volumes which list geographical features (towns, villages, crossroads, settlements, districts, rivers, streams, creeks, hills, mountains, valleys, coves, lakes, ponds), locate them, and sometimes give a few details concerning them. An atlas is a collection of maps in book form. Among the better gazetteer-type materials for PA are:

___J. Scott, THE US GAZETTEER, Bailey, Philadelphia, PA, 1795.

___S. A. Mitchell, AN ACCOMPANIMENT TO MITCHELL'S REF-ERENCE AND DISTANCE MAP OF THE US, Mitchell and Hinman, Philadelphia, Pa, 1834.

___T. F. Gordon, A GAZETTEER OF THE STATE OF PA, 1832, Polyanthos, New Orleans, LA, 1832 (1975).

___A. H. Espenshade, PA PLACE NAMES, Genealogical Publishing Co., Baltimore, MD, 1925 (1970).

___G. P. Donehoo, A HISTORY OF INDIAN VILLAGES AND PLACE NAMES IN PA, Gateway Press, Baltimore, MD, 1928 (1977).

___J. L. Kay and C. M. Smith, Jr., PA POSTAL HISTORY, Quarterman, Lawrence, MA, 1976. [1000 PA post offices 1775-1976.]

___J. Gioe, PA, HER COUNTIES, HER TOWNSHIPS, AND HER TOWNS, Ye Olde Genealogie Shoppe, Indianapolis, IN, 1980.

___G. Swetnam and H. Smith, A GUIDEBOOK TO WESTERN PA. [Over 1300 historic sites in Western PA.]

Atlases (collections of maps) published before 1904 are available for the state of PA, for practically every county, and for these cities: Allegheny, Bryn Mawr, Cheltenham, Erie, Harrisburg, Lancaster, Oil City, Philadelphia, Pittsburgh, Reading, Scranton, Shamokin, Sunbury, Wilkes-Barre, Williamsport, York. Some of the county and city atlases show the names of the landowners on the maps, and a few even have a list of all inhabitants. Listings of available atlases for PA are:

___J. M. Moak, ATLASES OF PA, A PRELIMINARY CHECKLIST OF COUNTY, CITY, AND SUBJECT ATLASES OF PA, The Author, Philadelphia, PA, 1976.

___R. M. Miller, PA MAPS AND ATLASES IN THE PA STATE UNIVERSITY LIBRARIES, The Libraries, University Park, PA, 1972.

___Research Publications, PA COUNTY AND REGIONAL HISTORIES AND ATLASES AVAILABLE ON MICROFILM, Research Publications, New Haven, CT, 1973.

___C. E. LeGear, US ATLASES, Library of Congress, Washington, DC, 1950-3, 2 volumes.

An early publication, three very valuable older PA atlases, two recent PA atlases, a recent US historical atlas, and a recent PA historical atlas are of exceptional utility in locating state land features:

___J. Scott, A GEOGRAPHICAL DESCRIPTION OF PA, ALSO OF THE COUNTIES, Philadelphia, PA, 1806.

___H. F. Walling and O. W. Gray, NEW TOPOGRAPHICAL ATLAS OF THE STATE OF PA, Stedman, Brown, and Lyon, Philadelphia, PA, 1872.

___J. R. Bien, ATLAS OF THE STATE OF PA, J. Bien and Co., New York, NY, 1900.

___G. F. Cram, DESCRIPTIVE REVIEW OF THE STATE OF PA WITH DETAIL MAPS, G. F. Cram Co., Chicago, IL, 1916.

___C. J. Puetz, PA COUNTY MAPS, County Maps, Lyndon Station, WI, 1985.

___COUNTY HISTORICAL MAPS, Archives Publishing Co., Harrisburg, PA. Maps of 28 PA counties with historical notes.

___J. H. Long, HISTORICAL ATLASES AND CHRONOLOGY OF COUNTY BOUNDARIES, 1788-1980, Hall and Co., Boston, MA, 1984, pp. 97-187 for PA.

___E. K. Muller, A CONCISE HISTORICAL ATLAS OF PA, Temple University Press, Philadeelphia, PA, 1989.

Many maps are available for PA, for its counties, for portions of the counties and for cities and towns. There are several nation-wide books which list PA maps and indicate sources of them or which give descriptions of map collections:

___National Archives and Records Service, GUIDE TO CARTO-GRAP-HIC RECORDS IN THE NATIONAL ARCHIVES, The Service, Washington, DC, 1971.

___National Archives and Records Service, GUIDE TO GENEALOGI-CAL RESEARCH IN THE NATIONAL ARCHIVES, The Service, Washington, DC, 1982, pp. 255-262.

___J. R. Hebert, PANORAMIC MAPS OF ANGLO-AMERICAN CITIES IN THE LIBRARY OF CONGRESS, The Library, Washington, DC, 1974. [Maps available for before 1900 for 166 PA cities and towns.]

___R. W. Stephenson, LAND OWNERSHIP MAPS IN THE LIBRARY OF CONGRESS, The Library, Washington, DC, 1967. [County maps before 1900 showing owners of the land, for practically every PA county.]

___Library of Congress, FIRE INSURANCE MAPS IN THE LIBRARY OF CONGRESS, The Library, Washington, DC, 1981, pp. 529-75. [Maps of 584 cities and towns used by fire insurance companies, much detail.]

___M. H. Shelley, WARD MAPS OF US CITIES, Library of Congress, Washington, DC, 1975. [Maps showing city ward divisions to assist you in census record searches in Allegheny, Philadelphia, and Pittsburgh.]

In addition, there are several volumes specifically devoted to listing PA maps (state, regional, county, township, city, town, borough):

___M. L. Simonetti, D. H. Kent, and H. E. Whipkey, DESCRIPTIVE LIST OF THE MAP COLLECTION IN THE PA STATE ARCHIVES, PA Historical and Museum Commission, Harrisburg, PA, 1976.

___R. M. Miller, PA MAPS AND ATLASES IN THE PA STATE UNIVERSITY LIBRARIES, University Park, PA, 1972.

___An Index to Maps Contained in the Ten Series of the Published PA Archives in H. H. Eddy and M. L. Simonetti, GUIDE TO THE

PUBLISHED ARCHIVES OF PA, PA Historical and Museum
Commission, Harrisburg, PA, 1976, pp. 35-45.

___Listing of PA Land Warrantee Maps in Southwest PA Genealogical
Services, PA LINE: A RESEARCH GUIDE TO PA GENEALOGY
AND LOCAL HISTORY, The Services, Laughlintown, PA, 1983, pp.
76-8.

Your attention needs to be drawn to several specialized types of maps
which can assist you as you attempt to locate your progenitor's land and
as you look for streams, roads, bridges, churches, cemeteries, towns, and
villages in the vicinity. The first of these are the highly detailed maps
issued by the US Geological Survey which has mapped the entire state of
PA and has issued a series of hundreds of maps, each covering a very
small area. These maps are available at very reasonable cost. Write the
following address and ask for the Index to Topographic Maps of PA and
a Map Order Form:

___Branch of Distribution, Eastern Region, US Geological Survey, 1200
South Eads St., Arlington, VA 22202.

A second type of map which is very useful are the landowner maps which
show the names of the persons who own each piece of property (see book
by Stephenson above). Another type of map is represented by the city
and town panorama maps which are careful depictions of cities as they
would be viewed from a balloon flying above (see book by Hebert above).
Detailed city maps were also drawn for fire insurance purposes (see book
mentioned above) and they constitute a fourth special type. A fifth type
of map is made up of those which have ward boundaries of larger cities
marked. These are useful when searching the unindexed census records
for city dwellers, especially when they are employed in conjunction with
city directories. A sixth special type is composed of maps which depict
original land grants made in PA. These are highly detailed maps,
hundreds and hundreds being available for many PA counties (see book
by Southwest Genealogical Services above). A seventh type of map is
represented by the county maps sold by the PA Department of
Transportation. Write them for a listing and prices:

___PennDOT Publication Sales Store, Bldg. No. 33, Harrisburg Interna-
tional Airport, Middletown, PA 17057.

An eighth type of map of great utility is represented by maps which show
churches, especially in the earlier years. Among them are these:

___J. Melish, MAP OF PA, 1822, The author, Philadelphia, PA, 1822.

___R. Howell, A MAP OF THE STATE OF PA, 1811.

___D. A. Sotzman, PA ENTWORFEN VON D. F. SOTZMAN, Carl
Ernst Bohn, Hamburg, 1797.

Finally, every PA genealogical researcher should own a copy of a map showing the development of PA counties, the dates of formation of each, and the derivation of each (from what previous counties it came):

___PA Department of Community Affairs, GENEALOGICAL MAP OF THE COUNTIES, The Department, Harrisburg, PA, 1933 (1978). [Available from PA Historical and Museum Commission Bookstore, PA State Museum, PO Box 1026, Harrisburg, PA 17120.]

An utterly invaluable set of maps which is of exceptional help in interpreting PA place locations during the period 1790-1920 is not to be overlooked. These maps give the census enumeration subdivisions and clearly show land locations for those listed in the census schedule:

___W. Thorndale and W. Dollarhide, MAP GUIDE TO THE US FEDERAL CENSUSES, PA, 1790-1920, Dollarhide Systems, Bellingham, WA, 1984.

The best collections for genealogically-related maps and atlases of PA are in SLP, PSA, LHS, PA State University [at University Park, PA], The Free Library of Philadelphia, The Library of Congress (LOC), and The National Archives (NA). When you seek gazetteers, atlases, and maps in these repositories, please be sure to look both in the main card catalogs and the special map catalogs, indexes, and listings. Most of the volumes mentioned in this section are available in SLP and LHS, and some will be found in LWP, CLP, LGL, RL, FHL, and through FHC.

---

17. Genealogical indexes and compilations for PA

There are a number of genealogical indexes and compilations for the colony and the state of PA which list very large numbers of names. These are of considerable utility because they may save you going through many small volumes and detailed records, especially in the early stages of your search for your PA forebears. The nation-wide indexes and compilations of this sort include:

___SURNAME INDEX and INTERNATIONAL GENEALOGICAL INDEX at FHL, Salt Lake City, UT, available also at FHC. [See section on FHL and FHC in Chapter 3.]

___ANCESTRAL FILE, FAMILY GROUP RECORDS ARCHIVES, and FAMILY REGISTRY at FHL, Salt Lake City, UT. Also through FHC. [See section on FHL and FHC in Chapter 3.]

___FAMILY ARCHIVES FAMILY FINDER INDEX, available from AGLL, PO Box 329, Bountiful, UT 84011. More than 115 million names on over 50 CD-ROMs of census, land, and marriage records.

___National Archives, GENERAL INDEX TO COMPILED MILITARY SERVICE RECORDS OF REVOLUTIONARY WAR SOLDIERS, SAILORS, AND MEMBERS OF ARMY STAFF DEPARTMENTS, The Archives, Washington, DC, Microfilm Publication M860, 58 rolls.

___F. Rider, AMERICAN GENEALOGICAL-BIOGRAPHICAL INDEX, Godfrey Memorial Library, Middletown, CT, 1942-, over 190 volumes so far.

___P. W. Filby and M. K. Meyer, PASSENGER AND IMMIGRATION LISTS INDEX, Gale Research Co., Detroit, MI, 1981-5, with annual supplements.

___New York Public Library, DICTIONARY CATALOG OF THE LOCAL HISTORY AND GENEALOGY DIVISION, NEW YORK PUBLIC LIBRARY, G. K. Hall, Boston, MA, 1974.

___Library of Congress, NATIONAL UNION CATALOG OF MANUSCRIPT COLLECTIONS, The Library, Washington, DC, annual volumes since 1962, index in each volume, also cumulative indexes. Also overall name and subject indexes.

___National Society Daughters of the American Revolution, LIBRARY CATALOG, VOLUME ONE: FAMILY HISTORIES AND GENE-ALOGIES, The Society, Washington, DC, 1982.

___Newberry Library, GENEALOGICAL INDEX OF THE NEWBERRY LIBRARY, G. K. Hall, Boston, MA, 1960, 4 volumes.

___Everton Publishers, COMPUTERIZED ROOTS CELLAR and COMPUTERIZED FAMILY FILE, The Publishers, Logan, UT.

In addition to the above nation-wide indexes and compilations, there are a sizable number of large indexes and compilations dealing exclusively with PA. Among the more notable of them are the following:

___INDEXES IN THE [PUBLISHED] PA ARCHIVES, AMS Press, New York, NY, 1838-1935 (1971-6): C(Volume entitled GENERAL INDEX TO THE COLONIAL RECORDS AND PA ARCHIVES) 1-433, 1(Volume entitled GENERAL INDEX TO THE COLONIAL RECORDS AND PA ARCHIVES) 437-653, 2(Indexes at end of each volume except 8-11 and 13), 3(27) i-33, 3(27) 337-790, 3(28-30), 4(Indexes at end of each volume), 4(12) 643-963, 6(15), 7(11-5), 8(No published index, manuscript index at PSA), 9(No published index, incomplete card file index at PSA). [Remember that the number or letter C before the parenthesis indicates the series, the numbers in the parentheses indicate the volumes in the series, and the numbers after the parentheses indicate the pages.]

___M. Dunn, INDEX TO PA'S COLONIAL RECORDS SERIES, Genealogical Publishing Co., Baltimore, MD, 1992.

___J. D. Stemmons and E. D. Stemmons, PA IN 1780: AN INDEX OF CIRCA 1780 PA TAX LISTS, The Authors, Salt Lake City, UT, 1978.

___INDEXES TO THE PA CENSUS SCHEDULES OF 1790, 1800/ 10/20/30/40/50/60, 1880/1900/10/20. [See section 6, this chapter.]

___CARD CATALOGS IN SLP, LHS, CLP, and RL. [See Chapter 3.]

___SPECIAL INDEXES, CATALOGS, AND LISTS IN SLP, PSA, LHS, LWP, CLP, and RL. [See Chapter 3.]

___R. B. Strassburger and W. J. Hinke, PA GERMAN PIONEERS, 1727-1808, PA German Society, Philadelphia, PA, 1934, 3 volumes.

___GENEALOGIES OF PA FAMILIES [From the PA Magazine of History and Biography and The PA Genealogical Magazine], Genealogical Publishing Co., Baltimore, MD, 1981-2, 4 volumes.

___PA GERMAN CHURCH RECORDS [From Proceedings of the PA German Society], Genealogical Publishing Co., Baltimore, MD, 1983, 3 volumes.

___PA VITAL RECORDS [From PA Periodicals], Genealogical Publishing Co., Baltimore, MD, 1983, 3 volumes.

___F. G. Hoenstine, GUIDE TO GENEALOGICAL AND HISTORICAL RESEARCH IN PA, The Authors, Hollidaysburg, PA, 1978,Index, pp. 275-604; Supplement I, 1985, pp. 75-214; Supplement II, 1990, pp. 75-126.

___John W. and W. Jordan, COLONIAL AND REVOLUTIONARY FAMILIES OF PA, Genealogical Publishing Co., Baltimore, MD, 1911-65 (1978), 17 volumes.

___R. V. Jackson, EARLY AMERICAN SERIES: PA, Accelerated Indexing Systems, North Salt Lake City, UT, 1983-4, 4 volumes.

___W. H. Egle, NOTES AND QUERIES: HISTORICAL, BIOGRAPHICAL, AND GENEALOGICAL, Genealogical Publishing Co., Baltimore, MD, 1881-1901 (1970), 12 volumes, with E. D. Schory, EVERYNAME INDEX TO EGLE'S NOTES AND QUERIES, Decatur Genealogical Society, Decatur, IL, 1982.

___D. O. Virdin, PA GENEALOGIES AND FAMILY HISTORIES, Heritage Books, Bowie, MD, 1992.

___C. C. Livengood, GENEALOGICAL ABSTRACTS OF THE LAWS OF PA AND THE STATUTES AT LARGE, Family Line Publns., Westminster, MD, 1990.

___CARD INDEX OF BIOGRAPHIES IN PA LOCAL HISTORIES,
PA Room, CLP, Pittsburgh, PA.
___PA WARRANT REGISTER INDEX ON MICROFILM, by county,
then by initial letter of surname, PSA Search Room, Harrisburg, PA.
___National Archives, MICROFILM INDEX OF COMPILED
SERVICE RECORDS FOR UNION ARMY VOLUNTEERS OF
PA, The Archives, Washington, DC, Microfilm Publication M554, 136
rolls.

Most of the published works mentioned above will be found in SLP
and LHS, many in CLP, and RL, and some in FHL (available through
FHC) and LL. The microfilms should be sought in SLP, PSA, LHS,
NAPF, and NA.

The importance of the PUBLISHED PA ARCHIVES (PPA) volumes
for PA genealogical research cannot be overemphasized. Even though
some of the materials have errors in them, these books contain a vast
amount of information especially up to about 1850. You should not fail
to carefully read and reread the following guidebook to the use of these
exceedingly valuable collections of data:
___H. E. Eddy and M. L. Simonetti, GUIDE TO THE PUBLISHED
ARCHIVES OF PA, PA Historical and Museum Commission, Harrisburg, PA, 1949.
Included in the 138 volumes are the following types of records: county,
baptism, bounty land, colonial, immigrant, land, Loyalist, marriage, mili-
tary, militia, naturalization, pension, Revolutionary War, tax, War of 1812,
and many others. Other guides to the PPA which you will find helpful
are:
___S. A. Weikel, GENEALOGICAL RESEARCH IN THE PPA, SLP,
Harrisburg, PA, 1976.
___J. S. Morris, USE OF THE PPA IN GENEALOGICAL RE-
SEARCH, Western PA Genealogical Society, Pittsburgh, PA, 1978.
___IN State Library, GUIDE TO GENEALOGICAL MATERIAL IN
THE PPA, The Library, Indianapolis, IN, 1937.
___Eastern WA Genealogical Society, TIPS TO THE USE OF THE
PPA, The Society, Spokane, WA, 1979.
___SLP, A GUIDE TO THE GENEALOGY/LOCAL HISTORY SEC-
TION OF THE SLP, The Library, Harrisburg, PA, 1985.

18. Genealogical periodicals

Several genealogical periodicals and
historical periodicals carrying some
genealogical data have been or are

being published for PA. These journals or newsletters contain genealogies, local history data, genealogical records, family queries and
answers, book reviews, and other pertinent information. If you had a PA
progenitor, you will find it of great value to subscribe to one or more of
the state-wide periodicals, as well as any periodicals published in the
region and/or county where he/she lived. Periodicals pertinent to PA research may be divided into four classes: (1) those that have state-wide
coverage, (2) those that are state-wide but apply only to special groups,
(3) those that have regional coverage, and (4) those that cover individual
counties. Lists of PA genealogical periodicals are published in these
references:

___V. D. Brow and D. M. Miller, PA DIRECTORY OF HISTORICAL
ORGANIZATIONS, 1976, PA Historical and Museum Commission,
Harrisburg, PA, 1976.

___V. N. Chambers, editor, GENEALOGICAL HELPER, Everton Pub-
lishers, Logan, UT, latest July-August issue.

___State Library of PA, A GUIDE TO THE GENEALOGY/LOCAL
HISTORY SECTION OF THE STATE LIBRARY OF PA, The
Library, Harrisburg, PA, 1989.

___DIRECTORY OF HISTORICAL SOCIETIES AND AGENCIES IN
THE US AND CANADA, American Association of State and Local
History, Nashville, TN, latest edition.

___E. P. Bentley, GENEALOGICAL ADDRESS BOOK, Genealogical
Publishing Co., Baltimore, MD, 1996.

Chief among the periodicals which have state-wide coverage of PA
are:

___PA GENEALOGICAL MAGAZINE (Quarterly), The Genealogical
Society of PA, 1301 Locust St., Philadelphia, PA 19107, since 1895.

___PA GENEALOGIST AND HISTORIAN, Heritage Society of PA, PO
Box 146, Laughlintown, PA 15655.

___PA MAGAZINE OF HISTORY AND BIOGRAPHY, The Historical
Society of PA, 1300 Locust St., Philadelphia, PA 19107, since 1977.
[Very little genealogical data after volume 60 (1936).] Index to
volumes 1-75.

___THE PA TRAVELER-POST (Quarterly), R. T. and M. C. Williams,
PO Box 307, Danboro, PA 18916, since 1964.

___STAGECOACH LIBRARY BULLETIN (Quarterly), G. T. Haw-
baker, PO Box 207, Hershey, PA 17033.

___YOUR FAMILY TREE (Quarterly), Hoenstine Rental Library, PO
Box 208, Hollidaysburg, PA 16648, 1948-83.

___NATIONAL GENEALOGICAL SOCIETY QUARTERLY, The Society, 4527 Seventeenth St., North, Arlington, VA 22207, since 1912. [Contains much PA data.]

Included in the major periodicals which carry genealogical data on special groups in the state of PA are:

___ASSOCIATION FOR THE ADVANCEMENT OF POLISH STUDIES, Newsletter/Bulletin, Alliance College Library, Cambridge Springs, PA.

___JOURNAL OF PRESBYTERIAN HISTORY, Presbyterian Historical Assn., Philadelphia, PA.

___PUBLICATIONS OF THE PA GERMAN SOCIETY (succeeded PROCEEDINGS AND ADDRESSES OF THE PA GERMAN SOCIETY), PA German Society, PO Box 397, Birdsboro, PA 18508, since 1891.

___MENNONITE FAMILY HISTORY (Quarterly), L. and L. A. Mast, PO Box 171, Elverson, PA 19520, since 1982.

___PA MENNONITE HERITAGE (Quarterly), Lancaster Mennonite Historical Society, 2214 Hillstream Rd., Lancaster, PA 17602, since 1978.

___DER REGGEBOGE (Quarterly), PA German Society, Breinigsville, PA 18031.

___Jewish Genealogical Society of Philadelphia. Elkins Park, PA 19117.

___JEDNOTA, 1st Catholic Slovak Union, Middletown, PA 17057.

___PA MINUTEMAN (Quarterly), PA Society, Sons of the American Revolution, 110 Ashford Ave., Pittsburgh, PA 15229.

___PALATINE IMMIGRANT (Quarterly), National Society, Palatines to America, 4115K Fawn Dr., Harrisburg, PA 17112.

___DER KURIER, Mid-Atlantic Germanic Soc., Dillsburg, PA 17019.

Among the very useful regional periodicals of PA are the ones listed below:

___CENTRAL PA GENEALOGICAL PIONEERS, Northumberland, PA 17857.

___CENTRAL PA GENEALOGICAL MAGAZINE, M. B. Lontz, 608 Broadway, Milton, PA 17847.

___KEYHOLE TO THE WEST (Quarterly), Genealogical Society of Southwestern PA, PO Box 894, Washington, PA 15301, since 1973.

___KEYSTONE SEEKERS GENEALOGICAL QUARTERLY, Capital Area Genealogical Society, PO Box 4502, Harrisburg, PA 17111-4502.

___NORTHEASTERN PA (Quarterly), Sheffield Publications, PO Box 1161, Carbondale, PA 18407, since 1980.

___OUR NAMES THE GAME, South Central PA Genealogical Society, PO Box 1824, York, PA 17405.

___SPECIAL PUBLICATIONS OF THE SOUTH CENTRAL PA GENEALOGICAL SOCIETY, The Society, PO Box 1824, York, PA 17405.

___WESTERN PA GENEALOGICAL SOCIETY QUARTERLY, The Society, 4338 Bigelow Blvd., Pittsburgh, PA 15213, since 1974.

___HISTORICAL JOURNAL: A QUARTERLY RECORD OF LOCAL HISTORY AND GENEALOGY (CHIEFLY NORTHWEST PA), J. F. Meginness, Williamsport, PA, 1888-94.

___SOUTHWEST PA GENEALOGICAL SERVICES, PO Box 253, Laughlintown, PA 15655.

In addition to the above journals, many PA county historical and/or genealogical societies and some city/town historical societies publish periodicals which contain sizable amounts of genealogical information, particularly for their regions. These periodicals will be indicated in Chapter 4 where the 67 PA counties will be treated individually. The periodicals are also listed in the reference works cited in the first paragraph of this section. Good collections of PA genealogically-oriented periodicals will be found in SLP, LHS, and CLP, and those relating to specific local regions will be found in RL and LL.

Not only do articles pertaining to PA genealogy appear in the above publications, they are also printed in other genealogical periodicals. Fortunately, indexes to major genealogical periodicals are available:

___For periodicals published 1858-1952, consult D. L. Jacobus, INDEX TO GENEALOGICAL PERIODICALS, Genealogical Publishing Co., Baltimore, MD, 1973.

___For periodicals published 1847-1985, then annually 1986-present, consult Fort Wayne and Allen County Public Library Foundation, PERIODICAL SOURCE INDEX, Fort Wayne and Allen County Library Foundation, Fort Wayne, IN, 1986-.

___For periodicals published 1957-present, consult the annual volumes by various editors, I. Waldemaier, E. S. Rogers, G. E. Russell, L. C. Towle, and C. M. Mayhew, GENEALOGICAL PERIODICAL ANNUAL INDEX, various publishers, most recently Heritage Books, Bowie, MD, 1957-.

These index volumes should be sought in SLP, LHS, and FHL (available through FHC), most LGL, some RL, and a few LL. In them, you should consult all general PA listings, then all listings under the counties which

concern you, as well as listings under family names (if included in the in
dexes).

---

19. Genealogical and historical societies

In the state of PA various societies for the study of genealogy, the discovery of hereditary lineages, the accumulation of data, and the publication of the materials have been organized. In addition to these genealogical societies, there are many historical societies which devote much time and effort to genealogical data collection and publication. These organizations are listed in:

___1991 DIRECTORY OF MUSEUMS AND HISTORICAL ORGANIZATIONS IN PA, PA Federation of Museums and Historical Societies, Harrisburg, PA, 1991.

___J. P. Bentley, GENEALOGICAL ADDRESS BOOK, Genealogical Publishing Co., Baltimore, MD, 1996.

___M. K. Meyer, DIRECTORY OF GENEALOGICAL SOCIETIES IN THE USA AND CANADA, The Author, Pasadena, MD, 1982.

___V. N. Chambers, editor, GENEALOGICAL HELPER, Everton Publishers, Logan, UT, latest July-August issue.

___DIRECTORY OF HISTORICAL SOCIETIES AND AGENCIES IN THE US AND CANADA, American Association of State and Local History, Nashville, TN, latest edition.

The PA societies which have a genealogical focus are of four types: (1) state-wide, (2) state-wide with special interests, (3) regional, and (4) local [county, city, town, township, borough].

The major state-wide society for genealogical research in PA is:
___GENEALOGICAL SOCIETY OF PA, 1300 Locust St., Philadelphia, PA 19107.

Among the specialized societies on the state-wide level are:
___American Catholic Historical Society of Philadelphia, 263 South Fourth St., Philadelphia, PA 19105.

___American Swedish Historical Foundation, 1900 Pattison Ave., Philadelphia, PA 19145.

___Evangelical and Reformed Historical Society, 555 West James St., Lancaster, PA 17603.

___Friends Historical Association, Haverford College Library, Haverford, PA 19041.

___German Society of PA, 611 Spring Garden St., Philadelphia, PA 19123.

___Huguenot Society of PA, 1300 Locust St., Philadelphia, PA 19107.

___Lancaster Mennonite Historical Society, 2215 Millstream Rd., Lancaster, PA 17602.

___Moravian Historical Society, 2114 East Center St., Nazareth, PA 18064.

___National Society of Colonial Dames of PA, 231 North Ithan Ave., Rosemont, PA 19010.

___Palatines to America, PO Box 21112, Columbus, OH 43221. [Includes a PA Chapter.]

___PA Dutch Folk Culture Society, Bauer Memorial Library Lenhartsville, PA 19534.

___PA Folklore Society, 411 Logan Hall, University of PA, Philadelphia, PA 19174.

___PA German Society, PO Box 397, Birdsboro, PA 18508.

___PA Scotch-Irish Society, 20th Floor, Three Parkway, Philadelphia, PA 19102.

___PA Society, Sons of the American Revolution, 6715 East Lake Rd., Erie, PA 16511.

___PA Society, Sons of the Revolution, 1300 Locust St., Philadelphia, PA 19107.

___Philadelphia Jewish Archives Center, 625 Walnut St., Philadelphia, PA 19106.

___Presbyterian Historical Society, 425 Lombard St., Philadelphia, PA 19147.

___Society of Mayflower Descendants in PA, 1300 Locust St., Philadelphia, PA 19107.

___Society of the War of 1812 in PA, 108 Avon Rd., Haverford, PA 19041.

___Sons of Union Veterans of the Civil War, Camp 200, 4278 Griscom St., Philadelphia, PA 19124.

___Swedish Colonial Society, 1300 Locust St., Philadelphia, PA 19107.

___Military Order of the Loyal Legion of the US, 1805 Pine St., Philadelphia, PA 19103.

___Valley Forge Historical Society, PO Box 122, Valley Forge, PA 19481.

In addition to the above organizations which have state-wide (or nation-wide) coverage, there are some important regional societies which concentrate on genealogical matters:

___Capital Area Genealogical Society, PO Box 4502, Harrisburg, PA 17111.

___Central PA Genealogical Society, PO Box 1135, State College, PA 16801.

___Genealogical Society of Southwestern PA, PO Box 894, Washington, PA 15301.
___North Central PA Historical Association, c/o Columbia County Historical Society, PO Box 197, Orangeville, PA 17815.
___South Central PA Genealogical Society, PO Box 1824, York, PA 17405.
___Western PA Genealogical Society, 4338 Bigelow Blvd., Pittsburgh, PA 15213.

There are also many <u>local</u> genealogical and historical societies in PA which can be of immense help to you in your quest for your PA ancestor(s). Many of the resident members of these societies are generally very knowledgeable about the background, the early families, and the available records of their local areas. By consulting them, you can often save valuable time as they guide you in your work. The local societies are also the best organizations to contact in order to find if someone else is working or has worked on your family lines. These local societies are named in the publications mentioned in the first paragraph of this chapter. Many of the most important of them will be listed under the counties in Chapter 4, where their addresses will be given so that you can contact them. It is advisable for all PA genealogical searchers to join the PA Genealogical Society as well as any regional and/or county organization which is in your ancestor's area. All correspondence with such societies should be accompanied by an SASE.

20. Land records

One of the most important types of PA genealogical records is that type which deals with land. This is because throughout most of its history a very large fraction of the PA population was made up of land owners. In addition, during the earlier years of the development of PA, land was widely available and quite inexpensive. From its very beginning in 1682, PA has had a land office which has sold the lands of the commonwealth to the first private land owners (individuals or groups). There are basically four types of land records in PA. (1) The <u>first</u> kind involves transactions by which the government of PA (colonial or state) originally transferred land to private groups or individuals. These transactions made use of documents and records called applications, requests, warrants, surveys, resurveys, and patents (or grants). (2) The <u>second</u> kind of land records involves the transfer of PA land as military land grants to PA Revolutionary War (and some French and Indian War) veterans. These records involve documents very similar to those previously mentioned, except that the lands were surveyed before applications were called for. This meant that the patent could be applied for at the time of application. (3) The third kind of land records involves land warranted and/or patented to private individuals or groups by DE, MD, VA, OH, NY, and CT in areas of present-day PA which were at one time claimed by these states or were at one time in disputed territory. (4) The fourth kind of land records involves land transferred from one private individual to another private individual (after the original transfer of the land by PA). The documents in these transactions include deeds and mortgages, and sometimes wills and estate administration papers.

The first category of land records (transfers from the proprietary, colonial, or state government to the first private owner) dates from 1682. Early land was sold in large tracts to people called Masters, who in turn rented the land to tenants or rented the land to immigrants who worked for a given number of years to pay for their transportation to PA. After a period of time these tenants and immigrants received the land on which they worked. As the number of squatters (people who just settled on the land) increased, an application system was started. This arrangement, which continued into this century, involved a prospective land owner making an application for the land he desires. The government then issued a warrant for a survey of the selected land to be made by the deputy or county surveyor. This survey, including a map or plat of the piece of property, was then submitted to the land office. If the land office approved, payment was made and a patent was issued. This patent was effectively a deed which conveyed to the purchaser clear title to the property. After the Revolutionary War, there became another way to acquire land. A person could settle on a piece of property and proceed to improve it, then file a request for a survey, then have the survey sent in to the land office, then finally make payment and receive the patent. A very good reference book to PA land records is available. It goes into great detail concerning the disposition and character of lands granted by the colony and the state of PA.

___D. B. Munger, PA LAND RECORDS, Scholarly Resources, Wilmington, DE, 1991.

The records for this first category of land transfers are found in original form in the PSA, and in the Philadelphia City Hall. There are also survey and patent records to be found in the counties. In addition, a number of published records appear in the PPA. The original records are as follows:

__PA APPLICATIONS, WARRANTS, SURVEYS, RESURVEYS, AND PATENTS, SINCE 1682, with indexes and other finding aids, PSA, Harrisburg, PA.

__RECORDS OF GENERAL LOAN OFFICE AND STATE TREASURER, Record Group 8, includes MORTGAGE BOOKS (1774-88, 4 volumes) indexed, and MORTGAGE RECORDS (1773-93, 5 boxes) indexed, PSA, Harrisburg, PA.

__RECORDS OF BUREAU OF LAND, Record Group 17, includes MORTGAGE RECORDS (1773-93) partially indexed, RENT RECORDS (1683-1776) partially indexed, WARRANT RECORDS (1684-1864) indexed, UNPATENTED LAND RECORDS (1820-37) unindexed, PATENT RECORDS (1781-1809) unindexed, LAND PAYMENT AND PURCHASE RECORDS (1781-1809) unindexed, SURVEY RECORDS (1675-9, 1701-1874) partially indexed, PSA, Harrisburg, PA.

__RECORDS OF THE OFFICE OF THE COMPTROLLER GENERAL, Record Group 4, includes WARRANT BOOKS (1791-1808, 6 volumes) unindexed, WARRANT COUNTERPARTS (1792-9, 1806-8, 6 boxes), WARRANT REGISTERS (1782-1807, 8 Volumes) indexed, and WARRANTS (1778-1809, 16 cartons) unindexed.

__WARRANTS AND SURVEYS OF THE PROVINCE OF PA, 1682-1759, 9 volumes, Philadelphia City Hall, Philadelphia, PA, indexed by A. Weinberg, T. E. Slattery, and C. E. Hughes, Jr, WARRANTS AND SURVEYS OF THE PROVINCE OF PA, Department of Records, City of Philadelphia, Philadelphia, PA, 1965.

__COUNTY LAND APPLICATION SURVEY, AND PATENT BOOKS AND PAPERS, from origin of each county, usually indexed, Offices of County Surveyor and Recorder of Deeds, County Court Houses or Local Historical or Genealogical Society or Local Library, in each individual county.

The pertinent records which have been published in the PPA are as follows, along with information on the indexing:

__LAND WARRANTS, 1682-1898, PPA C(8), 3(2-3, 24-26), indexed in C(General Index to C and 1st Series) 1-433, 3(2-3, at end of each volume), 3(27-30).

__LAND WARRANTEES BY COUNTY, 1733-1896, PPA 3(24-26), indexed in 3(27-30).

__BOARD OF PROPERTY RECORDS, CAVEAT BOOKS, 1748-84, PPA 3(2) INDEXED AT END OF VOLUME, also minutes including early land records, 1685-1795, PPA 2(19), 3(1) 25-773, 3(2) 1-158, indexed at end of each volume. PPA 2(19) published as W. H. Egle,

EARLY PA LAND RECORDS, Genealogical Publishing Co., Baltimore, MD, 1976.

The records in PSA, the Philadelphia City Hall, and the counties are generally available for your use. And the PPA will be found in SLP, LHS, CLP, FHL (available through FHC), many LGL, most RL, and some LL. The records and indexes of the PA Division of Land Records, are in the PSA. You especially need to examine a microfilm index in the PSA:

___MICROFILM INDEX OF LAND WARRANTEES BY COUNTY, Search Room, PSA, Harrisburg, PA.

The Division of Land Records was involved for a number of years in a very difficult project which can provide immense help to genealogists. They developed many Warrantee Township Maps. These maps show all the original tracts of land granted by the state along with the names of the warrantees. They were completed for 24 counties (Allegheny, Beaver, Bradford, Cameron, Dauphin, Elk, Erie, Fayette, Greene, Lackawanna, Lancaster, Lawrence, Luzerne, McKean, Mercer, Pike, Potter, Sullivan, Susquehanna, Tioga, Venango, Warren, Washington, Wayne) and partially completed for 4 counties (Berks, Fulton, Huntingdon, Schuylkill). The maps are available for a small fee from PSA. Copies of the maps may be seen in SLP and LHS, and those for individual counties have been deposited in the court houses.

The second category of land records consists of transfers of PA land as military land grants to PA Revolutionary War and some French and Indian War veterans. The state of PA set aside a sizable amount of land in northwestern PA for rewarding its Revolutionary War and French and Indian War veterans. Veterans were permitted to apply for tax-free property (known as Donation Lands) in Crawford and Mercer Counties and parts of present-day Armstrong, Butler, Erie, Forest, Lawrence, Venango, and Warren Counties. Also legislation was passed to permit veterans to purchase land at very cheap prices to compensate for the depreciation of money which was owed them from the War. These lands, known as Depreciation Lands were located in parts of present-day Allegheny, Armstrong, Beaver, Butler, and Lawrence Counties. These plots of land were surveyed before being offered, and thus a veteran's application lead directly to a patent.

The original records for these Donation and Depreciation Lands are located in the PSA. There are also patent records to be found in the counties. In addition, a number of published lists appear in the PPA. The original records are as follows:

___PA DONATION AND DEPRECIATION LAND APPLICATIONS AND PATENTS, with indexes and other finding aids, PSA, PSA Microfilm Roll No. 3429, Harrisburg, PA.

___RECORDS OF THE OFFICE OF THE COMPTROLLER GENERAL, Record Group 4, includes RETURN OF OFFICERS AND SOLDIERS TO WHOM PATENTS WERE NOT ISSUED, alphabetically arranged, and RETURN OF PA LINE ENTITLED TO DONATION LANDS, indexed, PSA, Harrisburg, PA.

___COUNTY LAND APPLICATION AND PATENT BOOKS AND PAPERS, usually indexed, Office of Recorder of Deeds, County Court Houses or Local Historical or Genealogical Society or Local Library, in counties listed in previous paragraph.

The pertinent records which have been published in the PPA are as follows, along with location of the indexes:

___DEPRECIATION LANDS, PPA C(14-16), 1(11), 3(3), indexed in C(General Index to C and 1 Series), 3(3, end of volume).

___DONATION LANDS, PPA C(14-16), 1(11), 3(39) 575-757, 3(7) 659-757, 4(4) 171, 6(4) 44-7, indexed in C(General Index to C and 1 Series), 3(3 and 7, at end of each volume), 4(12) 643-963, 7(1-5).

The records in PSA and the counties are generally available for your use. And the PPA will be found in SLP, LHS, CLP, FHL (available through FHC), many LGL, most RL, and some LL.

As you delve into the original transfers of land from PA to the first private owners, you need to realize that the applicant or warrantee is not always the same person as the patentee, that is, the person receiving the land. This is usually because the person who applied for and received the right to claim or purchase the land sold this right to someone else who used it to receive the patent. It also often occurred that the purchaser of the land may never see it, that is, that he sold it rather than settled on it. Another special consideration that you need to recognize is that after several years following the military land offer, all land that had not been taken up was opened to general purchase. Thus, just because a person obtained land in the military land districts does not mean he served in the military.

An excellent detailed guide to the two types of PA colonial and state land records discussed above is:

___D. B. Munger, PA LAND RECORDS, A HISTORY AND GUIDE FOR RESEARCH, Scholarly Sources, Wilmington, DE, 1991.

The <u>third</u> category of land record involves land warranted and/or patented to private owners by CT, VA, MD, and NY areas of present-day PA which were at one time claimed by these colonies/states or were thought by inhabitants to belong to them. During 1753-82, CT settlers came into northeastern PA. Up until about 1784, there was the VA District of West Augusta (which split into Monongalia, Ohio, and Yohogania Counties) in southwestern PA. The MD-PA border was in dispute until about 1767, but some people near the line were in ambiguity about where they belonged up until about 1800. And the NY-PA border was not firmly established until 1787. Should you suspect that your ancestors were caught up in any of these, you need to make careful inquiries at the appropriate State Archives (CT, VA, MD, NY) and in the counties of these states near or in your ancestors' area. Some references to these contested regions and their records are as follows:

__W. A. Russ, Jr., PA'S BOUNDARIES, PA Historical Association, Philadelphia, PA, 1966.

__J. S. Morris, THE MD-PA CONTROVERSY, THE PA-CT CONTROVERSY, and THE VA-PA CONTROVERSY, Bibliographies and Maps, The Author, Pittsburgh, PA, 1985.

__J. P. Boyd and R. J. Taylor, THE SUSQUEHANNA COMPANY PAPERS, Cornell University Press, Ithaca, NY, 1930-71, 11 volumes. [CT]

__PAPERS ON THE CT SETTLERS, PA Surveyor General's Office, Harrisburg, PA, numerous microfilms with index.

__CONNECTICUT CLAIMS, PPA C(5, 12-16), 1(2, 4, 6, 9, 11), 2(18), 4(2-4), indexed in C(General Index to C and 1 Series), 2(18, index at end of volume), 4(12) 643-963.

__W. H. Egle, DOCUMENTS RELATING TO THE CT SETTLEMENT IN THE WYOMING VALLEY, Heritage Books, Bowie, MD, 1990.

__G. E. McCracken, The American Genealogist 55 (1979) 81-7; D. B. Munger, New England Historic and Genealogical Register 139 (April 1985) 112-225.

__B. Crumrine, VA COURT RECORDS IN SOUTHWESTERN PA, Genealogical Publishing Co., Baltimore, MD, 1902-5 (1981).

__R. M. Bell, VA Genealogist 7 (1963) 78-83, 103-7, 152-62, 11 (1967) 126-7; J. F. Valentine, Genealogical Journal 4 (1975) 141-7; R. M. Bell, National Genealogical Society Quarterly 45 (1957) 132-6.

__VA CLAIMS, PPA 3(3) 483-574.

For the PA counties along the MD border, special attention should be paid to records of the MD counties (in parentheses) just across the line: Chester and Lancaster (Cecil), York and Adams (Frederick), Franklin

(Washington), Bedford and Somerset (Allegheny). The Holland Company also had land in PA. Their records should be sought in the Buffalo and Erie County Historical Society in Buffalo, NY. The following article should also be read:

___W. J. McClintock, Western PA Historical Magazine <u>21</u> (1938) 119-38.

The <u>fourth</u> category of land records involves land transferred from one private owner to another. These are records which are kept at the county level, and they will be found in the county court houses in the Office of the Recorder of Deeds. The most important documents are deeds which are almost always indexed. Also to be found in this office are mortgage records which are also usually indexed. For many counties microfilm copies of deed and mortgage records and their indexes will be found in PSA, LHS, and FHL (available through FHC). These microfilm holdings will be listed under the counties in Chapter 4. As you search deed and mortgage records for land sales and purchases involving your forebears, please don't forget that sometimes land transfers were made by a will, in which case there often is no deed or mortgage record.

21. Manuscripts

One of the most useful and yet one of the most unused sources of genealogical data are the various manuscript collections relating to PA. These collections will be found in state, regional, and private libraries, archives, museums, and repositories located in numerous places in PA, including universities, colleges, and church agencies. Manuscript collections consist of all sorts of records of religious, educational, patriotic, business, social, civil, professional, governmental, and political organizations; documents, letters, memoirs, notes and papers of early settlers, ministers, politicians, business men, educators, physicians, dentists, lawyers, judges, and farmers; records of churches, cemeteries, mortuaries, schools, corporations, and industries; works of artists, musicians, writers, sculptors, photographers, architects, and historians; and records, papers, letters, and reminiscences of participants in various wars, as well as records of military organizations and campaigns.

The major sources of manuscripts relating to PA are PSA, LHS, LWP, The Van Pelt Library of the University of PA, and the various religious organization repositories mentioned in section 7 of this chapter. In addition, many PA colleges and universities, and many PA county historical societies have notable collections. The holdings of these repositories are described in the following volumes and reference aids:

___J. C. Parker, A USER'S GUIDE TO THE MANUSCRIPT COLLECTION OF THE GENEALOGICAL SOCIETY OF PA, Marietta Publishing Co., Turlock, CA, 1986.
___I. Richman, HISTORICAL MANUSCRIPT DEPOSITORIES IN PA, The PA Historical and Museum Commission, Harrisburg, PA, 1965. [Needs to be updated, but still very useful for identifying PA collections.]
___H. E. Whipkey, GUIDE TO MANUSCRIPT GROUPS IN THE PSA, PA Historical and Museum Commission, Harrisburg, PA, 1976.
___F. J. Dallett, GUIDE TO THE ARCHIVES OF THE UNIVERSITY OF PA FROM 1740 TO 1820, University of PA Archives, Philadelphia, PA, 1978.
___Historical Society of PA, GUIDE TO THE MANUSCRIPT COLLECTIONS OF THE HISTORICAL SOCIETY OF PA, The Society, Philadelphia, PA, 1949.
___CARD CATALOGS, LHS, Philadelphia, PA.
___THE MAIN, MANUSCRIPT, AND SPECIAL CATALOGS, Van Pelt Library, University of PA, Philadelphia, PA.
___CARD CATALOG, LWP, Pittsburgh, PA.

There are several important national-level catalogs of manuscript repositories and their contents which will lead you to manuscript materials, both in PA and outside PA, which could refer to your ancestors. These are:
___US Library of Congress, THE NATIONAL UNION CATALOG OF MANUSCRIPT COLLECTIONS, The Library, Washington, DC, annual volumes since 1959-, index in each volume, also cumulative indexes; these indexes are by names, places, and historical periods, be sure and look also for surnames listed under the heading Genealogy. See the following listing for another index.
___E. Altham and several others, INDEX TO PERSONAL NAMES IN THE NATIONAL UNION CATALOG OF MANUSCRIPT COLLECTIONS, 1959-84, Chadwyck-Healey Publishing Company, Arlington, VA, 1988, 2 volumes.
___P. M. Hamer, A GUIDE TO ARCHIVES AND MANUSCRIPTS IN THE US, Yale University Press, New Haven, CT, 1961.
___US National Historical Publications and Records Commission, DIRECTORY OF ARCHIVES AND MANUSCRIPT REPOSITORIES IN THE US, The Commission, Washington, DC, 1978.
___National Society Daughters of the American Revolution, LIBRARY CATALOG, FAMILY HISTORIES AND GENEALOGIES, The Society, Washington, DC, 1982.

___H. Cripe and D. Campbell, AMERICAN MANUSCRIPTS, 1763-1815, Scholarly Resources, Wilmington, DE, 1977.

The reference books mentioned in the previous paragraphs are available in SLP, LHS, CLP, and in many other larger libraries including LGL and RL. If you find in these volumes materials which you suspect may relate to your ancestor, write to the appropriate repository asking for details. Don't forget to send an SASE and to ask for names of researchers if you cannot go in person. In PSA, LHS, and some other PA repositories there are special indexes, catalogs, and other finding aids to facilitate your search. In some cases, there are several indexes, not just one, so you need to be careful to examine all of them.

22. Marriage records

During the early formative years of the colony of PA (1647-82) a law was passed requiring marriage registration, but the regulation was largely ignored. The result was that during the period 1682-1851 not many official state or county records of marriages were kept. The most important of the few surviving compilations are:

___MARRIAGES RECORDED BY THE PA REGISTRAR GENERAL, 1685-9, PPA 2(8) v-viii.

___MARRIAGES IN THE PA GOVERNORS' ACCOUNTS, 1742-52, 1759-62, 4 volumes, Record Group 21, originals and 2 microfilms, PSA, Harrisburg, PA.

___EARLY PA MARRIAGE RECORDS, 1743-1821, PPA 2(2) 3-344, 2(8) 1-790, 2(9) 1 ff., 6(6) 285-310.

___MARRIAGE BONDS, PHILADELPHIA COUNTY, 1784-6, 9 folders, Record Group 27, PSA, Harrisburg, PA. [Same as PPA 6(6) 285-310.]

___J. B. Linn and W. H. Egle, PA MARRIAGES PRIOR TO 1790, Genealogical Publishing Co., Baltimore, MD, 1979. [From the above PPA listings.]

___J. B. Linn and W. H. Egle, RECORD OF PA MARRIAGES PRIOR TO 1810, Genealogical Publishing Co., Baltimore, MD, 1968. [From the above PPA listings.]

___PA MARRIAGE LICENSES, 1742-8, 1762-76, PA Magazine of History and Biography, 1915-7, volumes 39-41.

In the above listings PPA stands for the [PUBLISHED] PA ARCHIVES, a 128-volume set of records of the PSA which is discussed in detail in section 10. The reference PPA 2(2) 3-344 means [PUBLISHED] PA AR-

CHIVES, series 2, (volume 2), pp. 3-344. Do not forget that much of the material in PPA is indexed, as described in sections 10 and 17.

In the years 1852-4, the Register of Wills in each county was required to maintain marriage records and to send duplicates to the state. However, reporting to the Register was often not done, so the records are far from being complete, and some of them have since been lost. The entries in these records include names, parents' names, residence of husband, date, and place. The surviving originals of these marriage reports are in CH, LL, or PSA. Microfilm copies of many of them are in PSA and FHL, the latter being available through FHC. The records in PSA have been gathered together and are available as:

___RECORD AND INDEXES OF BIRTHS, DEATHS, AND MARRIAGES, 1852-4, Record Group 26, PSA, Harrisburg, PA, originals and 6 microfilm rolls.

Not all counties are included in this collection and hence it may be necessary for you to search the CH, LL, and FHL holdings for the counties whose records are not there. In Chapter 4, those counties whose 1852-4 vital records are in PSA and/or FHL are indicated.

For the time span 1855-84, no official state or county marriage records were kept, but some cities maintained registers. Chief among these are the following:

___LANCASTER MAYOR'S RECORD BOOK, MARRIAGES 1858-61, Record Group 48, PSA, Harrisburg, PA.

___PHILADELPHIA MARRIAGE REGISTERS, 1860-85, 23 volumes, indexed, Vital Statistics, Philadelphia Department of Public Health, City Hall Annex, Philadelphia, PA 19107.

___PITTSBURGH MARRIAGE RECORDS, 1870-85, Office of Biostatistics, Pittsburgh Health Department, City-County Bldg., Pittsburgh, PA 15219; microfilm in CLP.

Since 01 October 1885, marriage records have been kept in the Office of the Clerk of the Orphans' Court in each county. These records consist of applications for marriage licenses and returned marriage licenses. The applications contain names, age, birthplace, and residence of each of the parties, and the date of the license. The returned licenses show the names and addresses of the parties, the date of the marriage, and the person performing the ceremony. The originals of these records are to be found in the local CH and/or LL. Microfilm copies of records for many counties may be found in PSA, FHL, LGL, and LL. The PSA has collected the records for all counties for 1885-9 and has grouped them alphabetically by grooms' and brides' names:

__RECORD OF MARRIAGES, 1885-9, Record Group 14, 4 volumes, 2 microfilm rolls, PSA, Harrisburg, PA.

As you can see from the above, very few official marriage data are available before 1885. This means that information needs to be sought from other non-official sources. The most likely sources for such information (with the section in this chapter where they are discussed) are as follows: Bible (section 2), biography (section 3), cemetery (5), census (6), church (7), manuscripts (22), military pension (25-27), mortuary (28), newspaper (30), published genealogies (31), tax lists (33), and will-probate records (34). The most fruitful of these sources are usually the church and newspaper records. There is a useful compilation of PA vital records which have been published in two major PA genealogical journals. This compilation contains many marriage data:

__PA Magazine of History and Biography and PA Genealogical Magazine, PA VITAL RECORDS, Genealogical Publishing Co., Baltimore, MD, 1983, 3 volumes. [Over 100000 names.]

Numerous non-official sources of PA marriages, both at the state and county levels are listed in

__J. D. and E. D. Stemmons, THE VITAL RECORD COMPENDIUM, Everton Publishers, Logan, UT, 1979.

When you are seeking marriage date and place information in archives and libraries, be certain to explore all the above mentioned sources, and don't fail to look under the county listings and the following headings in library card catalogs: Marriage licenses, and Registers of births, etc.

23. Military records: colonial

Before going into detail on sources of military records (sections 23, 24, 25, 26) you need to understand the types of records which are available and what they contain. There are five basic types which are of value to genealogists: (a) service, (b) pension, (3) bounty land, (d) claims, and (e) military unit history. Service records contain a number of the following: name, rank, military unit, personal description, plus dates and places of enlistment, mustering in, payrolls, wounding, capture, death, imprisonment, hospital stay, release, oath of allegiance, desertion, promotion, battles, heroic action, re-enlistment, leave of absence, mustering out, and discharge. Pension records (applications and payment documents) contain a number of the following: name, age, rank, military unit, personal description, name of wife, names and ages of children, residences during pension period, plus dates and places of service, wartime experiences, birth, marriage, pension payments, and death. <u>Bounty land</u> records (applications and awards of land) contain the same sort of data that pension records do. <u>Claims</u> of military participants for back pay and of civilians for supplies or services contain some of the following: name, details of claim, date of claim, witnesses to claim, documents supporting claim, action on claim, amount awarded. <u>Military unit history</u> records trace the detailed events of the experiences of a given military unit throughout a war, often referring to officers, enlisted personnel, battles, campaigns, deaths, plus dates and places of organization, mustering in, reorganization, mustering out and other pertinent events. Now, with this background, you are ready to learn where these records may be found.

The Quakers who established PA were opposed to war. They dominated the provincial Assembly and stood against all efforts to establish a provincial militia or to raise provincial troops. On several occasions the proprietors tried to establish a militia but the Quaker Assembly squelched the action. However, even though there was no militia law, citizens of PA were free to enter the British military forces in the colonies and to establish volunteer militia groups. In King William's War (1689-97), Queen Anne's War (1702-13), the War of Jenkins' Ear (1739-), and King George's War (1744-8) PA either raised volunteer militia for the British or gave money to support the war effort. The French and Indian War, which began in 1755 and ended in 1763, and Pontiac's War (1763-5) were essentially the only military actions in which pre-Revolutionary PA organized and paid troops to defend the colony.

The records related to these wars which contain names of participants and describe the activities include:

___PPA C(4) 468, C(5) 174-94, 209-10, 248-9, 325, 1(1), 1(49), 1(12) 323-467, 2(1-2, 4-7), 4(1-4, 11-12), 5(1), indexed as C and 1(General Index), 2(index at end of each volume), 4(index in volume 12), 5(index in Series 6(15))).

___M. J. Buckalew and others, FRONTIER FORTS PRIOR TO 1783, The Authors, Philadelphia, PA, 1916.

___B. Laverty, COLONIAL MUSTER ROLLS AT LHS, Historical Society of PA, Philadelphia, PA, 1983.

___M. Dunn, INDEX TO PA'S COLONIAL RECORDS SERIES, Genealogical Publishing Co., Baltimore, MD, 1992.

A useful discussion of pre-Revolutionary military activity in PA is provided by:

___W. A. Hunter, PRE-REVOLUTIONARY MILITARY SERVICE IN
PA, Information Leaflet No. 2, PA Historical and Museum Commission, Harrisburg, PA, 1969.

_____

24. Military records: Revolutionary War

_____

As mentioned in Chapter
1, PA had a heavy
involvement in the
American War of Inde-
pendence, particularly in
the middle years. Over 26000 PA patriots fought with the Continental
(united colonies) Army and well over this number of state-related military
personnel (associators, militia, rangers, privateers, state regulars) fought
in state units. Note carefully that there were two types of service: 1st
federal or national or Continental service in which the military units were
under the control of the Continental Congress, and 2nd state service in
which the military units were under the control of PA. Continental
service was rendered in regiments or battalions in which men enlisted for
long periods of service. State service was rendered in units of several
different types. Early in the war, there was no law requiring service, so
volunteer units known as associators (part-time, short-term duty during
1775-7) were formed. In 1777, a law making military service compulsory
was passed, and militia (part-time, short-term duty during 1777-84) units
replaced the volunteer associators. All through the war, there were also
two other volunteer types of state service, namely, State Regulars
(full-time, long-term duty) and Rangers (full-time duty against the frontier
Indians for terms of about 6 months). There were also over 1000 men
who served in the PA Navy. Records for the Continental soldiers were
kept on both the national and state levels, but records for the
state-related personnel were kept only in PA. Further details on these
military service arrangements will be found in:
___PA Historical and Museum Commission, THE MILITARY SYSTEM
OF PA DURING THE REVOLUTIONARY WAR, Leaflet No. 3,
The Commission, Harrisburg, PA, 1968.
___J. B. B. Trussell, UNDERSTANDING PA'S REVOLUTIONARY
WAR ORGANIZATION AS AN AID IN GENEALOGICAL
RESEARCH, Western PA Genealogical Society Quarterly, Volume
8, No. 4, pp. 187-97.

Quite a large volume of records relating to this war is available for
you to investigate: national service records, national pension records, national bounty land records, state service records, state bounty land re-
cords, state pension records, and some county records. Again, please

recognize that you will usually find both national and state records on Continental personnel, but there are only state records (no national ones) on the associators, militia, rangers, and state regulars.

The first step you should take in searching for your PA ancestor who may have served in this War or supported it is to employ the following indexes and look for him in them:

___National Archives, GENERAL INDEX TO COMPILED SERVICE RECORDS OF REVOLUTIONARY WAR SOLDIERS, The Archives, Washington, DC, Microfilm Publication M860, 58 rolls. [Continental only, copies in PSA, NA, NAFB, FHL, FHC, can be borrowed through your LL or through AGLL, PO Box 244, Bountiful, UT 84010]

___National Archives, INDEX TO THE COMPILED SERVICE RECORDS OF AMERICAN NAVAL PERSONNEL DURING THE REVOLUTIONARY WAR, The Archives, Washington, DC, Microfilm Publication M879, 1 roll. [Includes Marines, copies in PSA, NA, NAFB, FHL, FHC]

___National Genealogical Society, INDEX TO REVOLUTIONARY WAR PENSION [AND BOUNTY LAND] APPLICATIONS IN THE NATIONAL ARCHIVES, The Society, Washington, DC, 1976. [Copies in SLP, LHS, CLP, LGL, some RL, FHL, FHC]

___F. Rider, AMERICAN GENEALOGICAL INDEX, Godfrey Memorial Library, Middletown, CT, 1942-52, 48 volumes; and F. Rider, AMERICAN GENEALOGICAL AND BIOGRAPHICAL INDEX, Godfrey Memorial Library, Middletown, CT, 1952-85, over 190 volumes, more to come. [Continental and state service]

___US Pay Department, War Department, REGISTERS OF CERTIFICATES ISSUED BY JOHN PIERCE TO OFFICERS AND SOLDIERS OF THE CONTINENTAL ARMY, Genealogical Publishing Co., Baltimore, MD, 1983.

___National Society of the DAR, DAR PATRIOT INDEX, The Society, Washington, DC, latest edition. [Continental, state, public service, military aid]

If you discover from these sources that your ancestor served in the Continental forces, you may then proceed to obtain his records from the National Archives. The service records are:

___The National Archives, COMPILED SERVICE RECORDS OF SOLDIERS WHO SERVED IN THE AMERICAN ARMY DURING THE REVOLUTIONARY WAR, The Archives, Washington, DC, Microfilm Publication M881, 1097 rolls.

__The National Archives, COMPILED SERVICE RECORDS OF AMERICAN NAVAL, QUARTERMASTER, AND COMMISSARY PERSONNEL WHO SERVED DURING THE REVOLUTIONARY WAR, The Archives, Washington, DC, Microfilm Publication M880, 4 rolls.

And the pension and bounty land records are:

__The National Archives, REVOLUTIONARY WAR PENSION AND BOUNTY LAND WARRANT APPLICATION FILES, The Archives, Washington, DC, Microfilm Publication M804, 2670 rolls.

These films are available at NA, NAFB, FHL, FHC, and may be borrowed from your LL or though AGLL, PO Box 244, Bountiful, UT 84010. Or you may write the NA (Reference Service Branch, National Archives, 8th and PA Ave., NW, Washington, DC 20408) for 3 copies of NATF Form 80 which you can use to request service, pension, and bounty land records by mail. A third alternative is to hire a researcher in Washington, DC to go to the NA for you. Lists of such searchers will be found in

__J. N. Chambers, editor, THE GENEALOGICAL HELPER, Everton Publishers, Logan, UT, latest September-October issue.

The second step that you should take, especially if you failed to find your progenitor in the first step is to look into state sources. Even if you did find your ancestor in the first step, you should not neglect this second possible source of data. Foremost among these state sources is

__PPA C(5, 10-16), 1(7-12), 2(1-7, 10-15), 3(3, 5-7, 23), 4(2-4, 10-12), 5(1-8), 6(1-2, 4, 9, 14) indexed as follows: 1(General Index to C and 1) 1-653, 2(indexes at ends of volumes 1, 3-7, 11, 12, 14, 18-19), 3(indexes at ends of each volume and in volumes 27-30), 4(indexes at end of each volume and in volume 12), 6(15), 7(1-5).

Remember that numbers before the parentheses refer to series in the PPA, numbers in parentheses refer to volumes, and numbers after parentheses refer to pages. Included in these references are records referring to Associators, Continental Line, Depreciation Lands, Depreciation Pay, Donation Lands, Militia, Muster Rolls, the PA Navy, the PA Line, Pension Applications, Pensioners, Rangers, and PA Regulars. Be a bit cautious in searching these published records because there are some duplications of lists, some errors in which some men are listed in the wrong county or township, and some transcription errors. Many other PA Revolutionary War records are held by PSA and are listed in:

__R. M. Dructor, GUIDE TO GENEALOGICAL SOURCES AT THE PSA, PA Historical and Museum Commission, Harrisburg, PA, 1981.

___R. M. Baumann and D. S. Wallace, GUIDE TO MICROFILM COLLECTIONS IN THE PSA, PA Historical and Museum Commission, Harrisburg, PA, 1980.

Especially important among these are:

___REVOLUTIONARY WAR ASSOCIATORS, LINE, MILITIA, AND NAVY ACCOUNTS, 1775-1809, Record Group 4, PSA, Harrisburg, PA.

___REVOLUTIONARY WAR MILITARY ABSTRACT CARD FILE, 1775-83, alphabetically by name, PSA, Harrisburg, PA.

___REVOLUTIONARY WAR PENSION ACCOUNTS AND FILES, Record Group 2, Microfilm, 7 rolls, alphabetically by name, PSA, Harrisburg, PA.

Also be sure to make use of the card index in PSA which lists over 100000 persons who gave military service to PA during 1775-1809.

___MILITARY ABSTRACT CARD FILE, PSA, Harrisburg, PA.

And do not fail to examine the following books:

___H. E. Cope, SOLDIERS AND WIDOWS OF REVOLUTIONARY WAR PENSIONS GRANTED BY PA, The Author, n.p., n.d.

___M. F. Lloyd, PA SOCIETY OF SONS OF THE AMERICAN REVOLUTION CENTENNIAL REGISTER, 1888-1988, The Society, Harrisburg, PA, 1988.

The third step that you may take is to look into the records of the PA county where your veteran was buried. The specific source you should seek is the County Veterans' Grave Register which dates from 1775 forward. Finally mention needs to be made of some PA Loyalist records. Important among these are some PPA records of confiscated and forfeited estates and of prisoners:

___PPA C(11-16), 1(7-10), 2(1), 6(12-13) indexed in 1(General Index to C and 1) 1-653, 2(index at end of volume 1), 7(1-5).

Also notable are records of claims of Loyalists for their property losses and records of some other types:

___Bureau of Archives for Ontario, SECOND REPORT FOR THE PROVINCE OF ONTARIO, The Bureau, Ontario, 1904.

___Public Record Office, AUDIT OFFICE SERIES 12 AND 13, The Office, London, England. [Copies in FHL and Library of Congress]

___M. J. Clark, LOYALISTS IN THE SOUTHERN CAMPAIGN OF THE REVOLUTIONARY WAR, Genealogical Publishing Co., Baltimore, MD, 1980-1, especially volumes 2-3.

___A. M. Ousterhouk, CONFISCATED PA ESTATES, PA Genealogical Magazine 30 (1978) 237-253.

___FORFEITED ESTATES ACCOUNTS, PPA 6(12-13).

___MUSTER ROLLS, PA LOYALIST REGIMENTS, Public Archives of
   Canada, Ottawa, Ontario, Canada, and Library of Congress,
   Washington, DC.

For considerably more detail about genealogical data which can be
gleaned from Revolutionary War records, you may consult a book especially dedicated to this:

___Geo. K. Schweitzer, REVOLUTIONARY WAR GENEALOGY,
   Geo. K. Schweitzer, 407 Ascot Court, Knoxville, TN 37923-5807.

This volume goes into detail on local, state, and national records, discusses both militia and Continental Army service, deals in detail with service,
pension, bounty land, and claims records, and treats the subjects of regimental histories, battle accounts, medical records, courts-martial, foreign
participants, Loyalist data, maps, museums, historic sites, patriotic organizations, and many other related topics. Another very useful detailed
source book listing many Revolutionary War records is:

___J. C. and L. L. Neagles, LOCATING YOUR REVOLUTIONARY
   WAR ANCESTOR, Everton Publishers, Logan, UT, 1983.

---

25. Military records: War of 1812

After the Revolution, the PA
militia continued quite actively.
One of the major duties was the
defense of the frontier against
Indian attacks. A number of
their personnel records, especially during 1783-1817, will be found in the
PPA as follows:

___PPA 5(3, 5) and 6(3-5) indexed in 6(15) and 7(1-5).

There are also other militia records in the PSA which may be located by
looking in:

___R. M. Baumann and D. S. Wallace, GUIDE TO MICROFILM COL-
   LECTIONS IN THE PSA, PA Historical and Museum Commission,
   Harrisburg, PA, 1980.

Not to be overlooked during the post-Revolutionary War period are some
federal records relating to federal service 1784-1811. These are indexed
and the notations in the index lead to further documents:

___National Archives, INDEX TO COMPILED MILITARY SERVICE
   RECORDS OF VOLUNTEER SOLDIERS WHO SERVED FROM
   1784 TO 1811, The Archives, Washington, DC, Microfilm Publication
   M694, 9 rolls.

In the period 1812-60, the US was involved in two major foreign wars: The War of 1812 (1812-5) and the Mexican War (1846-8). A number of PA men were participants in the War of 1812. They served both in national and in state organizations, and therefore several types of national records (service, bounty land, pension) as well as state records (service, pension) need to be sought. Only a few national pensions were given before 1871, and state pension records did not begin until 1866. To obtain national records (only for men who served in national units) you may write the NA and request copies of NATF Form 80, which may be used to order military service, bounty land, and pension information. Or you may choose to visit the NA or to have a hired researcher do the work for you. Instructions for these approaches are the same as given for the Revolutionary War records in the previous section. Among the microfilm indexes and alphabetical files which the NA employees will search, or which you or your hired researcher should search are:

___The National Archives, INDEX TO COMPILED SERVICE RECORDS OF VOLUNTEER SOLDIERS WHO SERVED DURING THE WAR OF 1812, The Archives, Washington, DC, Microfilm Publication M602, 234 rolls. [Leads to service records.]

___The National Archives, INDEX TO WAR OF 1812 PENSION APPLICATION FILES, The Archives, Washington, DC, Microfilm Publication M313, 102 rolls.

___The National Archives, WAR OF 1812 MILITARY BOUNTY LAND WARRANTS (WITH INDEXES), 1815-58, The Archives, Washington, DC, Microfilm Publication M848, 14 rolls.

___The National Archives, POST-REVOLUTIONARY WAR BOUNTY LAND WARRANT APPLICATION FILE, The Archives, Washington, DC, arranged alphabetically.

Copies of the three microfilm publications mentioned above are available at NA, some NAFB, some LGL, and at FHL (and through FHC). The microfilms are available on interlibrary loan from your local library or directly through AGLL (PO Box 244, Bountiful, UT 84010). Among published national sources for War of 1812 data are:

___F. I. Ordway, Jr., REGISTER OF THE GENERAL SOCIETY OF THE WAR OF 1812, The Society, Washington, DC, 1972.

___F. S. Galvin, 1812 ANCESTOR INDEX, National Society of the US Daughters of 1812, Washington, DC, 1970.

___C. S. Peterson, KNOWN MILITARY DEAD DURING THE WAR OF 1812, The Author, Baltimore, MD, 1955.

Among the state source volumes, records, and microfilms which you should search for PA military service and pension records are:

___PPA 2(12), 4(5), 6(7-10), indexed in 2(end of volume 12), 7(1-59).

___WAR OF 1812 LIST OF SOLDIERS, Record Group 2, Microfilm, 2 rolls, PSA, Harrisburg, PA, alphabetical by name.

___WAR OF 1812 PENSION FILE, 1866-96, Record Group 2, Microfilm, 27 rolls, PSA, Harrisburg, PA, alphabetical by name.

___WAR OF 1812 MILITIA ACCOUNTS, 1812-27, Record Group 2, Microfilm, 7 rolls, PSA, Harrisburg, PA.

___J. B. Linn and W. H. Egle, MUSTER ROLLS OF THE PA VOLUNTEERS IN THE WAR OF 1812, Genealogical Publishing Co., Baltimore, MD, 1890 (1967).

Do not fail to look in the county Veterans' Grave Register for the burial place of your veteran forebear. For considerably more detail about genealogical information which can be derived from War of 1812 records, you may consult a book especially dedicated to this:

___Geo. K. Schweitzer, WAR OF 1812 GENEALOGY, Geo. K. Schweitzer, 407 Ascot Court, Knoxville, TN 37923-5807.

This volume goes into detail on local, state, and national records, discusses service, pension, bounty land, and claims records, and treats the subjects of regimental histories, hospital records, courts-martial, prisoners, militia activity, battle sites, museums, officer biographies, and many other related topics.

The Mexican War was fought 1846-8. As before NATF Form 80 should be obtained and used, or you should visit the NA, or you should hire a researcher as indicated in previously-given instructions (see section 24). Again, military service, pension, and bounty land records should be asked for. The NA indexes which lead to the records and some alphabetized national records include:

___The National Archives, INDEX TO THE COMPILED SERVICE RECORDS OF VOLUNTEER SOLDIERS DURING THE MEXICAN WAR, The Archives, Washington, DC, Microfilm Publication M616, 41 rolls.

___The National Archives, INDEX TO MEXICAN WAR PENSION FILES, The Archives, Washington, DC, Microfilm Publication T317, 14 rolls.

___The National Archives, POST-REVOLUTIONARY WAR BOUNTY LAND APPLICATION FILE, The Archives, Washington, DC, arranged alphabetically.

Two useful publications, one a roster of troops in the Mexican War, another a list of the dead, are:

___W. H. Roberts, MEXICAN WAR VETERANS, 1846-8, Washington, DC, 1887.

___C. S. Peterson, KNOWN MILITARY DEAD DURING THE MEXI-
CAN WAR, The Author, Baltimore, MD, 1957.

Among state sources available for the Mexican War are the following,
all of which are in PSA:
___PPA 6(10) indexed in 7(1-5).
___INDEX TO RECRUITS, 1ST AND 2ND REGIMENTS, PA
VOLUNTEERS, 1847-8, Record Group 2, PSA, Harrisburg, PA.
___MEXICAN WAR ACCOUNTS AND RELATED PAPERS, 1846-80,
Record Group 2, Microfilm, 6 rolls, PSA, Harrisburg, PA. [Muster
rolls, claims for pay.]
___MEXICAN SERVICE INDEX, 1846-8, Record Group 19, PSA,
Harrisburg, PA. [1st PA Volunteer Regiment only.]

---

26. Military records: Civil War

Records which are available for PA participants in the Civil War
(1861-5) include national service records for soldiers, sailors, and
marines, national pension records for the same participants, national claims records, numerous state records,
and a number of county records. No bounty land awards were made for
service in this war. A major index lists PA military service records which
are in the NA:
___The National Archives, INDEX TO COMPILED SERVICE RE-
CORDS OF VOLUNTEER UNION SOLDIERS WHO SERVED
IN ORGANIZATIONS FROM THE STATE OF PA, The Archives,
Washington, DC, Microfilm Publication M554, 136 rolls.
This index leads to the compiled service records which are in files in the
NA. The index to Union veteran pension applications is:
___The National Archives, GENERAL INDEX TO PENSION FILES,
1861-1934, The Archives, Washington, DC, Microfilm Publication
T288, 544 rolls.
The pension file index points to pension records which are filed in the
NA. The first index may be consulted in SLP, NA, NAPB, FHL, and
FHC. Or you may choose to have the indexes examined and to obtain
the service and pension records on your PA Civil War veteran by employing NATF Form 80 in a mail request, or by going to NA personally,
or by employing a researcher to do the work at the NA for you. Instructions for these three possibilities are given in section 24. Details of
many other Civil War records which are in the NA will be found in:

___National Archives Staff, GUIDE TO GENEALOGICAL RE
SEARCH IN THE NATIONAL ARCHIVES, The Archives,
Washington, DC, 1982, Chapters 4-10, 16.

The most important published materials on Civil War personnel of PA
are:
___S. P. Bates, HISTORY OF PA VOLUNTEERS, 1861-5, PA State
Legislature, Harrisburg, PA, 1869-71, 5 volumes.
This volume lists PA soldiers in the Civil War under their regiments (1st
through 215th). The volume should be used in conjunction with the
microfilm index which is listed below as the first item among the more
important state Civil War records:
___VETERANS' NAME LISTING, CIVIL WAR, 1861-6, Record Group
19, Microfilm, 80 rolls, PSA, Harrisburg, PA. [Much information on
individual soldiers.]
___RECORDS OF DRAFTED MEN, SUBSTITUTES, DESERTERS,
AND CONSCIENTIOUS OBJECTORS, 1862-5, Record Group 19,
Microfilm, 7 rolls, and Original Records, 7 boxes, PSA, Harrisburg,
PA.
___DESCRIPTIVE BOOKS OF THE G.A.R., 1866-1933, Manuscript
Groups 60 and 272, PSA, Harrisburg, PA. [Records of the Grand
Army of the Republic, a very active post-war veterans' organization].
___MILITARY CLAIMS FILE AND REGISTER WITH INDEX,
1862-1905, Record Group 1, PSA, Harrisburg, PA.
For many other state Civil War records in PSA, see:
___R. M. Dructor, GUIDE TO GENEALOGICAL SOURCES AT THE
PSA, PA Historical and Museum Commission, Harrisburg, PA, 1980.
County records which may be looked for since they are often quite helpful
with reference to military service are the County Veterans' Grave Regis-
ter, Commissioners' Enrollment Book, Bounty Records, Records of
Soldiers' Relief, Veterans' Burials, and Widows' Burials.

For a detailed in-depth discussion of Civil War records as genealogical
sources, consult:
___Geo. K. Schweitzer, CIVIL WAR GENEALOGY, Geo. K.
Schweitzer, 407 Ascot Court, Knoxville, TN 37923-5807.
This book treats local, state, and national records, service and pension
records, regimental and naval histories, enlistment rosters, hospital records, court-martial reports, burial registers, national cemeteries, gravestone allotments, amnesties, pardons, state militias, discharge papers,
officer biographies, prisons, prisoners, battle sites, maps, relics, weapons,

museums, monuments, memorials, deserters, black soldiers, Indian soldiers, and many other topics.

There is in the National Archives an index to service records of the Spanish-American War (1898-9):

___The National Archives, GENERAL INDEX TO COMPILED SERVICE RECORDS OF VOLUNTEER SOLDIERS WHO SERVED DURING THE WAR WITH SPAIN, Microfilm Publication M871, The Archives, Washington, DC, 126 rolls, leads to service records in NA.

The pension records are indexed in:

___The National Archives, GENERAL INDEX TO PENSION FILE 1861-1934, Microfilm Publication T288, The Archives, Washington, DC, 544 rolls, leads to pension records in NA.

Again properly submitted NATF Forms 80 (see section 24 for instructions) will bring you both military service and pension records (there were no bounty land records). Or you may choose to hire a researcher, or even go yourself. State of PA sources which you may find of value include:

___SPANISH-AMERICAN WAR SERVICE RECORDS AND BONUS APPLICATIONS, 1898, Record Group 19, Microfilm, 22 rolls, PSA, Harrisburg, PA, alphabetical by name.

___SPANISH-AMERICAN WAR US VOLUNTEERS, 1898, Record Group 19, Microfilm, 11 rolls, PSA, Harrisburg, PA, alphabetical by name.

___MUSTER ROLLS AND RELATED RECORDS, 1898, Record Group 19, PSA, Harrisburg, PA.

___T. J. Stewart, RECORD OF PA VOLUNTEERS IN THE SPANISH-AMERICAN WAR, 1898, PA Adjutant General's Office, Philadelphia, PA, 1901.

Some national records for World War I and subsequent wars may be obtained from the following address. However, many documents were destroyed by an extensive fire in 1972. Write for Form 180:

___National Personnel Records Center (MPR), 9700 Page Blvd., St. Louis, MO 63132.

Draft records for World War I are in Record Group 163 (Records of the Selective Service System of World War I) at National Archives, Atlanta Branch, 1557 St. Joseph Ave., East Point, GA 30344.

There are also PA records relating to World Wars I and II which you will find listed in the two following reference works:

___R. M. Dructor, GUIDE TO GENEALOGICAL SOURCES AT THE
PSA, PA Historical and Museum Commission, Harrisburg, PA, 1980.
___F. M. Suran, GUIDE TO THE RECORD GROUPS IN THE PSA,
PA Historical and Museum Commission, Harrisburg, PA, 1980.

As we conclude these sections (23-26) on PA military records, there
is an exceptionally useful card file in PSA. This file lists all known war
veterans buried in PA and gives military and personal data on each.
___WAR VETERANS BURIED IN PA, CARD FILE, PSA, Harrisburg,
PA.
As has been mentioned, there are similar files in each county of the veterans buried in the county.

27. Mortuary records

Very few PA mortuary records have been transcribed or microfilmed, even though a few are to be found in manuscript form. This means that you must write directly to the mortuaries which you know or suspect were involved in burying your ancestor. Sometimes a death account will name the mortuary; sometimes it is the only one nearby; sometimes you will have to write several to ascertain which one might have done the funeral arrangements. And you need to realize that before there were mortuaries, the furniture or general merchandise store in some communities handled burials, especially the supplying of coffins. You may discover that the mortuary that was involved is now out of business, and so you will have to try to discover which of the existing ones may have inherited the records. Mortuaries for PA with their addresses are listed in the following volumes:

___C. O. Kates, editor, THE AMERICAN BLUE BOOK OF FUNER-
AL DIRECTORS, Kates-Boyleston Publications, New York, NY,
latest issue.
___NATIONAL DIRECTORY OF MORTICIANS, The Directory,
Youngstown, OH, latest issue.
One or both of these reference books will usually be found in the offices
of most mortuaries. In general the older mortuaries should be the more
likely sources of records on your ancestor. In all correspondence with
mortuaries be sure to enclose an SASE and make your letters brief and
to the point.

28. Naturalization records

In the earliest years of the colonial period, many of the immigrants to the territory that later became the US were from the British Isles and since the colonies were British, they were citizens. When immigrants of other nationalities began to arrive, English traditions, customs, governmental structures, and language had become firmly established. The immigrant aliens were required to give oaths of allegiance and abjuration and/or to become naturalized by presenting themselves in court. In a few instances, naturalizations were by special acts of the Assembly. In 1740, the English Parliament passed a law setting requirements for naturalization: 7 years residence in one colony plus an oath of allegiance to the Crown.

In 1776-7, all those who supported the Revolution were automatically considered to be citizens. During the period 1777-91, immigrants were obligated to take an oath of allegiance. In 1788, the Articles of Confederation of the newly established US made all citizens of states citizens of the new nation. The US Congress in 1790 enacted a national naturalization act which required one year's state residence, two years' US residence, and a loyalty oath taken in a court. In 1795, a five years' residence came to be required along with a declaration of intent three years before the oath. Then in 1798, these times became 14 and 5 years respectively. Revised statutes of 1802 reverted to the 5 and 3 years of 1795. The declaration and oath could be carried out in any court of record (US, PA, county). Wives and children of naturalized males usually became citizens automatically. And persons who gave military service to the US and received an honorable discharge also received citizenship.

In 1906, the Bureau of Immigration and Naturalization was set up, and this agency has kept records on all naturalizations since then. Thus, if you suspect your ancestor was naturalized after September 1906, write to the following address for a Form 6641 which you can use to request records:
___Immigration and Naturalization Service, 425 I St., Washington, DC 20536.
For naturalization records before October 1906, you need to realize that the process could have taken place in any of several courts. Fortunately, many of these records have been preserved, and a sizable portion have been microfilmed, published, and/or indexed.

Among the oath and naturalization records which are available in published form are the following PA compilations:
___OATHS OF ALLEGIANCE, 1727-94, PPA C(11), 1(5, 6), 2(3, 14, 17), indexed in C(General Index), 1(General Index), 2(end of 3, 14, 15, 17).

___NATURALIZATIONS, 1740-73, PPA 2(2) indexed in 2(end of 2).

___M. S. Guiseppi, NATURALIZATIONS OF FOREIGN PROT-
ESTANTS, 1740-73, Huguenot Society of London, London, England,
1921.

___P. W. Filby, PHILADELPHIA NATURALIZATIONS, 1789-1880,
Gale Research Co., Detroit, MI, 1942 (1982).

___PA SUPREME COURT, PERSONS NATURALIZED IN THE
PROVINCE OF PA, 1740-73, Genealogical Publishing Co., Baltimore, MD, 1876 (1967).

___T. Westcott, NAMES OF PERSONS WHO TOOK THE OATH OF
ALLEGIANCE TO THE STATE OF PA, 1777-89, Genealogical
Publishing Co., Baltimore, MD, 1865 (1965).

___W. H. Egle, NAMES OF FOREIGNERS WHO TOOK THE OATH
OF ALLEGIANCE TO PA, 1727-55, WITH FOREIGN ARRIVALS,
1786-1808, Genealogical Publishing Co., Baltimore, MD, 1890 (1976).

___NATURALIZATIONS BY SPECIAL ACTS OF THE LEGISLA-
TURE, Statutes at Large of PA, Volumes 2-8, AMS Press, New York,
NY, 1896-1915.

___Western PA Genealogical Society, A LIST OF IMMIGRANTS WHO
APPLIED FOR NATURALIZATION PAPERS IN THE DISTRICT
COURTS OF ALLEGHENY COUNTY, PA, The Society, Pittsburgh,
PA, 1978-81, 6 volumes. [Covers 1798-1891.]

___South Central PA Genealogical Society, ABSTRACT OF PA
RECORDS OF NATURALIZATION, 1695-1773, FOUND IN PPA
C(1-3, 9, 10), 1(1, 3, 4) AND STATUTES AT LARGE OF PA (2-8),
The Society, York, PA, 1983.

There are also some microfilmed and original records in the PSA which
must not be overlooked:

___PA SUPREME COURT NATURALIZATION RECORDS, 1794-18-
68, Record Group 33, Microfilm, 41 rolls, PSA, Harrisburg, PA,
partially indexed.

___INDEX TO NATURALIZATION PAPERS OF THE EASTERN
DISTRICT OF THE STATE SUPREME COURT, 1794-1824,
1842-68, Record Group 33, Microfilm, 1 roll, PSA, Harrisburg, PA.

___NATURALIZATION DOCKET, WESTERN DISTRICT, 1812-67,
Record Group 33, PSA, Harrisburg, PA.

___DECLARATIONS OF INTENTIONS, EASTERN DISTRICT,
1832-70, 1873-5, 1881-1906, Record Group 33, Microfilm, 5 rolls,
PSA, Harrisburg, PA.

There are also naturalization records for PA immigrants who used federal courts. These records include both declarations of intention and petitions for naturalization.

___US DISTRICT COURT, EASTERN DISTRICT OF PA, NATURALIZATION RECORDS, 1795-1951, partially indexed, NAPB, Philadelphia, PA. On NA Microfilm M1248, 51 rolls.

___US CIRCUIT COURT, EASTERN DISTRICT OF PA, NATURALIZATION RECORDS, 1790-1911, partially indexed, NAPB, Philadelphia, PA.

___US DISTRICT COURT, WESTERN DISTRICT OF PA, NATURALIZATION RECORDS, 1820-1935, NAPB, Philadelphia, PA. On NA Microfilm M1208, 3 rolls.

In addition, the Archives of the City and County of Philadelphia have two very important record groups, especially so because so very many immigrants entered PA through Philadelphia.

___DECLARATION OF ALIENS DOCKET, 1821-1911, 91 volumes, Archives of City and County, Philadelphia, PA.

___INDEX TO NATURALIZATION DECLARATIONS, 1811-1903, 72 boxes, indexed, Archives of City and County, Philadelphia, PA.

Finally, please do not fail to examine the county records for oath and naturalization materials. The more likely places for them are in the Court of Common Pleas before 1790 and in this court and the Court of Quarter Sessions and Oyer and Terminer after 1790.

29. Newspaper records

A sizable number of original and microfilmed newspapers are available for towns, cities, and counties of PA. These newspapers date from 1719 and carry valuable information including national news, local news, ads, marriages, and deaths. The first PA newspaper was the American Weekly Mercury which was started in Philadelphia in 1719. The second newspaper in PA also had its beginnings in Philadelphia; it was called the PA Gazette and dates from 1728. Then in 1739, a German language publication called Der Hoch Deutsch Pennsylvanische Geschicht Schreiber appeared in Germantown. This was followed by the PA Journal and Weekly Advertiser (1742), the Lancaster Gazette (1752-3), the PA Chronicle and Universal Advertiser (1767-73), the PA Packet or General Advertiser (1771), and the PA Evening Post (1775). When the Revolution started, there were 34 newspapers being published in the colonies, six of them in PA: in Philadelphia, the Gazette, the Journal, the Post, and the Packet, plus one in Germantown and one in Lancaster.

The largest collections of PA newspapers and microfilms of them are to be found in SLP (largest), LHS, and CLP. Other collections with good local and sometimes regional holdings are located in many LL, RL, and college and university libraries in PA. There are several important guides to original and microfilm PA newspapers which you can use to ascertain if newspapers are available for your ancestor's area:

___L. F. Rauco, PA NEWSPAPERS, SLP, Harrisburg, PA, 1984. [A list of newspapers held by SLP, the largest collection in existence.] Supplemented by newspapers listed in SLP Computer Index (LUIS).

___G. E. Rossell, PA NEWSPAPERS: A BIBLIOGRAPHY AND UNION LIST, PA Library Commission, Pittsburgh, PA, 1978.

___Pittsburgh Regional Library Center, NEWSPAPER LIST, The Center, Pittsburgh, PA, 1976.

Four national listings which contain many PA newspapers along with information on where the originals and/or microfilms of them can be found are:

___C. S. Brigham, HISTORY AND BIBLIOGRAPHY OF AMERICAN NEWSPAPERS, 1690-1820, American Antiquarian Society, Worcester, MA, 1961, 2 volumes.

___W. Gregory, AMERICAN NEWSPAPERS, 1821-1936, H. W. Wilson Co., New York, NY, 1937.

___Library of Congress, NEWSPAPERS IN MICROFORM, The Library, Washington, DC, 1973, plus SUPPLEMENTS, to date.

___K. J. R. Arndt and M. E. Olson, GERMAN-AMERICAN NEWSPAPERS AND PERIODICALS, 1732-1955, Johnson Reprint Corp., New York, NY, 1965.

Unfortunately, not too many newspapers have been indexed, so it is usually necessary that you have some idea of the time span of your ancestor, which will facilitate your page by page search. However, some early newspapers have been indexed or genealogical data have been abstracted from them and then indexed. Reference to many of these will be given in the next paragraph. Some existing newspaper indexes are listed in the following useful volumes:

___A. C. Milner, NEWSPAPER INDEXES, Scarecrow Press, Metuchen, NJ, 1977-82, 3 volumes.

___N. M. and M. L. Lathrop, LATHROP REPORT ON NEWSPAPER INDEXES, The Authors, Wooster, OH, 1979.

___B. M. Jarboe, OBITUARIES: A GUIDE TO SOURCES, Hall, Boston, MA, 1982.

Do not fail to ask in various libraries, particularly in pertinent LL, about newspaper indexes, since these often exist in card file or manuscript form in these places.

A considerable amount of work has been done in abstracting, indexing, and publishing genealogical information from early PA newspapers. Included among these valuable works are:

___K. Scott, GENEALOGICAL ABSTRACTS FROM THE AMERICAN WEEKLY MERCURY, 1719-46, Genealogical Publishing Co., Baltimore, MD, 1974. [3400 names.]

___K. Scott, GENEALOGICAL DATA FROM COLONIAL NY NEWSPAPERS, 1726-83, Genealogical Publishing Co., Baltimore, MD, 1977. [Includes PA data.]

___K. Scott, ABSTRACTS FROM BEN FRANKLIN'S PA GAZETTE, 1728-48, Genealogical Publishing Co., Baltimore, MD, 1975. [12000 names.]

___G. T. Hawbaker, RUNAWAYS, RASCALS, AND ROGUES: MISSING SPOUSES, SERVANTS, AND SLAVES, The Author, Hershey, PA, 1987.

___PA German Folklore Society, NEWSPAPER NOTICES BY GERMAN SETTLERS, 1742-61, The Society, Allentown, PA, 1938.

___E. W. Hocker, GENEALOGICAL DATA RELATING TO GERMAN SETTLERS OF PA, FROM ADS IN GERMAN NEWSPAPERS, 1743-1800, Genealogical Publishing Co., Baltimore, MD, 1981.

___M. Reamy, ABSTRACTS OF SOUTH CENTRAL PA NEWSPAPERS, 1791-1800, Family Line Publns, Westminster, MD, 1988-9, 2 volumes.

___MARRIAGES AND DEATHS FROM NEWSPAPERS OF LANCASTER COUNTY, 1821-30, Family Line Publns, Westminster, MD, 1988.

___K. Scott and J. R. Clarke, ABSTRACTS FROM THE PA GAZETTE, 1748-55, Genealogical Publishing Co., Baltimore, MD, 1977.

___K. Scott and K. Stryker-Rodda, BURIED GENEALOGICAL DATA, A COMPLETE LIST OF ADDRESSED LETTERS LEFT IN THE POST OFFICES OF PHILADELPHIA, CHESTER, LANCASTER, TRENTON, NEW CASTLE, AND WILMINGTON, 1748-80, Genealogical Publishing Co., Baltimore, MD, 1977. [27000 names from the PA Gazette.]

___K. Scott, GENEALOGICAL DATA FROM THE PA CHRONICLE, 1767-74, National Genealogical Society, Washington, DC, 1971.

___K. Scott, DEATH ABSTRACTS FROM THE PA GAZETTE, 1775-83, Genealogical Publishing Co., Baltimore, MD, 1976. [Over 600 names.]

___K. Scott, RUNAWAYS, EXCERPTS FROM THE PA GAZETTE, 1775-83, National Genealogical Society Quarterly, 1976-9, Volumes 64-7.

___J. H. Wion, DEATHS IN CENTRAL PA: AN INDEX TO OBITU-ARIES IN THE DEMOCRATIC WATCHMAN, BELLEFONTE, PA, 1889-1920, The Compiler, New York, NY, 1969.

___MARRIAGES AND DEATHS FROM PITTSBURGH NEWSPAPERS, 1786-, Card File, CLP, Pittsburgh, PA.

___C. Livengood, ABSTRACTS FROM THE KITTANNING GAZETTE, ABOUT 1835, The Author, Sarver, PA, 1982.

___C. E. Duer, THE PEOPLE AND TIMES OF WESTERN PA, PITTSBURGH GAZETTE ABSTRACTS, 1795-1806, Western PA Genealogical Society, Pittsburgh, PA, 1986-8, 3 volumes.

---

30. Published genealogies for the US

There are many published indexes, microfilm indexes, and card indexes which list large numbers of published genealogies at the national level. The most important indexes dealing exclusively with PA were listed in section 17. These listings included the card and microfilm catalogs in SLP, LHS, CLP, FHL, and FHC. This section sets out further indexes to genealogies all over the US. These indexes contain many references to genealogies of PA people and therefore you must not fail to look into them. Among the larger ones are:

___F. Rider, AMERICAN GENEALOGICAL INDEX, Godfrey Memorial Library, Middletown, CT, 1942-52, 48 volumes. [Millions of references]

___F. Rider, AMERICAN GENEALOGICAL & BIOGRAPHICAL INDEX, Godfrey Memorial Library, Middletown, CT, 1952-83, over 190 volumes. [Millions of references]

___The Newberry Library, THE GENEALOGICAL INDEX OF THE NEWBERRY LIBRARY, G. K. Hall, Boston, MA, 1960, 4 volumes. [500,000 names]

___The NY Public Library, DICTIONARY CATALOG OF THE LOCAL HISTORY & GENEALOGY DIVISION OF THE NEW YORK PUBLIC LIBRARY, G. K. Hall, Boston, MA, 1974, 20 volumes. [318,000 entries]

___J. Munsell's Sons, INDEX TO AMERICAN GENEALOGIES, 1711-1908, reprint, Genealogical Publishing Co., Baltimore, MD, 1967. [60,000 references]

___M. J. Kaminkow, GENEALOGIES IN THE LIBRARY OF
CONGRESS, Magna Carta, Baltimore, MD, 1972-7, 3 volumes, with
SUPPLEMENTS, plus A COMPLEMENT TO GENEALOGIES IN
THE LIBRARY OF CONGRESS, Magna Carta, Baltimore, Md,
1981. [Over 50,000 names in all.]

___FHL, FAMILY HISTORY LIBRARY CATALOG, SURNAME
SECTION, at FHL and every FHC. [Over 70,000 entries.]

___National Society of the DAR, DAR LIBRARY CATALOG, VOLU-
ME I, FAMILY HISTORIES AND GENEALOGIES, The Society,
Washington, DC, 1983. [Over 14800 titles.]

The above volumes are available in SLP, LHS, CLP, FHL (FHC), LGL,
some RL, and some LL. The FHL Catalog can be found in FHL (FHC).

---

31. Regional compilations

In addition to state and local publications, there are also some valuable
regional publications which should not
be overlooked by any PA researcher.
For the most part, these are volumes
which are basically historical in character, but carry much genealogical
information. They vary greatly in accuracy and coverage, so it is well to
treat the data cautiously. In general, they cover specific regions which are
usually made up of a few or many PA counties, usually ones which are
connected by river valleys. In deciding which ones of these books to
search for your forebears, you will need to make good use of the geographic and county maps of Chapter 1. The following works are ones
which apply to southeastern PA:

___A. C. Myers, WHARTON'S LAND SURVEY REGISTER, Helen
Harris, Pittsburgh, PA, 1955.

___I. D. Rupp, HISTORY OF LANCASTER AND YORK COUNTIES,
Historical Society of York County, York, PA, 1845 (1976).

___E. J. Fulton and B. K. Mylin, INDEX TO WILL BOOKS AND
INTESTATE RECORDS OF LANCASTER COUNTY, 1729-1850,
Genealogical Publishing Co., Baltimore, MD, 1936 (1981).

___A. Harris, A BIOGRAPHICAL HISTORY OF LANCASTER
COUNTY, Genealogical Publishing Co., Baltimore, MD, 1872 (1977).

___C. A. Fisher, EARLY PA BIRTHS, 1675-1875, Genealogical Publish-
ing Co., Baltimore, MD, 1947 (1979). [Berks, Northumberland,
Snyder, and Union Counties.]

___F. Ellis and A. N. Hunderford, HISTORY OF THE SUSQUE-
HANNA AND JUNIATA VALLEYS, Everts, Peck, and Richards,
Philadelphia, PA, 1886, 2 volumes.

___H. M. Kieffer, SOME OF THE FIRST SETTLERS OF THE FORKS OF THE DE AND THEIR DESCENDANTS, Genealogical Publishing Co., Baltimore, MD, 1902 (1973).

___J. W. Jordan, COLONIAL FAMILIES OF PHILADELPHIA, Lewis Historical Publishing Co., New York, NY, 1911, with SUPERIOR INDEX, Hamilton Computer Service, Park City, UT, 1980.

___H. A. Shenk, A HISTORY OF THE LEBANON VALLEY, National Historical Association, Harrisburg, PA, 1930, 2 volumes. [Berks and Dauphin Counties.]

___W. Jordan, COLONIAL AND REVOLUTIONARY FAMILIES OF PHILADELPHIA, Lewis Historical Publishing Co., New York, NY, 1933.

___C. Z. Mast and R. E. Simpson, ANNALS OF THE CONESTOGA VALLEY, The Authors, Scottsdale, PA, 1942. [Lancaster, Berks, and Chester Counties.]

___J. B. Nolan, SOUTHEASTERN PA, A HISTORY OF THE CO-UNTIES OF BERKS, BUCKS, CHESTER, DELAWARE, MONT-GOMERY, PHILADELPHIA, AND SCHUYLKILL COUNTIES, Lewis Historical Publishing Co., Philadelphia, PA, 1943, with V. G. Hamilton, EVERYNAME INDEX, Hamilton Computer Service, Park City, UT, 1976.

___G. T. Hawbaker and C. L. Graff, A NEW INDEX: LANCASTER COUNTY BEFORE THE FEDERAL CENSUS, The Authors, Hershey, PA, 1981 ff.

For the northeastern section of PA, these works are pertinent:

___I. A. Chapman, THE HISTORY OF WYOMING VALLEY, Polyanthos, New Orleans, LA, 1830 (1971).

___C. Miner, HISTORY OF WYOMING, J. Crissey, Philadelphia, PA, 1845.

___J. A. Clark, THE WYOMING VALLEY AND THE LACKA-WANNA COAL REGION, The Author, Scranton, PA, 1875.

___H. Hollister, HISTORY OF THE LACKAWANNA VALLEY, W. H. Tinson, Philadelphia, PA, 1885.

___G. B. Kulp, FAMILIES OF THE WYOMING VALLEY, Yordy, Wilkes-Barre, PA, 1885, 3 volumes.

___H. E. Hayden, A. Hand, and J. W. Jordan, GENEALOGICAL AND FAMILY HISTORY OF THE WYOMING AND LACKAWANNA VALLEYS, Lewis Publishing Co., New York, NY, 1906, 2 volumes.

___F. C. Johnson, THE HISTORICAL RECORDS OF THE WYOMING VALLEY, quarterly periodical, 1886-1908, 14 volumes.

___O. J. Harvey, HISTORY OF WILKES-BARRE, Raeder Press, Wilkes-Barre, PA, 1909-30, 6 volumes.

For the eastern portion of PA, these volumes should be consulted:
___I. D. Rupp, HISTORY OF NORTHAMPTON, LEHIGH, MONROE, CARBON, AND SCHUYLKILL COUNTIES, Arno Press, New York, NY, 1845 (1971), with V. G. Hamilton, NAME INDEX, Hamilton Computer Service, Park City, UT, 1976.
___J. W. Jordan, HISTORIC HOMES AND INSTITUTIONS AND GENEALOGICAL AND PERSONAL MEMOIRS OF THE LEHIGH VALLEY, Lewis Publishing Co., New York, NY, 1905, 2 volumes.

And for the south central PA area, some of the relevant publications are:
___I. D. Rupp, THE HISTORY AND TOPOGRAPHY OF DAUPHIN, CUMBERLAND, FRANKLIN, BEDFORD, ADAMS, AND PERRY COUNTIES, Cumberland County Historical Society, Carlisle, PA, 1846 (1975), with V. G. Hamilton, NAME INDEX, Hamilton Computer Service, Park City, UT, 1976.
___Mrs. G. A. Perkins, EARLY TIMES ON THE SUSQUEHANNA, Malette and Reid, Binghamton, NY, 1870.
___A. Nevin, MEN OF MARK OF CUMBERLAND VALLEY, 1776-1876 Philadelphia, PA, 1876.
___G. P. Donehoo, A HISTORY OF THE CUMBERLAND VALLEY, Susquehanna History Association, Harrisburg, PA, 1930, 2 volumes. [Cumberland and Franklin Counties.]
___South Central PA Genealogical Society, ANCESTRAL CHARTS, 1776-1977, The Society, York, PA, 1976-7, 2 volumes plus index volume.

This next listing of regional compilations which contain sizable genealogical information applies to central PA:
___I. D. Rupp, HISTORY AND TOPOGRAPHY OF NORTHUMBERLAND, HUNTINGDON, MIFFLIN, CENTRE, UNION, COLUMBIA, JUNIATA, AND CLINTON COUNTIES, Lancaster, PA, 1847, with V. G. Hamilton, NAME INDEX, Hamilton Computer Service, Park City, UT, 11976.
___F. Ellis and A. N. Hunderford, HISTORY OF THE SUSQUEHANNA AND JUNIATA VALLEYS, Everts, Peck, and Richards, Philadelphia, PA, 1886, 2 volumes.
___U. J. Jones, HISTORY OF THE EARLY SETTLEMENT OF THE JUNIATA VALLEY, Harrisburg Publishing Co., Harrisburg, PA, 1899.

___J. F. Meginness, BIOGRAPHICAL ANNALS OF DECEASED RESIDENTS OF THE WEST BRANCH VALLEY OF THE SUS-QUEHANNA, Gazette and Bulletin Printing House, Williamsport, PA, 1889.

___COMMEMORATIVE BIOGRAPHICAL ENCYCLOPEDIA OF THE JUNIATA VALLEY, Runk and Co., Philadelphia, PA, 1897, 1 volumes.

___COMMEMORATIVE BIOGRAPHICAL RECORD [CENTRAL PA], Beers and Co., New York, NY, 1898.

___J. W. Jordan, HISTORY OF THE JUNIATA VALLEY AND ITS PEOPLE, Lewis Historical Publishing Co., New York, NY, 1913, 3 volumes.

___National Historical Association, A HISTORY OF THE JUNIATA VALLEY, The Association, Harrisburg, PA, 1936, 3 volumes.

___F. A. Godcharles, CHRONICLES OF CENTRAL PA, Lewis Historical Publishing Co., New York, NY, 1944, 4 volumes.

___C. A. Fisher, EARLY CENTRAL PA LINEAGES, The Author, Selinsgrove, PA, 1948.

Of considerable significance for ancestor searching in the area of southwestern PA are these volumes:

___B. Crumrine, VA COURT RECORDS IN SOUTHWESTERN PA, 1775-80, Genealogical Publishing Co., Baltimore, MD, 1974.

___I. Waldenmaier, INDEX TO THE MINUTE BOOKS OF THE VA COURTS HELD WITHIN SOUTHWESTERN PA, 1775-80, The Author, Washington, DC, 1957.

___J. Doddridge, NOTES ON THE SETTLEMENT AND INDIAN WARS OF THE WESTERN PARTS OF VA AND PA, 1763-83, Burt Franklin, New York, NY, 1876 (1976).

___J. Veech, THE MONONGAHELA OF OLD, OR HISTORICAL SKETCHES OF SOUTHWESTERN PA TO 1800, Genealogical Publishing Co., Baltimore, MD, 1910 (1975).

___J. S. Van Voorhis, THE OLD AND NEW MONONGAHELA, Genealogical Publishing Co., Baltimore, MD, 1893 (1974).

___C. A. Hanna, OH VALLEY GENEALOGIES, Genealogical Publishing Co., Baltimore, MD, 1900 (1972). [Washington, Westmoreland, and Fayette Counties.]

___J. N. Boucher, A CENTURY AND A HALF OF PITTSBURGH AND HER PEOPLE, The Lewis Publishing Co., New York, NY, 1908, 4 volumes.

___J. W. Jordan, GENEALOGICAL AND PERSONAL HISTORY OF THE ALLEGHENY VALLEY, Lewis Historical Publishing Co., New York, NY, 1913, 3 volumes.

___L. C. Walkinshaw, ANNALS OF SOUTHWESTERN PA, Lewis Historical Publishing Co., New York, NY, 1939, 4 volumes.

___H. L. Leckey, THE TENMILE COUNTRY AND ITS PIONEER FAMILIES, A GENEALOGICAL HISTORY OF THE UPPER MONONGAHELA VALLEY, The Author, Waynesburg, PA, 1950, 9 volumes, with H. Chance, INDEX TO VOLUMES 1-7, The Author, Liberty, PA, 1972.

___H. Vogt, WESTWARD OF YE LAURALL HILLS, The Author, Brownsville, PA, 1976.

The region of western PA is represented by the publications listed below:

___I. D. Rupp, EARLY HISTORY OF WESTERN PA, A. P. Ingraham, Pittsburgh, PA, 1846.

___J. W. Jordan, GENEALOGICAL AND PERSONAL HISTORY OF WESTERN PA, Lewis Historical Publishing Co., New York, NY, 1915, 3 volumes with SUPERIOR INDEX, Hamilton Computer Service, Park City, UT, 1980.

___C. A. Rook, WESTERN PENNSYLVANIANS, Jones Co., Pittsburgh, PA, 1923.

___F. S. Helman and B. Heffelfinger, YOUR FAMILY TREE, 1948 ff., one volume per year.

___E. F. Throop, WESTERN PA GENEALOGICAL INDEXES, The Author, Saegertown, PA, 1974 ff., several volumes.

___J. J. Tabb, BITS AND PIECES, BOOKS AND STONES, The Author, Dallas, TX, 1976-8, 2 volumes.

___C. C. Hastings, Sr., PIONEER SETTLERS OF WESTERN PA, Custom Print Co., San Fernando, CA, 1976. [Allegheny and Washington Counties.]

___W. B. Duff, THE FOREFATHERS AND FAMILIES OF CERTAIN SETTLERS IN WESTERN PA, Moore, Pittsburgh, PA, 1976.

Also of note are these volumes which are useful in several other sections of PA:

___W. J. McKnight, A PIONEER OUTLINE HISTORY OF NORTHWESTERN PA, Lippincott, Philadelphia, PA, 1905.

___J. Riesenman, Jr., HISTORY OF NORTHWESTERN PA, Lewis Historical Publishing Co., New York, NY, 1943, 3 volumes.

___J. W. Jordan, GENEALOGICAL AND PERSONAL HISTORY OF NORTHERN PA, Lewis Historical Publishing Co., New York, NY, 1913, 3 volumes.

___ S. F. Weyburn, FOLLOWING THE CT TRAIL FROM THE DE
RIVER TO THE SUSQUEHANNA VALLEY, Anthracite Press,
Scranton, PA, 1932.

___ J. B. Linn, ANNALS OF BUFFALO VALLEY, 1755-1855, Hart,
Harrisburg, PA, 1877, with M. B. Lontz, INDEX, Polyanthos, New
Orleans, LA, 1965 (1975).

32. Tax lists Among the very useful records kept in PA counties from the time of origin are tax assessment rolls, maps of taxable property, tax payment records, delinquent tax returns, tax liens, lists of land sold for taxes, and tax exonerations (exemptions). Although a portion of these records have been lost, large numbers survive. The Board of County Commissioners administers the tax arrangements and the tax records are kept in the office of the Board. In some cases, older records have been placed in a local library (either county or historical society). In other cases, the originals of early records have gotten to the PSA or copies of them are located there. Microfilm copies of some of them will be found in LHS and FHL, and some have been published in the PPA. The taxes which are recorded in these documents are chiefly on land and on individual males, but from time to time tax was paid on other items: occupations, carriages, livestock, watches, and slaves. Many tax lists are divided into sections: one showing landowners, another listing inmates (married renters), and a third giving freemen (unmarried males over 21). The lists ordinarily show name, occupation (if other than farmer), acres of land, and amount of tax. There are often helpful notations added to the entries (gone, moved, deceased), a death is indicated when a name has the word heirs added to it, and a marriage is indicated when a freeman becomes a landowner or an inmate. The word seated means that a landowner was resident, the word unseated signifying non-residence.

There are several compilations which indicate the counties and dates for published and microfilmed tax records:

___ N. L.P. Fortna and F. M. Suran, GUIDE TO COUNTY AND
MUNICIPAL RECORDS ON MICROFILM IN THE PSA, PA
Historical and Museum Commission, Harrisburg, PA, 1982.

___ R. M. Dructor, GUIDE TO GENEALOGICAL SOURCES AT THE
PSA, PA Historical and Museum Commission, Harrisburg, PA, 1981.

___ F. M. Suran, GUIDE TO RECORD GROUPS IN THE PSA, PA
Historical and Museum Commission, Harrisburg, PA, 1980.

___ H. H. Eddy and M. L. Simonetti, GUIDE TO THE PPA, PA
Historical and Museum Commission, Harrisburg, PA, 1976.

___FHL, FAMILY HISTORY LIBRARY CATALOG, LOCALITY
SECTION, in FHL and every FHC.
___John D. Stemmons, THE US CENSUS COMPENDIUM, Everton
Publishers, Logan, UT, 1973.
___H. H. Woodroofe, A GENEALOGIST'S GUIDE TO PA RECORDS
[IN THE LHS], The Genealogical Society of PA, Philadelphia, PA,
1994.
These volumes will make you aware that the major repositories for published and microfilmed tax records are SLP, PSA, LHS, FHL (FHC), and
certain LL. In Chapter 4, the microfilmed tax records available for individual counties will be noted under the counties. However, please
remember that there are many tax records in the individual counties
which have not been copied, and so they must be searched out there at
the CH and/or LL (county or historical society). Among the more readily
accessible of the published and microfilmed tax lists are:
___TAX LISTS, PPA 3(11-22), 4(7), indexed in 3(27-30) and 4(end of
volume 7 and volume 12), dates 1767-88. [Records for various time
periods during 1767-88 for Allegheny, Bedford, Berks, Bucks, Chester,
Cumberland, Dauphin, Fayette, Huntingdon, Lancaster, Northampton,
Northumberland, Philadelphia, Washington, Westmoreland, and York
Counties.
___TAX AND EXONERATION LISTS, 1762-1801, Record Group 4,
Four different sets of Microfilm, 38 rolls, PSA, Harrisburg, PA. [Re-
cords for various time periods during 1762-1801 for the counties listed
in the previous item plus Franklin and Montgomery.]
___J. D. and E. D. Stemmons, PA IN 1780, The Compilers, Salt Lake
City, UT, 1978. [An index to tax lists of PA counties around 1780.]
___PHILADELPHIA CITY AND COUNTY TAXPAYERS, 1779, TLC
Genealogy, Miami Beach, FL, 1991.

Three other sets of tax records for PA are of importance to your research. Beginning in 1779 and then every seven years thereafter, PA
required an enumeration of taxpayers in each county so that representation in the PA Assembly could be properly apportioned. These documents have been referred to as Septennial Census Returns. Many have
perished, a few may still be in the counties, but the PSA has some during
the time span 1779-1863 for 29 counties and the city of Philadelphia.
___SEPTENNIAL CENSUS RETURNS, 1779-1863, Record Group 7,
Microfilm, 14 rolls, PSA, Harrisburg, PA. [Included are records for
these counties: Adams (1800), Allegheny (1800), Armstrong (1800),
Bedford (1779/86/1800), Berks (1779/86/93/1800), Bucks (1786/1800),
Centre (1800), Chester (1779/86/1800), Columbia (1821), Cumberland

(1793/1800), Dauphin (1786/1800/7), Delaware (1793/1800), Fayette (1786/1800), Franklin (1786/1800/7/14/21/28/35/42), Greene (1800), Huntingdon (1800/21), Lancaster (1779/86/93/1800), Luzerne (1800), Lycoming (1800), Mifflin (1800/21), Montgomery (1786/93/1800/7/42), Northampton (1786/1800), Northumberland (1800), Philadelphia City (1793/1800/63), Philadelphia (1793), Somerset (1800), Washington (1786/1800), Wayne (1800), Westmoreland (1786/1800), Wyoming (1849), and York (1786/93/1800/7).]

These records usually list only the taxpayer's names and occupations, although other data may appear in the later ones. Most of the data is arranged according to township with names alphabetized. The second set of records is the US Direct Tax Lists of 1798 for PA, these being a result of the first direct tax law of the US Government. The entries show names, value of real estate and slave properties, and amount of tax, along with detailed descriptions of dwellings. The microfilm copies are:

___The National Archives, US DIRECT TAX OF 1798: LISTS FOR PA, Microfilm Publication M372, 224 rolls, The Archives, Washington, DC. [Available in SLP, PSA, NA, and NAPB.]

The third set of records of taxpayers was generated during the Civil War when a federal tax was placed on goods, services, licenses, income over $600, and personal property. The assessment lists are alphabetized under the name of the place or area where the taxpayer owed tax. Numerous lists were made, since tax was often monthly, and many lists have survived. A descriptive pamphlet shows the counties in each assessment area, district, or division. A microfilm copy of the assessment lists for PA is available:

___The National Archives, INTERNAL REVENUE ASSESSMENT LISTS FOR PA, 1862-6, Microfilm Publication M787, 107 rolls, The Archives, Washington, DC. [Available in NA and NAPB.]

Please do not forget that though there are many published and microfilmed tax records, the majority of the very valuable county tax lists are still in the counties. They must be sought at the CH and/or LL.

---

33. Will and intestate records

When a person died leaving property (an estate), it was necessary for the county governmental authorities to see that it was properly distributed according to the law. If a will had been written, it had usually been filed in the office of the Register of Wills. Upon the death of the person, the will was presented for authentication to the Orphans' Court. When this process, called probate, had been carried through, the executor(s) named in the will did the actual work of distributing the estate under the supervision of the Orphans' Court and the Register of Wills. If the will had not been previously filed and copied into the records, this was done. If no will had been written, this being called an intestate situation, the authorities appointed an administrator who carried out the distribution of the estate in accordance with the requirements of the law. Very early, PA passed laws that in the case of intestates equal parts of the estate were to be granted to heirs with a double share to the eldest son. In the various actions by which executors and administrators distributed the estate, many records were generated because complete accounting to the authorities was required. These records may include appointments and bonds of executors and administrators, papers, accounts, inventories, appraisals, sales, settlements, guardian records, land divisions, petitions, and inheritance tax information. In general, the office of the Register of Wills keeps these records: original wills, probated wills, unrecorded wills, will books containing copied wills, executors' and administrators' bonds and papers, inventories, appraisals, and inheritance tax records. Among other matters the Orphans' Court handles judicial matters applying to estates, and the Clerk of the Orphans' Court (often the same as the Register of Wills) keeps records of these matters: probate records, contested estate, papers dealing with division of estates, guardian records. The matters will be found in the minute books, dockets, indexes to the dockets, and papers filed in court proceedings. In early times and in counties with small populations, the estate records were sometimes intermingled with other court records, particularly the Court of Common Pleas.

Items of genealogical import which are often found in will and intestate records are date of death and/or probate, occupation, property owned, religion, citizenship, residence, wife's name, whether wife is living or not, parents' names, childrens' names, order of childrens' births, children which are minors, names of childrens' spouses, slaves, family friends, and associates. For the most part, original PA estate records are to be found in CH and LL. You should seek the records there paying special attention to attempting to locate the executor's or administrator's papers and to ascertain if there were extensive Orphans' Court records due to court action in settlement of the estate. The PSA, LHS, and FHL (FHC) have microfilm copies of many will and intestate records for numerous PA counties. These will be listed in Chapter 4 under the individual counties. In addition, some estate records have been transcribed and published. They will be found in SLP, LHS, CPL, some LGL, and those for certain regions and local areas in the pertinent RL and LL. Among the published materials are:

___B. and M. Closson, PA WILL BOOKS, available for over 25 PA counties, Closson Press, Apollo, PA, 1979-.

___E. J. Fulton and B. K. Mylin, AN INDEX TO THE WILL BOOKS AND INTESTATE RECORDS OF LANCASTER COUNTY, Genealogical Publishing Co., Baltimore, MD, 1936 (1974).

___PA German Folklore Society, PA GERMAN WILLS, The Society, Allentown, PA, 1950.

___R. T. and M. C. Williams, INDEXES TO WILLS AND ADMINISTRATIVE RECORDS OF BERKS (1752-1850), BUCKS (1682-1850), DELAWARE (1789-1850), MONTGOMERY (1784-1850), NORTHAMPTON (1752-1850), LEHIGH (1812-50), AND PHILADELPHIA (1682-1850) COUNTIES, The Compilers, Danboro, PA, 1971-4, 9 volumes.

Chapter 3

RECORD LOCATIONS

━━━━━━━━━━

1. Court houses (CH)

━━━━━━━━━━

As was mentioned at the beginning of Chapter 2, the major repositories for PA genealogical records are the State Library of PA (SLP), the PA State Archives (PSA), the Library of the Historical Society of PA (LHS), the Library of the Historical Society of Western PA (LWP), the Carnegie Library of Pittsburgh (CLP), the Genealogical Society of UT (FHL) and its many branches (FHC), the National Archives (NA) and its eleven Field Branches (NAFB), PA regional libraries (RL), PA local libraries (LL), large genealogical libraries over the US (LGL), and PA court houses (CH). All these will be treated in detail in this chapter beginning with the court houses (CH).

The place in which you are likely to find the greatest amount of primary genealogical information relating to your PA ancestor(s) is in the court house of the county where he/she/they lived. This is because county record keeping had far more to do with the lives of individuals than any other agency. The county offices and the possible pertinent records, along with the approximate dates from which they were kept, are listed here. Please bear in mind that there were some losses, and therefore not all the records may be available today. In addition, not all of these categories of records were kept in all counties, and not all of them were labelled exactly as given here. In other words, this is not a list of precisely what you will find, but a list of what should be looked for.

___The County Commissioners: Minutes (1715-), Tax Assessors' Oaths (1799-), Tax Collectors' Oaths (1841-), Tax Assessments (origin-), Personal Property Tax (origin-), Military Roll (1858-1921), Veterans Burials (1885-1921), Veterans' Graves (1775-).

___Registration Commission: Voters' Registry Lists (1874-1937).

___Recorder of Deeds: Deed Books (origin-), Deed Indexes (origin-), Patent Books (1818-), Mortgage (origin-), Mortgage Indexes (origin-), Corporation Charters (1874-), Warrantee Tract Maps.

___Prothonotary [Clerk of the Court of Common Pleas]: Minutes (origin-), Trial List (origin-), Appearance Docket (origin-), Appearance Docket Papers (origin-), Justices of the Peace and Aldermans Docket (origin-), Partition Docket (1849-), Equity Docket (origin-), Divorce Index, Case Files and Packets (origin-).

__Clerk of the Court of Quarter Sessions and Oyer and Terminer: Minutes (origin-), Trial Lists (origin-), Quarter Sessions Docket (origin-), Oyer and Terminer Docket (origin-), Quarter Sessions Papers (origin-), Oyer and Terminer Papers (origin-), Naturalization (1790-), Case Files.

__Register of Wills: Wills (origin-), Executors' and Administrators' Papers (origin-), Inventories and Appraisements (origin-), Inheritance Tax (1826-), Marriage (1852-5), Birth (1852-5), Death (1852-5), Probate Case files and Packets (origin-).

__Clerk of Orphans' Court: Minutes (origin-), Papers (origin-), Docket (origin-), Partition Docket (1889-), Distribution Docket (origin-), Marriage License (1885-), Birth (1893-1905), Death (1893-1905), Soldiers' Pensioned by PA (1783-5).

__Coroner: Inquests.

__Jail Warden: Prisoners' Records, Prisoners of War (1814-).

__County Surveyor: Land Grant Applications (origin-), Land Grants (origin-), Surveys (origin-), Warrantee Maps.

Practically all of the surviving original county court house records in PA remain in the courthouses, although some have been transferred to the local county library or to the library of a local historical society., and a few are in the PSA. Some of the more genealogically important records (such as wills, intestate records, deeds, birth, deaths, marriages, tax) have been microfilmed for over 60 PA counties, and all or part of them are available in PSA, LHS, and FHL (FHC). These microfilmed records are listed under the counties in Chapter 4. There are also some published record transcripts, many of which can be located in SLP, LHS, LWP, and CLP, with those pertaining to given counties being available in the respective RL and LL (LL including both public and local historical society libraries). Many of the published records and some of the microfilmed ones are also available in numerous large genealogical libraries (LGL) located throughout the US. A valuable guide to available PA county records is:

__PA Historical and Museum Commission, COUNTY RECORDS SURVEY, 1985-6, The Commission, Harrisburg, PA, 1987.

2. The State Library of PA (SLP)

The State Library of PA (hereafter abbreviated SLP) is located in the Forum Building, Commonwealth Ave. and Walnut St., Harrisburg, PA 17105. The mailing address is PO Box 1601, Harrisburg, PA 17105, and the telephone number for information about the Genealogy/Local History Collection is 1-717-787-4440. The number for the Map Collection is 1-717-787-4440, for Law/Government Publications is 1-717-787-3273, and for the Newspaper Collection is 1-717-787- 3883. This institution, along with the PA State Archives (PSA), makes Harrisburg the best single place in the world to start a PA genealogical search, especially if you do not know your ancestor's county. The library, as is the character of libraries, is largely a repository for <u>published</u> materials (books, microfilms, microfiche), but they also have a number of typescript works. The genealogy and local history collection and associated collections in SLP consist of 13500 genealogy microform titles, many unpublished compilations, over 13000 maps and atlases, more than 75000 newspaper microfilm reels, over 2000 bound volumes of newspapers, over 40000 titles of PA governmental publications, numerous periodicals, and much other material. These include vital records (birth, baptism, marriage, divorce, death, burial, cemetery), censuses, church records, county records (court, deed, land, tax, probate, will), state and county histories and biographies, immigration and naturalization records, ethnic sources, periodicals, military information, newspapers, published family histories, Bible records, and manuscript genealogies. Before you visit the SLP, write them, sending two dollars for postage, and request these items:

___THE STATE LIBRARY OF PA, GENERAL INFORMATION, PA Dept. of Education, Harrisburg, PA, latest edition.

___STATE LIBRARY OF PA, RECORDS OF INTEREST TO GENE-ALOGISTS, PA Dept. of Education, Harrisburg, PA, latest edition.

___"CONSIDER THIS -- GUIDES TO GENEALOGICAL RECORDS IN THE SLP, SLP, Harrisburg, PA, latest editions. Numerous guide sheets to holdings.

They all should be read very carefully before you arrive at SLP.

Near the SLP there are two hotels, the Ramada Inn Harrisburg (Second and Chestnut Sts., Harrisburg, PA 17101, telephone 1-717-234-5021 or 1-800-228-2828) which is about five blocks away, and the Hilton Harrisburg (1 North Second St., Harrisburg, PA 17101, telephone 1-717-233-6000 or 1-800-445-8667) which is about four blocks away. There is public parking in several places approximately two blocks from SLP, there being parking lots or garages at the corner of Strawberry and Fifth Sts. (just southwest of SLP) and on the corner of Commonwealth and North Sts. (just northeast of SLP).

When you enter the main door of the Forum Bldg., turn right, walk down the hall, and go in the door at the end of the hall (Room 102). Go through the security gate, and if you have not obtained the guide leaflets mentioned above, ask for them at the Reference Desk. Take a seat, and read through them carefully. Remind yourself of the general rules that apply to library use, namely, no drinking, eating, smoking, loud talk, or other distracting behavior, care in using all materials, use only of pencils, and no reshelving of volumes (place them on trucks). Then glance around a bit. To the right of the Reference Desk as you face it, you will see Alcove 19, which is where the Genealogy/Local History Collection begins. Next to Alcove 19, you will see Alcove 20, behind which is the First Genealogy Room, the Second Genealogy Room, then the Third Genealogy Room (Room 101). Walk down through these rooms to get their general layout.

Now return to Alcove 19. In this area you will find US and PA history, and PA historical serials, periodicals, and monographs. Then move on to Alcove 20 which contains more PA periodicals and serials, PA biography, and PA county and city histories on one wall, and on the other wall a long row of microfilm cabinets. These cabinets contain PA county and regional histories and atlases, PA city directories, PA censuses (1790-1920), a genealogical surname card index (a microfilm copy of the one to be discussed later), an index to biographies in some state and local histories in the Library of Congress, Port of Philadelphia Maritime Records (1766-1880) including a Naturalization Records Index (1794-1880), 1820 and 1850-80 Manufactures Census, 1850-80 Agricultural Censuses, 1850-80 Non-population Censuses, 1862-6 Internal Revenue Assessment lists, microfilmed genealogies and periodicals, and local histories and primary sources with author and title and geographic and name indexes, Philadelphia passenger lists (1800-1948) with index, indexes to compiled service records of Union Civil War soldiers of PA, US Direct Tax of PA (1798), a coat of arms index and numerous microfiche of genealogical works.

Continuing on, walk now into the First Genealogy Room which contains more volumes of PA county and city histories and a number of microfilm readers. Proceed into the Second Genealogy Room, and there you will see a large card cabinet and several file cabinets. The file cabinets contain manuscript family genealogies and unbound genealogical periodicals. On the walls will be found US and PA genealogical reference works, genealogical guidebooks and compendiums, and a large number of family genealogy books (continuing on the balcony). You will also see a special reference shelf containing PA census indexes and passenger list indexes. Now go into the Third Genealogy Room. Notice the computer terminals (for the Computer Catalog LUIS), and the bookshelves which contain special reference materials, immigration and colonial materials, early PA genealogical records, published PA county records, records for other states, and surname and heraldry volumes.

Several other areas in SLP contain records of genealogical importance. These include the Main Reading Room (Room 102), the Newspaper Room (Room 120), and the Law/Government Publications Reading Room (Room 116) for PA statutes and appeals records and the American State Papers. Also there is a noon-time snack bar in Room 216 and women's rest rooms on the east and men's rest rooms on the west on both the first and second floors. Now, let's discuss the quickest way to find what you need in the SLP without overlooking any important source of ancestral information. The proper route is to use the card indexes, computer catalog, and files in the SLP. These are as follows, along with their locations:

__PA SURNAME CARD FILE, Second Genealogy Room, Genealogy/Local History Area, SLP, Harrisburg, PA.

__PA PLACE CARD FILE, Second Genealogy Room, Genealogy/Local History Area, SLP, Harrisburg, PA.

__MAIN COMPUTER CATALOG, Third Genealogy Room, Room 102, SLP, Harrisburg, PA. (By author, subject, title, key word)

__FAMILY GENEALOGY VERTICAL FILE (ALPHABETICAL), Second Genealogy Room, Genealogy/Local History Area, SLP, Harrisburg, PA.

__MAP COLLECTIONS (PA MAP BY PLACE, USGS MAP INDEX, LAND WARRANTEE MAPS), Alcoves 12 and 13, Main Reading Room, Room 102, SLP, Harrisburg, PA.

__MISCELLANEOUS GENEALOGICAL CARD INDEXES (SEILHAMER GENEALOGICAL NOTES INDEX, PA GENERAL INDEX, PA SUBJECT FILE INDEX, others), Second Genealogical Room, Genealogy/Local History Area, SLP, Harrisburg, PA.

In addition, there is a very good publication which describes many of the holdings of the Newspaper Room (Room 120).

__L. F. Rauco, PA NEWSPAPERS, PA Dept. of Education, Harrisburg, PA, 1984. Newspapers also listed in SLP Computer Catalog (LUIS).

Be sure and consult it for recent acquisitions.

There is a supplemental listing in the Newspaper Room which gives newspapers added after Rauco's book was published.

The question now becomes how you go about making maximum use of the card or computer indexes listed above. A very easy way to recall the procedure is to remember the word SLANT. S stands for subject, L stands for locality, A stands for author, N stands for name, and T stands for title. And these are the five things you need to look under in a card or computer catalog, unless that catalog is a special one which is arranged by only one or two of these. However, you should do your research not in the order S-L-A-N-T, but in the order N-L-S-A-T since this is a faster approach. In other words, <u>FIRST</u>, look up all the <u>N</u>ames you are interested in to see what materials there are. Copy the numbers and titles from the cards or the screen which you think pertain to your ancestor(s) because these numbers (referred to as call numbers) will let you find the material. Then, <u>SECOND</u>, look in the card index or computer catalog under the <u>L</u>ocality where your ancestor(s) lived, more particularly in the county, the township, the city, the town, and/or the borough. Be sure to examine <u>every</u> card or listing and copy the call numbers and titles of all materials which you think have even a remote chance of being useful. <u>THIRD</u>, examine the index or catalog with reference to <u>S</u>ubjects which might lead you to sources which will give data on your forebear(s). The headings to the sections in Chapter 2 are some that you need to look under. In some indexes, these headings occur after the word PA (such as Pennsylvania--Bible records) and in other cases they occur as headings themselves (such as Bible records). Other useful subject headings (sometimes following Pennsylvania--, sometimes standing alone) are American Loyalists, Bounties, military--PA (and -US), Cemeteries--PA, Deeds, Epitaphs--PA, Gravestone inscriptions, Immigrants, Land titles, Marriage licenses, Mortgages, (Name of cemetery), (Name of church), (Name of denomination), (Name of ethnic group), Oaths, Obituaries, Orphans' Court records, Passenger lists, Pastoral records, PA--History--(Name of war), PA--Militia, Pensions, Military--PA (and --US), Probate records, Registers of births, etc., Surveys, Undertakers' records, US--History--(Name of war), Warrants.

    <u>FOURTH</u>, if there are volumes mentioned in Chapter 2 which you need to find (there should be many), you may locate them by looking under the name of the author. And <u>FIFTH</u>, since some of the volumes in Chapter 2 are referred to with no author, you can find them by looking under the title. This procedure will ensure you locating all the materials pertinent to your genealogy which the SLP holds. When you get the call numbers and title of materials you need, look for those having call numbers beginning with 929, 973, 974, 975, 976, and 977 on the shelves in the Genealogy/Local History area. For volumes with other call numbers, ask for them in the Main Reading Room (102). Look for microfilms in the cabinets in Alcove 20, except for the American State Papers (Room

116). Look for newspapers in Room 120. And for maps and atlases which you found listed in the catalog or the indexes, ask the attendants at the desk in Room 102 to obtain them for you. Do not try to get them for yourself. We will now suggest the order for your work.

Begin your use of the indexes by using the PA SURNAME CARD FILE (you will need only to look up names), then the PA PLACE CARD FILE (you will need only to look under the localities), then the MAIN COMPUTER CATALOG (all five categories must be used: Name, Locality, Subject, Author, Title). Next glance through the FAMILY GENEALOGY VERTICAL FILE (only names), then the MAP COL-LECTION (only the locality), then the MISCELLANEOUS GENEA-LOGICAL CARD INDEXES, also the listings of newspapers in the book mentioned above in the newspaper update list, and in the Computer Catalog. These procedures will let you put your hands on much of the material mentioned in Chapter 2 with only a few major exceptions. These exceptions are: some US governmental records (chiefly National Archives microfilms and records), many PA state governmental records (chiefly records held in the PA State Archives [PSA], and many PA county governmental records (some held by PSA, LHS, and FHL, and more held by the counties themselves).

The staff members at SLP will be very helpful to you in locating the indexes, files, and Computer Catalog. However, these knowledgeable people cannot do your research for you; they can only guide and assist you because of their obligations to serve state officials and other state residents.

3. The PA State Archives (PSA)

The PA State Archives (here-after abbreviated PSA) is located at Third and Forster Sts., Harris-burg, PA 17108-1026, just four blocks from the State Library of PA (SLP). The mailing address is PO Box 1026, Harrisburg, PA 17120, and the telephone number is 1-717-783-3281. The two institutions, SLP and PSA, supplement each other so as to make Harrisburg the best single place to start the genealogical search for a PA ancestor whose county you do not know. The primary function of the PSA is to collect, preserve, and make available to PA state officials the records of the PA state government. It does not do genealogical research for persons who visit it, neither does it search unindexed records in response to mail or telephone inquiries. However, as time permits, they are willing to assist genealogical searchers who come to the PSA with a knowledge of what records they want to look into. Therefore before you visit the PSA, you need to write The PA Historical and Museum Division Bookstore, PO Box 1026, Harrisburg, PA 17120, and order the following book:

__R. M. Dructor, GUIDE TO THE GENEALOGICAL SOURCES IN THE PSA, PA Historical and Museum Commission, Harrisburg, PA, 1981.

Also send a long SASE to the PSA and ask them for their leaflet:

__GENEALOGICAL RESEARCH AT THE PSA, PA State Archives, PO Box 1026, Harrisburg, PA 17120.

You may be able to find the above book in a large genealogical library, but it can be more readily studied if you own it. The volume and the leaflet should be carefully gone through. When you do so, you will find that the holdings of PSA include microfilm county records (deeds, marriages, court, wills, tax records) for many PA counties, census records and indexes (1790-1920), PA military service records, PA naturalization records (1740-73, 1794-1906), passenger lists (1727-1808), taxpayer enumerations (1779-1863), vital records (1852-5), military pension records (Revolutionary War, War of 1812), supreme court records (1740-1971), over 2000 maps (1681-), oaths of allegiance (1777-90), rent rolls (1683-1776), quit rent books (1741-76), church records, prison records, family papers, and numerous manuscripts. The PSA also holds many documents (warrants, surveys, patents, land applications) relating to the original transfer of land (1682-1940s) from the colony or state of PA to the first individual owner.

Hotel facilities and parking areas for PSA are the same as those for SLP since the two repositories are so close. When you enter the main door of the PSA, you will see an entry desk just to the right. Stop there, identify yourself, ask for a registration form and a copy of the regulations, and then fill the form out. The regulations, which you should read carefully, provide that available lockers and coat racks must be used for storage of personal belongings (brief cases, cameras, bags, oversize handbags, coats), that eating, drinking, smoking, loud talk, and boisterous conduct are not permitted, that call slips are to be filled out to obtain records and manuscripts, that records and manuscripts are not to be marked, traced, rearranged, or damaged, that microfilm rolls may be removed from the cabinets but are not to be replaced, that only pencils may be used, that copies of most materials may be obtained, that permission to use reproduction equipment (typewriters, computers, tape recorders, cameras) must be obtained, and that removal of any materials from the Search room is a crime. Rest rooms are located in the hall where the Entry Desk sits.

Next, glance straight ahead at the facilities: a glassed-in Manuscript Reading Room, and to its left and behind it, a Microfilm Reading Room. Now, proceed into the Microfilm Reading Room by entering it through the passageway to the left of the Manuscript Reading Room. Take a seat at the Research Table, and glance around the room. On bookshelves in the passageway through which you entered, there are guidebooks (GB) and guide leaflets (GL) to the microfilms, original materials, and manuscripts held by the PSA. These include:

__(GB-1) R. M. Dructor, GUIDE TO THE GENEALOGICAL SOURCES IN THE PSA, PA Historical and Museum Commission, Harrisburg, PA, 1981.

__(GB-2) N. L. Fortna and F. M. Suran, GUIDE TO COUNTY AND MUNICIPAL RECORDS ON MICROFILM IN THE PSA, PA Historical and Museum Commission, Harrisburg, PA, 1982.

__(GB-3) R. M. Baumann and D. S. Wallace, GUIDE TO THE MICROFILM COLLECTION IN THE PSA, PA Historical and Museum Commission, Harrisburg, PA, 1980.

__(GB-4) M. L. Simonetti, DESCRIPTIVE LIST OF THE MAP COLLECTION IN THE PSA, PA Historical and Museum Commission, Harrisburg, PA, 1976.

__(GB-5) F. M. Suran, GUIDE TO THE RECORD GROUPS IN THE PSA, PA Historical and Museum Commission, Harrisburg, PA, 1980.

__(GB-6) H. E. Whipkey, GUIDE TO THE MANUSCRIPT GROUPS IN THE PSA, PA Historical and Museum Commission, Harrisburg, PA, 1976.

__(GB-7) D. B. Munger, PA LAND RECORDS, A HISTORY AND GUIDE FOR RESEARCH, Scholarly Resources, Wilmington, DE, 1991.

__(GB-7) Rosters of PA Civil War participants.

__(GB-8) Published PA Census Indexes, 1790-1870.

__(NB-1) Notebooks of the PA County Records Survey Inventory.

__(GL-1) Guide Leaflets to the PSA: American Revolution, Beginning Your Civil War Research, County Records, Finding Your Way at the PSA, French and Indian War, Genealogical Records, Genealogical Research at the PSA, Getting Started in the State Land Records of PA, Mexican War, Military Records, Military Records on Microfilm at the PSA, Naturalization Records, Naturalizations and Oaths of Allegiance, PA Census Records, Pre-1790 Naturalizations and Oaths of Allegiance in PA, (Published) PA Archives Quick Reference

Guide, Ships Lists of German Passengers, Spanish-American War, State Land Records of PA: A Beginners Guide, Vital Statistics, War of 1812, available in Microfilm Reading Room, PSA, Harrisburg, PA. Also on these shelves are the Published PA Archives (PPA), the National Union Catalog of Manuscript Collections and some other archives volumes, an index to the 8th Series of the Published PA Archives, and a number of PA historical and genealogical books.

Along the walls you will see many microfilm cabinets, labelled as follows:

___County Records,

___State Records,

___Miscellaneous Records,

___State Land Records, and

___Census Microfilm.

On the tops of several of these cabinets there are guides to their contents. Adjacent to the Research Table and next to one of the large pillars, there is a small Guidebook Table, which holds:

___(NB-2) GUIDES TO OFFICIAL COUNTY RECORD MICRO-FILMS, 10 black looseleaf notebooks, PSA Microfilm Reading Room, Harrisburg, PA.

These guides refer you to PSAs large holdings of microfilms of county records which are in the County Records microfilm cabinets. On top of the Miscellaneous Records and State Records microfilm cabinets are two black notebooks which list many microfilms in those cabinets (including a few more county records):

___(NB-3) SPECIAL COLLECTIONS MICROFILM NOTEBOOK, Microfilm Reading Room, PSA, Harrisburg, PA.

___(NB-4) MANUSCRIPT GROUPS NOTEBOOK, Manuscript Group 4, Microfilm Reading Room, PSA, Harrisburg, PA.

In the microfilm cabinets, there will be found a number of major indexes (MI) which will in turn lead you to numerous documents and/or micro-films of documents. These indexes are listed here with their Microfilm Roll Numbers given in parentheses. The numbers are the numbers under which the rolls are filed in the microfilm cabinets.

___(MI-1) Microfilms of the Soundex Indexes to the 1880, 1900, 1910, and 1920 Census Indexes, Census Microfilm Cabinets, PSA, Harrisburg, PA.

___(MI-2) Microfilm Indexes of Land Purchased from the Government Before 1733: Old Rights Index (1.21), Patents (1.16), Purchases from Penn (1.21), Leases and Releases (25.33).

___(MI-3) Microfilm Indexes of Land Purchased from the Government After 1733: Warrant Registers (1.1-1.5), Patents (1.16-1.20), East and West Side Purchases (1.8-1.9), New Purchase Applications (1.9), Last Purchases (1.9), Donation and Depreciation Lands (3429).

___(MI--4) Microfilm Indexes to Military Records: Revolutionary War (1733-1738, 4444-4497), Revolutionary War Pensions (20-22, 191-195), War of 1812 (1, 35-61), Mexican War (33, 492, 3573), Civil War (3176-3251), Spanish-American War (569, 3393).

___(MI-5) Microfilm Index of Births, Deaths, and Marriages, 1852-54 (668-673).

___(MI-6) Microfilm Index to Philadelphia Deaths, 1803-60 (3497-3511).

The guidebooks listed above (GB-1 through GB-8), the guide leaflets listed above (GL-1), the notebooks listed above (NB-1 through NB-4), and the Microfilm Indexes listed above (MI-1 through MI-6) will lead you to two types of items: (1) microfilms and (2) original documents and manuscripts. For the microfilms, Microfilm Roll Numbers will be given. This will allow you to find the microfilms in the cabinets in the Microfilm Reading Room, and to read them there on the microfilm readers. For the original documents and manuscripts, you will find Record Group numbers (RG) or Manuscript Group Numbers (MG) which will let you request the materials from an Archivist in the Manuscript Reading Room. These items must be read in the Manuscript Reading Room under the supervision of the Archivist.

The staff members at PSA are dedicated, efficient experts at their work, but you must respect the demands upon their time. Do them the courtesy of knowing exactly what you want before you go. This can be done by familiarizing yourself with the publication mentioned in the first paragraph. They will be glad to help you, especially if you can ask them brief, precise questions. Likewise, they will respond to a single, brief question by mail if they can answer it by looking in a readily-available index, and if you enclose a long SASE and a 5$ fee. They will send you a list of their fees for more extensive services.

---

4. Library of the Historical Society of PA (LHS)

The best genealogical resource repository in eastern PA is the Library of the Historical Society of PA (abbreviated LHS). This facility, which houses the largest private manuscript collection in the US, is located at

1300 Locust St., Philadelphia, PA 19107. The telephone number is 1-215-732-6200. The library is a repository for both the published and manuscript holdings of the Historical Society of PA and many items contributed by the Genealogical Society of PA. Its holdings include many census schedules, county records (such as court, deed, probate, tax, will), over 2700 newspapers, more than 10000 reels of microfilm, over 20000 published genealogies, about 30000 manuscript genealogies, more than 50000 volumes and pamphlets, about 15 million manuscript items, church and cemetery records, Bible records, vital data (birth, divorce, marriage, death), military records, naturalization and immigration lists, and much other material. Before you go to the LHS, study very carefully the listings of county records held by the LHS as published in the following book, paying careful attention to the counties of your ancestor(s):

___H. Woodroofe, GENEALOGIST'S GUIDE TO PA RECORDS (IN THE LHS), Genealogical Society of PA, Philadelphia, PA 1994.

This volume can be found in many medium and large-sized genealogical libraries throughout the US.

The open hours are 10 am-5 pm Tuesday, 1 pm-9 pm Wednesday, 10 am-5 pm Thursday, 10 am-5 pm Friday, and 10 am-5 pm Saturday with the library being closed Sundays, Mondays, and holidays. Always call ahead before visiting them because times are subject to change. There are commercial parking lots and buildings in several places within a few blocks of the LHS, one of the most convenient being one block away at the corner of Juniper and Locust Sts. Among the hotels which are within walking distance are the Holiday Inn Express Midtown (1305 Walnut St., Philadelphia, PA 19107, telephone 1-215-735-9300 or 1-800-465-4329), the Doubletree Hotel Philadelphia (Broad and Locust Sts., Philadelphia, PA 19107, telephone 1-215-893-1600), the Warwick Philadelphia (17th and Locust Sts., Philadelphia, PA 19103, telephone 1-215-735-6000 or 1-800-523-4210), the Latham Hotel (17th and Walnut Sts., Philadelphia, PA 19103, telephone 1-215-563-7474), and the Abigail Adams B&B Hotel (1208 Walnut St., Philadelphia, PA 19107, telephone 1-215-546-7336 or 1-800-887-1776).

When you walk in the front door of the LHS, you will find a registration desk on your right. Present yourself to the attendant, show some identification, fill out the registration form, read the regulations, sign the register, and pay the small daily research fee. As you will see, the regulations forbid beverages, food, smoking, ask you to exercise care with all materials, and instruct you to deposit coats, umbrellas, brief cases, and other personal items in the nearby lockers. Now take the elevator up to the second floor. When you arrive, you will see the door to the Reading Room/Reference Materials Area on your right. Ahead, then on your left, you will see the entrance to the Assistance/Public Catalogs Area. Go into the Assistance/Public Catalogs Area and take a seat. Glance around the Assistance/Public Catalogs Area to get your bearings. Then stroll around the Area and identify the following card catalogs:

___Historical Catalog (prior to 1960),

___Genealogical Catalog,

___Historical/Genealogical Catalog,

___Manuscripts Catalog, and

___Map and Atlas Catalog.

These five catalogs are the major keys to the contents of the LHS. You need also to identify some smaller index catalogs which are located in orange drawers placed in between the Historical and Genealogical Catalogs: Periodicals Index, Philadelphia Newspapers List, Non-Philadelphia Newspapers List, and the Inscription File. Not to be overlooked is a volume sitting on top of the Manuscripts Catalog:

___GUIDE TO THE MANUSCRIPT COLLECTIONS OF THE HISTORICAL SOCIETY OF PA, The Society, Philadelphia, PA, 1991.

Now, proceed into the Reading Room/Reference Materials Area. Many of the enormous holdings of LHS are in this Area, but there are many more in closed stacks. Beginning at the bookshelves to the left of the entrance door, you will find on the west wall Family Histories R-to-Z, and in a room behind the west wall Family Histories A-to-R. Then turning the corner to the north wall, there are General Reference books, including the Biographical and Genealogy Master Index. Following this, there are PA Reference volumes including Philadelphia city directories, biographical compilations, genealogical compilations, PA directories, regional and county biographical works, county histories, city biographical works, and city histories. Turning the corner to the east wall, you will find more PA Reference volumes, including the (Published) PA Archives series. You are now at the south wall (the southeast corner of it). As you move westward along it you will observe Genealogical Reference works including PA genealogical periodicals, genealogical guidebooks, genealogical periodical indexes, ethnic works, passenger lists, immigration books, and PA historical periodicals. Beyond these, you will come to an African-American reference section, and then a door into the Open Stacks. Entering the Open Stacks, you will find on your left Military Reference materials and DAR volumes. In front of you, there will be microfilm readers, and behind them over 55 book stacks. To your far right will be Census Indexes and many cabinets of micrrofilms. These microfilms include PA censuses, PA county deeds, PA newspapers, PA church records, PA tax lists, PA county wills, PA orphans court records, PA city directories, and the microfiche IGI.

As has been stated, the keys to all these riches (and more in the closed stacks) are the five catalogs, the lists of county record holdings in the book by Woodroofe, and the guidebook to manuscripts (see first paragraph of this section). Using the memory word SLANT, examine the card catalogs (all of them), first looking under Name, then Location, then Subject, and finally Author and Title. Details of this procedure and the use of the location and subject categories were described in section 2 of this chapter (the section on SLP). Do not overlook the periodical and the newspaper lists mentioned above. When you find items you wish to examine, copy the call numbers and the title from the index card onto a piece of scrap paper. If the call number begins with Gen, Fa, Ref, U, V, W, or X, you can retrieve the items for yourself in the Reading Room/ Reference Materials/Open Stacks Area. All other items must be requested at the Desk in the Reading Room by presenting a properly filled-out request form. You can use the published materials at the reading tables, and the microfilms can be read on the readers in the Open Stacks Area. When you are finished, leave the published materials at your desk. Do not reshelve them. And leave the microfilms on the designated table in the Open Stacks Area. Do not return them to the cabinets. Manuscripts, original documents, and other restricted items must be used in a special area in the Reading Room. If you wish photocopies, they may be purchased at the Desk for materials which are in good enough condition to copy. Most of the publications mentioned in Chapter 2, many of the microfilms, and many of the microfilms to be listed in Chapter 4 are available at LHS. In addition, LHS holds numerous church record microfilms not generally available elsewhere. Since LHS is located in Philadelphia, its collection is best for eastern PA, the holdings thinning somewhat with distance.

The staff at LHS is exceptionally busy, and they are thus unable to do genealogical searching for you. They are glad to advise you and to suggest approaches, but you must carry out the work yourself. The LHS offers a research service to those who cannot visit the facility. Details may be obtained by calling 1-215-732-6200.

5. The Carnegie Library of Pittsburgh (CLP)

There is a major repository and two secondary record repositories in Pittsburgh which have sizable genealogical resources for the state of PA, even though the emphasis is on the western half. These institutions are the Carnegie Library of Pittsburgh (CLP), the Hillman Library of the University of Pittsburgh, and the Library of the Historical Society of Western PA (LWP). The first two of them are within a few blocks of each other just three miles west of downtown Pittsburgh in an area called Oakland. Within walking distance are two motels: Holiday Inn Heart of Oakland, 100 Lytton Ave., Pittsburgh, PA 15213 [1-(412)-6826200 or 1-800-465-4329], and Best Western University Center, 3401 Boulevard of the Allies, Pittsburgh, PA 15213 [1-(412)- 683-6100 or 1-(800)-528-1234].

The Carnegie Library of Pittsburgh (CLP) is located at 4400 Forbes Ave., Pittsburgh, PA 15213 [1-(412)-622-3154 for the PA room and 1-(412)-622-3158 for the Microfilm Room]. Hours are 9 am-9 pm (Monday, Tuesday, Wednesday, Thursday), 9 am-5:30 pm (Friday, Saturday), and 1-5 pm (Sunday). The library is closed on Sunday from May to October. The library is a free public library supported by Pittsburgh, Allegheny County, and the Commonwealth of PA. Hours are subject to change and therefore it is best to call Library Information [1-(412)-622-3131] to make sure they will be open when you plan your visit. Parking for CLP is available in a lot located behind the library. This lot can be entered at the corner of Forbes Ave. and South Craig St. by turning south. A discount is available if you have your ticket validated at the Main Desk on the first floor.

Three rooms in CLP are of chief interest to genealogical searchers: the PA Room, the Microfilm Room, and the Main Reference Room, all located on the second floor. When you enter the front door of the library, go through the security gate then up the stairs to the second floor. Turn right, and walk straight to the end of the hall, then enter the door on your right which takes you into the PA Room, where the majority of the genealogical materials (except the microfilms) are to be found. The Main Desk which is staffed by professional librarians will be on your left as you enter. Make yourself known to one of the staff and then briefly indicate to her/him the subject(s) of your search. Bear in mind the general rules that apply in genealogical research libraries: no food, drink, or smoking, no loud conversation, no use of any writing instruments other than pencils, no marking of any materials, no re-shelving of volumes (place them on designated carts or shelves).Now find yourself a seat at one of the worktables. Notice that along the walls of the room are many bookshelves. Directly in front of the Main Desk are shelves designated as the Special Shelves because they contain the most frequently used general reference works. The other shelves contain published works largely on the history and genealogy of PA, but there are also many more volumes in the room on the east and still others back in the restricted stacks (librarians must bring them out for you).

Just to the right of the Main Desk (as you face it), you will find a large card file which contains three major card indexes. These indexes list practically all the PA holdings of CLP which are useful to genealogists: books, microforms (microfilms, microfiche), transcripts, unpublished materials. The first card index you must look into lists the older holdings of CLP according to the Dewey Decimal System (a numbering and labelling system used to identify and arrange books and other library materials). Included in this file (under the heading GENEALOGY) are over 2000 family histories and genealogies, plus a large listing of family histories and genealogies under the localities to which they apply (also under the heading GENEALOGY). The second card index you need to examine lists the recent holdings of CLP according to the Library of Congress System (another numbering and labelling system). Using the previously-described procedure based on the word SLANT (Subject, Location, Author, Name, Title), look for materials relating to your ancestor(s), doing them in this order: Name, Location, Subject, Author, Title. Be sure and search both indexes. When you find books pertinent to your search, record the call numbers, then go to the shelves in the room and locate the volume. If you cannot find it, then it is probably in the stacks, so fill out a call slip (on top of the card file) and hand it to a librarian. The book will be brought to you. When there are microforms pertinent to your search, record the call numbers. Then go to the Microform Room at the northeast corner of the second floor where you can ask an attendant for the material and can read it on one of the readers. If you are unfamiliar with the operation of the reader, please do not hesitate to request assistance.

Among other finding aids in the PA Room is the third card index in the large card file. This is an index to persons whose biographies are in PA local history books. A very large number of these histories have been included and they are listed in a loose-leaf notebook on the Special Shelves. The three major indexes which you must use are therefore:

___PA HISTORY AND GENEALOGY CARD INDEX, Dewey System, PA Room, CLP, Pittsburgh, PA. Can also be accessed through CAROLINE, the CLP on-line computer catalog.

___PA HISTORY AND GENEALOGY CARD INDEX, Library of Congress System, PA Room, CLP, Pittsburgh, PA. Can also be accessed through CAROLINE, the CLP on-line computer catalog.

___CARD INDEX OF BIOGRAPHIES IN PA LOCAL HISTORIES, PA Room, CLP, Pittsburgh, PA.

In addition to these card indexes, there are a number of loose-leaf or pamphlet-like finding aids on the Special Shelves: US Censuses (1790-1910 regular, 1850/60/70 Mortality), Church histories and Records and Cemeteries by County, Books on the Special Shelf List (marriage, court, birth, baptism, obituaries, military, cemetery, passenger lists, genealogy guides), PA County and Valley Histories. Further, at the Main Desk will be found the Inventory of the CLP Manuscript Collection, which is not too large a group of documents. Behind the Main Desk is a card file cabinet with several useful Pittsburgh card indexes in it.

To the right of the Main Desk and behind it is a doorway leading to book shelves, the Genealogical Collection of the Western PA Genealogical Society (book stacks 1-3), and the Microfilm Room. In the area of the Genealogical Collection of the Western PA Genealogical Society will be found two important card catalogs, one to their collection, and the other to lineage charts of their members:

___Card Catalog to the Genealogical Collection of the Western PA Genealogical Society, search by name, location, subject, author, title.

___Western PA Genealogical Society Ancestor Chart Index, search by name.

On top of the Ancesstor Chart Index are binders which contain the charts, and four notebooks which list available church histories. In the Microfilm Room, there is a small 4-drawer card cabinet sitting on the Service Desk. This finding aid will lead you to many of the microfilms in the CPL Collection:

___Patron's Guide to Alphabetical List of Microfilms, search by title and subject of the microfilm.

This guide is supplemented by several other lists to which staff members have access.

Among the most valuable of the published materials in CLP you will find county histories for all PA counties, state and local biographical volumes, church and cemetery records for many counties, numerous atlases and maps, the [Published] PA Archives, Civil War records and regimental histories, hundreds of genealogies, census indexes (1790-1870), and PA local genealogical periodicals. The microfilm collection contains census indexes (1880, 1900-20), censuses (1790-1920), many western PA newspapers, county and regional histories and atlases, periodicals, the 1798 PA Direct Tax List, Federal Land Papers, family histories, and private papers. As you might imagine, the CLP holdings are especially rich for Pittsburgh and Allegheny County. In addition to the above-mentioned types of records, the special records for the local area (Pittsburgh, Allegheny County) include city directories (1813-), estate and will indexes and records (1788-1975), death and marriage notices from newspapers (1786-1910), marriage licenses (1885-1970), ministers' returns (1875-1886), death records (1874-1903), over 16000 manuscript items on Pittsburgh history, and a 5-volumed set on founding families compiled by Foulson (containing an index to Allegheny County wills up to 1867).

The library staff at CLP is an exceptionally competent one, but they are quite busy with maintaining the collection and assisting researchers who visit the facilities. They, therefore, do not have the time to do research for individuals, but they will be glad to advise those who come in person, and they will reply to short, simple, one-question mail requests for information which can be readily found in indexes. If you write them, please do not forget to enclose an SASE. Should you need to have someone do extensive research for you, they will name some people who offer to do work of this sort.

Just across the front parking area from the CLP is the Hillman Library of the University of Pittsburgh. While school is in session, it is open 7:30 am-midnight weekdays, 7:30 am-5 pm on Saturday, and Sunday afternoons. To check on the times, call 1-412-648-7700. This facility is not a genealogical library, but it has many resources that are often helpful to PA family researchers. Included are many US censuses (including the 1790-1910 regular schedules, the US Direct Tax of 1798, the manufacturer's schedules 1820/50/60/70/80, the agricultural schedules for 1850/60/70/80), PA military records (1775-90), county and municipal council minutes for numerous localities, a few other PA county records, city directories for several PA cities (1793-1901), many regional newspapers (including numerous ethnic ones), and western PA manuscript records of businesses, organizations, associations, societies, clubs, churches, individuals, and families. The Pittsburgh and Allegheny County holdings are especially rich, including Allegheny city records (1830-1907), Pittsburgh birth, marriage, and death records (1870-1905), Allegheny County jail records (1863-1932), voters registration records, coroners records (1887-1973), church records, and organizational records. Locating these records in Hillman Library can be carried out by examining the main card catalog, the serials printout, the computer catalog PITTCAT, and the specialized finding aids (listings, inventories, and catalogs). These are to be found on the ground floor of the building, in the Microform Area (2nd floor), in the Special Collections and Archives Service Center (3rd floor), and in the Old Newspapers Area (4th floor). Other important sections of the library are the Government Publications Collection and the Map Collection.

6. The Library of the Historical Society of Western PA (LWP)

The Library of the Historical Society of Western PA (LWP) is located at 1212 Smallman St., Pittsburgh, PA 15222 in the Senator John Heinz Pittsburgh Regional History Center. The hours are 10:00 am-5:00 pm Tuesday through Saturday, closed Sunday and Monday. The telephone number is 1-412-454-6407. There is a parking lot across the street from the library. The excellent collection in this repository has been gathered under the auspices of the Historical Society of Western PA. The extensive library (published) holdings and the large archival (manuscripts) materials constitute a valuable resource for persons searching in Pittsburgh, Allegheny County, and/or the western counties of the state of PA. As is the case for practically any library or archives, times are subject to alteration, so don't fail to call before you make a research trip.

When you enter the main door of the Center, you will find yourself standing in the Great Hall of the museum area. Register at the desk, then take the elevator to the 6th floor. When you arrive, enter the door which will put you in the Reading Room of the library. You will find the Main Desk straight ahead. Make yourself known to the librarian, show some identification, and sign the register. Finally, remember the rules for researching. These rules are those you will usually find in libraries and archives: no food, drink, or smoking, no loud conversation, no use of any writing instruments other than pencils, no marking of or defacing of materials, no reshelving of materials (place them on designated shelves or carts).

The LWP contains over 35000 volumes (histories, family materials, atlases, military rosters, lineage books, compiled records, church records, cemetery readings, research guides), newspapers, historical periodicals, county records, Pittsburgh city records, maps, manuscripts, church records, family papers, organization records, and pictures. Although the materials in the LWP are pertinent to all of PA, the collection has a strong bias toward the western section. All periods of PA history are represented: colonial, Revolutionary, early statehood, Civil War, late 19th century, early 20th century.

The major finding aids which will lead you to the materials pertinent to your ancestor search are two very large indexes located in the Reading Room:
___LIBRARY AND ARCHIVES CARD CATALOG, LWP, Pittsburgh, PA.
___ON-LINE COMPUTER LIBRARY AND ARCHIVES CATALOG, LWP, Pittsburgh, PA.
You should examine the listings in both these catalogs using the SLANT system which we have discussed previously. Your searches should be done in the order: Name, Location, Subject, Author, Title. When you locate materials you want to examine, record the call numbers on call slips. Then ask a librarian to obtain them for you. Likewise, in the cases of manuscripts and other archival materials, ask the librarian for them. The manuscript holdings have been summarized in a series of periodical articles and in a recent guidee:
___The Manuscript and Miscellaneous Collections of the Historical Society of Western PA, WESTERN PA HISTORICAL MAGAZINE, Volumes 49-55 (1966-72).
___C. Seeman, GUIDE TO ARCHIVAL PAPERS, RECORDS, AND COLLECTIONS, LWP, Pittsburgh, PA, 1995.

In addition to the two large indexes, there are a number of special card indexes which you need to know about, so you can go through pertinent ones carefully. In the Main Card Index Cabinet, you will find:
___BIOGRAPHY AND BUSINESS INDEX, LWP, Pittsburgh, PA.
___SERIALS (PERIODICALS) INDEX, LWP, Pittsburgh, PA.
___ARCHIVES MAPS AND PLATS, LWP, Pittsburgh, PA.
___ARCHIVES NEWSPAPER INDEX, LWP, Pittsburgh, PA.
___OBITUARIES INDEX, 1910-91, LWP, Pittsburgh, PA.
___VERTICAL FILE INDEX, LWP, Pittsburgh, PA.
___INDEX OF CHURCH RECORDS ON MICROFILM, LWP, Pittsburgh, PA.
___ALLEGHENY CEMETERY LIST, LWP, Pittsburgh, PA.

There are several important loose-leaf binder finding aids available at the Main Desk by request:
___PHOTOGRAPH COLLECTIONS INVENTORY,
___GUIDE TO PHOTOGRAPH AND POSTCARD COLLECTIONS,
___GUIDE TO SELECTED PHOTOGRAPH COLLECTIONS.
And on several of the work tables are copies of:
___INVENTORIES OF ARCHIVAL PAPERS, RECORDS, AND COLLECTIONS, 5 volumes, LWP, Pittsburgh, PA.

The hard-working staff at the LWP is very busy, which means that they are unable to do any detailed genealogical research for anyone. They will be glad to assist you or your hired researcher when you visit them, but they must limit themselves to suggestions and guidance. In general, they will respond to mail requests provided that your letter is brief, asks one or two simple, straight-forward questions which can be looked up in indexes, and is accompanied by a long SASE. If you require extensive investigations in their records, they will send you names of people who do research for hire.

7. The Family History Library (FHL) & Its Branch Family History Centers (FHC)

The largest genealogical library in the world is the Family History Library of the Genealogical Society of UT (FHL). This library, which holds well over a million rolls of microfilm plus a vast number of books, is located at 50 East North Temple St., Salt Lake City, UT 84150. The basic keys to the library are composed of six indexes. (1) The International Genealogical Index, (2) The Surname, Index in the FHL Catalog, (3) The Indexes to the Family Group Records Collection, (4) The Ancestral File, (5) The Social Security Death Index, and (6) The Locality Index in the FHL Catalog. In addition to the main library, the Society maintains a large number of Branches called Family History Centers (FHC) all over the US. Each of these branches has microfiche and computer copies of the International Genealogical Index, the Surname Index, the Index to the Family Group Records Collection, the Ancestral File, the Social Security Death Index, and the Locality Index. In addition each FHC has a supply of forms for borrowing microfilm copies of the records from the main library. This means that the astonishingly large holdings of the FHL are available through each of its numerous FHC branches. The FHC in PA are as follows:

___Altoona FHC, 842 Whitehall Road, State College, PA.
___Broomall FHC, 721 Paxon Hollow Road, Broomall, PA.
___Clarks Summit FHC, Leach Hill and Griffin Road, Clarks Summit, PA.
___Erie FHC, 1101 South Hill Road, Erie, PA.
___Kane FHC, 30 Chestnut St., Kane, PA.
___Philadelphia FHC, 721 Paxon Hollow Road, Broomall, PA.
___Pittsburgh FHC, 46 School St., Pittsburgh, PA.
___Reading FHC, 3344 Reading Crest Ave., Reading PA.
___Scranton FHC, Leach Hill and Griffin Road, Clarks Summit, PA.
___State College FHC, 842 Whitehall Road, State College, PA.
___York FHC, 2100 Hollywood Drive, York, PA.
Other FHC are to be found in the cities listed below. They may be located by looking in the local telephone directory under the listing CHURCH OF JESUS CHRIST OF LATTER-DAY SAINTS-GENEALOGY LIBRARY or in the Yellow Pages under CHURCHES-LATTER-DAY SAINTS.
___In AL: Bessemer, Birmingham, Dothan, Huntsville, Mobile, Montgomery, Tuscaloosa, in AK: Anchorage, Fairbanks, Juneau, Ketchikan, Kotzebue, Sitka, Sodotna, Wasilla, in AZ: Benson, Buckeye, Camp Verde, Casa Grande, Cottonwood, Eagar, Flagstaff, Glendale, Globe, Holbrook, Kingman, Mesa, Nogales, Page, Payson, Peoria, Phoenix, Prescott, Safford, Scottsdale, Show Low, Sierra Vista, Snowflake, St. David, St. Johns, Tucson, Winslow, Yuma, in AR: Fort Smith, Jacksonville, Little Rock, Rogers,
___In CA (Bay Area): Antioch, Concord, Fairfield, Los Altos, Menlo Park, Napa, Oakland, San Bruno, San Jose, Santa Clara, Santa Cruz, Santa Rosa, In CA (Central): Auburn, Clovis, Davis (Woodland), El Dorado (Placerville), Fresno, Hanford, Merced, Modesto, Monterey (Seaside), Placerville, Sacramento, Seaside, Stockton, Turlock, Visalia, Woodland, In CA (Los Angeles County): Burbank, Canoga Park, Carson, Cerritos, Chatsworth (North Ridge), Covina, Glendale, Granada Hills, Hacienda Heights, Huntington Park, La Crescenta, Lancaster, Long Beach (Los Alamitos), Los Angeles, Monterey Park, Northridge, Norwalk, Palmdale, Palos Verdes (Rancho Palos Verdes), Pasadena, Torrance (Carson), Valencia, Van Nuys, Whittier, In CA (Northern): Anderson, Chico, Eureka, Grass Valley, Gridley, Mt. Shasta, Quincy, Redding, Susanville, Ukiah, Yuba City, In CA (Southern, except Los Angeles): Alpine, Anaheim, Bakersfield, Barstow, Blythe, Buena Park, Camarillo, Carlsbad, Corona, Cypress (Buena Park), El Cajon (Alpine), Escondido, Fontana, Garden Grove (Westminster), Hemet, Huntington Beach, Jurupa (Riverside), Los

Alamitos, Mission Viejo, Moorpark, Moreno Valley, Needles, Newbury Park, Orange, Palm Desert, Palm Springs (Palm Desert), Poway (San Diego), Redlands, Ridgecrest, Riverside, San Bernardino, San Diego, San Luis Obispo, Santa Barbara, Santa Maria, Simi Valley, Thousand Oaks (Moorpark), Upland, Ventura, Victorville, Vista, Westminster,

___In CO: Alamosa, Arvada, Aurora, Boulder, Colorado Springs, Columbine, Cortez, Craig, Denver, Durango, Fort Collins, Frisco, Grand Junction, Greeley, La Jara, Littleton, Louisville, Manassa, Meeker, Montrose, Longmont, Northglenn, Paonia, Pueblo, in CT: Bloomfield, Hartford, Madison, New Canaan, New Haven, Waterford, Woodbridge, in DC: Kensington, MD, in DE: Newark, Wilmington, in FL: Boca Raton, Cocoa, Ft. Lauderdale, Ft. Myers, Gainesville, Hialeah, Homestead, Jacksonville, Lake City, Lake Mary, Lakeland, Miami, Orange Park, Orlando, Palm City, Panama City, Pensacola, Plantation, Rockledge, St. Petersburg, Tallahassee, Tampa, West Palm Beach, Winterhaven, in GA: Atlanta, Augusta, Brunswick, Columbus, Douglas, Gainesville, Jonesboro, Macon, Marietta, Powder Springs, Roswell, Savannah, Tucker, in HI: Hilo, Honolulu, Kaneohe, Kauai, Kona, Laie, Lihue, Miliani, Waipahu,

___In ID: Basalt, Blackfoot, Boise, Burley, Caldwell, Carey, Coeur D'Alene, Driggs, Emmett, Firth, Hailey, Idaho Falls, Iona, Lewiston, McCammon, Malad, Meridian, Montpelier, Moore, Mountain Home, Nampa, Pocatello, Paris, Preston, Rexburg, Rigby, Salmon, Sandpoint, Shelley, Soda Springs, Twin Falls, Weiser, in IL: Champaign, Chicago Heights, Fairview Heights, Nauvoo, Peoria, Rockford, Schaumburg, Wilmette, in IN: Bloomington, Evansville, Fort Wayne, Indianapolis, New Albany, Noblesville, South Bend, Terre Haute, West Lafayette, in IA: Ames, Cedar Rapids, Davenport, Sioux City, West Des Moines, in KS: Dodge City, Olathe, Salina, Topeka, Wichita, in KY: Hopkinsville, Lexington, Louisville, Martin, Paducah, in LA: Alexandria, Baton Rouge, Denham Springs, Monroe, Metairie, New Orleans, Shreveport, Slidell,

___In ME: Augusta, Bangor, Cape Elizabeth, Caribou, Farmingdale, Portland, in MD: Annapolis, Baltimore, Ellicott City, Frederick, Kensington, Lutherville,in MA: Boston, Foxboro, Tyngsboro, Weston, Worcester, in MI: Ann Arbor, Bloomfield Hills, East Lansing, Escanaba, Grand Blanc, Grand Rapids, Hastings, Kalamazoo, Lansing, Ludington, Marquette, Midland, Muskegon, Traverse City, Westland, in MN: Anoka, Duluth, Minneapolis, Rochester, St. Paul, in MS: Clinton, Columbus, Gulfport, Hattiesburg, in MO: Cape Girardeau, Columbia, Farmington, Frontenac, Hazelwood, Independence, Joplin, Kansas City, Liberty, Springfield, St. Joseph, St. Louis, in MT: Billings, Bozeman, Butte, Glasgow, Glendive, Great Falls, Havre, Helena, Kalispell, Missoula, Stevensville, in NE: Grand Island, Lincoln, Omaha, Papillion,

___In NV: Elko, Ely, Henderson, LaHonton Valley, Las Vegas, Logandale, Mesquite, Reno, Tonapah, Winnemucca, in NH: Concord, Exeter, Nashua, Portsmouth, in NJ: Caldwell, Dherry Hill, East Brunswick, Morristown, North Caldwell, in NM: Albuquerque, Carlsbad, Farmington, Gallup, Grants, Las Cruces, Santa Fe, Silver City, in NY: Albany, Buffalo, Ithaca, Jamestown, Lake Placid, Liverpool, Loudonville, New York City, Pittsford, Plainview, Queens, Rochester, Scarsdale, Syracuse, Vestal, Williamsville, Yorktown, in NC: Asheville, Charlotte, Durham, Fayetteville, Goldsboro, Greensboro, Hickory, Kinston, Raleigh, Skyland, Wilmington, Winston-Salem, in ND: Bismarck, Fargo, Minot, in OH: Akron, Cincinnati, Cleveland, Columbus, Dayton, Dublin, Fairborn, Kirtland, Perrysburg, Reynoldsburg, Tallmadge, Toledo, Westlake, Winterville,

___In OK: Lawton, Muskogee, Norman, Oklahoma City, Stillwater, Tulsa, in OR: Beaverton, Bend, Brookings, Central Point, Coos Bay, Corvallis, Eugene, Grants Pass, Gresham, Hermiston, Hillsboro, Keizer, Klamath Falls, LaGrande, Lake Oswego, Lebanon, Minnville, Medford, Newport, Nyssa, Ontario, Oregon City, Portland, Prineville, Roseburg, Salem, Sandy, The Dallas, in RI: Providence, Warwick, in SC: Charleston, Columbia, Florence, Greenville, North Augusta, in SD: Gettysburg, Rapid City, Rosebud, Sioux Falls, in TN: Chattanooga, Franklin, Kingsport, Knoxville, Madison, Memphis, Nashville, in TX: Abilene, Amarillo, Austin, Bay City, Beaumont, Bryan, Conroe, Corpus Christi, Dallas, Denton, Duncanville, El Paso, Ft. Worth, Friendswood, Harlingen, Houston, Hurst, Katy, Kileen, Kingwood, Longview, Lubbock, McAllen, Odessa, Orange, Pasadena, Plano, Port Arthur, Richland Hills, San Antonio, Sugarland,

___In UT: American Fork, Altamont, Beaver, Blanding, Bloomington, Bluffdale, Bountiful, Brigham City, Canyon Rim, Castle Dale, Cedar City, Delta, Duchesne, Escalante, Farmington, Ferron, Fillmore, Granger, Heber, Helper, Highland, Holladay, Hunter, Huntington, Hurricane, Hyrum, Kanab, Kaysville, Kearns, Laketown, Layton, Lehi, Loa, Logan, Magna, Manti, Mapleton, Midway, Moab, Monticello, Moroni, Mt. Pleasant, Murray, Nephi, Ogden, Orem, Panguitch, Parowan, Pleasant Grove, Price, Provo, Richfield, Riverton, Roosevelt, Rose Park, Salt Lake City, Sandy, Santaquin, South Jordan, Springville, St. George, Syracuse, Tooele, Trementon, Tropic, Vernal, Wellington, Wendover, West Jordan, West Valley City, in VA:

Annandale, Bassett, Charlottesville, Chesapeake, Dale City, Falls
Church, Fredericksburg, Hamilton, Martinsville, McLean, Newport
News, Norfolk, Oakton, Pembroke, Richmond, Roanoke, Salem,
Virginia Beach, Waynesboro, Winchester, in VT: Berlin, Montpelier,
___In WA: Auburn, Bellevue, Bellingham, Bremerton, Centralia, Colville,
Edmonds, Ellensburg, Elma, Ephrata, Everett, Federal Way,
Ferndale, Lake Stevens, Longview, Lynnwood, Marysville, Moses
Lake, Mt. Vernon, North Bend, Olympia, Othello, Port Angeles,
Pullman, Puyallup, Quincy, Renton, Richland, Seattle, Silverdale, Spo-
kane, Sumner, Tacoma, Vancouver, Walla Walla, Wenatchee,
Yakima, in WV: Charleston, Fairmont, Huntington, in WI: Appleton,
Eau Clair, Hales Corner, Madison, Milwaukee, Shawano, Wausau, in
WY: Afton, Casper, Cheyenne, Cody, Gillette, Green River, Jackson
Hole, Kemmerer, Laramie, Lovell, Lyman, Rawlins, Riverton, Rock
Springs, Sheridan, Urie, Worland.

The FHL is constantly adding new branches so this list will probably be
out-of-date by the time you read it. An SASE and a $2 fee to FHL (ad-
dress in first paragraph above) will bring you an up-to-date listing of
FHC.

When you go to FHL or FHC, first ask for the PA International
Genealogical Index and examine it for the name of your ancestor, then if
you are at FHL, request the record. If you are at FHC, ask them to
borrow the microfilm containing the record from FHL. The cost is only
a few dollars, and when your microfilm arrives (usually 4 to 6 weeks), you
will be notified so that you can return and examine it. Second, ask for
the Surname Catalog. Examine it for the surname of your ancestor. If
you think any of the references relate to your ancestral line, and if you
are at FHL, request the record. If you are at FHC, ask them to borrow
the record for you. Third, ask for the Indexes to the Family Group
Records Collection which will be found in the Author/Title Section of the
FHL Catalog. Locate the microfilm number which applies to the surname
you are seeking. If you are at FHL, request the microfilm. If you are at
FHC, ask them to borrow the microfilm for you. When it comes, examine
the microfilm to see if any records of your surname are indicated. If so,
obtain them and see if they are pertinent.

Fourth, ask for the Ancestral File and look up the name you are seeking. If it is there, you will be led to sources of information, either people
who are working on the line, or records pertaining to the line. Fifth, if
you are seeking a person who died after 1937, request the Social Security
Death Index and look her/him up in it. Sixth, ask for the PA Locality

Catalog.   Examine all listings under the main heading of PENN-
SYLVANIA.   Then examine all listings under the subheading of the
county you are interested in. These county listings will follow the listings
for the state of PA. Toward the end of the county listings, there are
listed materials relating to cities and towns in the county. Be sure not to
overlook them. If you are at FHL, you can request the materials which
are of interest to you. If you are at FHC, you may have the librarian
borrow them for you. A large number of the records referred to in
Chapter 2 and those listed under the counties in Chapter 4 will be found
in the PA locality catalog.

The FHL and each FHC also have a set of Combined Census Indexes.
These indexes are overall collections of censuses and other records for
various time periods. Set 1 covers all colonies and states 1607-1819, Set
2 covers all states 1820-9, Set 3 covers all states 1830-9, Set 4 covers all
states 1840-9, Set 5 covers the southern states 1850-9, Set 6 covers the
northern states 1850-9, Set 7 covers the midwestern and western states
1850-9, Set 7A covers all the states 1850-9, and further sets cover various
groups of states 1860 and after. If you happen to be at FHL, there is
another important set of indexes that you should have examined. These
are the Temple Ordinance Indexes, especially the Temple Records Index
Bureau Files. If you are at a FHC, you may request a form to send to
the FHL along with a small fee. The FHL will examine the Temple Ordinance Indexes for you. Further details concerning the records in FHL
and FHC along with instructions for finding and using them will be found
in:
___J. Cerny and W. Elliott, THE LIBRARY, A GUIDE TO THE LDS
     FAMILY HISTORY LIBRARY, Ancestry Publishing, Salt Lake City,
     UT, 1988.

---

8. National Archives (NA) and its Branches (NAFB)

The Na-
tional Ar-
chives and
Records
Service
(NA), located at Pennsylvania Ave. and 8th St., Washington, DC 20408,
is the national repository for federal records, many being of importance
to genealogical research. The NA does not concern itself with colonial
records (pre-1776) or with state records or with records of smaller local
regions, such as counties. Among the most important records which
pertain to PA are the following ones (with the section in Chapter 2 where
they were discussed): census 1790-1920 (section 6), emigration and

immigration (section 14), military (sections 25-27), and naturalization (section 29). Please recall that there are many types of records under the military category (military service, bounty land, pension, claims, civilian). Extensive detail on these records is provided in:

___NA Staff, GENEALOGICAL RESEARCH IN THE NATIONAL ARCHIVES, National Archives and Records Service, Washington, DC, 1982.

The many records of the NA may be examined in Washington in person or by a hired researcher. Microfilm copies of many of the major records and/or their indexes may also be seen in the Field Branches of the National Archives (NAFB) which are located in or near Atlanta, Boston, Chicago, Denver, Fort Worth, Kansas City, Los Angeles, New York, Philadelphia (NAFB), San Francisco, and Seattle. They may be located by looking in the telephone directories of these cities under FEDERAL ARCHIVES AND RECORDS CENTER. The National Archives Philadelphia Branch is particularly rich in microfilm copies of federal records applying to PA. Many of the more important PA records available in the NA and the NAFB are also available as microfilm copies in PSA and PSL, especially the census and military records.

9. Regional Libraries (RL)

In the state of PA there are a number of regional libraries (RL) which have sizable genealogical collections. Their holdings are larger than those of most local libraries, but are smaller than the holdings of SLP, LHS, LWP, and CLP. As might be expected, the materials in each RL are best for the immediate and surrounding counties. Among the best of these RL are:

___Berks County Historical Society Library, 940 Centre Ave., Reading, PA 196053. [1-(215)-375-4375 to check open times.]

___Bucks County Historical Society Library, 84 South Pine St., Doylestown, PA 18901. [1-(215)-345-0210 to check open times.]

___Chester County Historical Society Library, 225 North High St., West Chester, PA 19380. [1-(215)-692-4800 to check open times.]

___Crawford County Genealogical Society Library, 848 North Main St., Meadville, PA 16335. [1-(814)-724-6080 to check open times.]

___Lancaster County Historical Society Library, 230 North President Ave., Lancaster, PA 17603. [1-(717)-392-4633 to check open times.]

___Lebanon County Historical Society Library, 924 Cumberland St., Lebanon, PA 17042. [1-(717)-272-9203 to check open times.]

___(Luzerne County) Wyoming Historical and Genealogical Society Library, 49 South Franklin St., Wilkes-Barre, PA 18701. [1-(717)-823-6244 to check open times.]

___Historical Society of Montgomery County Library, 1654 DeKalb St., Norristown, PA 19401. [1-(215)-272-0297 to check open times.]

___(Northampton County) Easton Public Library, 515 Church St., Easton, PA 18042. [1-(215)-258-2917 to check open times.]

___Warren County Historical Society Library, PO Box 427, Warren, PA 16365. [1-(814)-723-1795 to check open times.]

___(Washington County) Citizens Library, 55 South College St., Washington, PA 15301. [1-(412)-222-2400 to check open times.]

___Historical Society of York County Library, 250 East Market St., York, PA 17403. [1-(717)-848-1587 to check open times.]

When a visit is made to any of these libraries, your first endeavor is to search the card catalog. You can remember what to look for with the acronym SLANT, the use of which was described in section 2 of this chapter. This procedure should give you very good coverage of the library holdings which are indexed in the card catalog.

The second endeavor at any of these libraries is to ask about any special archives, indexes, catalogs, collections, manuscripts, or materials which might be pertinent to your search. You should make it your aim particularly to inquire about Bible, cemetery, church, map, manuscript, military, mortuary, and newspaper materials. In some cases, microform (microfilm, microfiche, microcard) records are not included in the regular card catalog but are separately indexed. It is important that you be alert to this possibility.

In addition to the RL mentioned above, there are several libraries in PA which have highly-specialized collections which are pertinent to facets of PA genealogy. Many of these have been listed in section 7 of chapter 2 which names church record centers. Other specialized collections are mentioned in:

___AMERICAN LIBRARY DIRECTORY, Bowker, New York, NY, latest edition.

10. Local libraries (LL)

Listed under the PA counties in Chapter 4 are many of the important local libraries (county, city, consolidated, local society) in the state. These libraries are of a very wide variety, some having sizable holdings of genealogical materials, some having practically none. However, you must never overlook a LL in a county or city of your interest since quite often they have local records or collections available nowhere else. In addition, local librarians are frequently very knowledgeable concerning genealogical sources in their areas. Further, they are also usually acquainted with people in the county who are experts in the county's history and genealogy. Thus, both local libraries and local librarians can be of exceptional value to you. A good listing of them is provided in:

___DIRECTORY OF PA LIBRARIES, SLP, Harrisburg, PA, latest edition.

When you visit a LL, the general procedure described previously should be followed: First, search the card catalog. Look under the headings summarized by SLANT: subject, location, author, name, title, doing them in the order L-N-S-A-T. Then, second, inquire about special indexes, catalogs, collections, materials, and microforms. Also ask about any other local sources of data such as cemetery records, church records, maps and atlases, genealogical and historical societies, mortuary records, and old newspaper records and indexes.

If you choose to write a LL, please remember that the librarians are very busy people. Always send them an SASE and confine your questions to one straight-forward item. Librarians are usually glad to help you if they can employ indexes to answer your question, but you must not expect them to do research for you. In case research is required, they will usually be able to supply you with a list of researchers which you may hire.

---

11. Large genealogical libraries (LGL)

Spread around the US there are a number of large genealogical libraries (LGL) which have at least some PA genealogical source materials. In general, those libraries nearest PA (DE, MD, NJ, NY, OH, VA) are the ones that have the larger PA collections, but there are exceptions. Among these LGL are:

___In AL: Birmingham Public Library, Library at Samford University in Birmingham, AL Archives and History Department in Birmingham, in AZ: Southern AZ Genealogical Society in Tucson, in AR: AR Genealogical Society in Little Rock, AR History Commission in Little Rock, Little Rock Public Library, in CA: CA Genealogical Society in San Francisco, Los Angeles Public Library, San Diego Public Library, San Francisco Public Library, Sutro Library in San Francisco,

___In CO: Denver Public Library, in CT: CT State Library in Hartford, Godfrey Memorial Library in Middletown, in FL: FL State Library in Tallahassee, Miami-Dade Public Library, Tampa Public Library, in GA: Atlanta Public Library, in ID: ID Genealogical Society, in IL: Newberry Library in Chicago, in IN: IN State Library in Indianapolis, Public Library of Fort Wayne, in IA: IA State Department of History and Archives in Des Moines, in KY: KY Historical Society Library in Frankfort,

___In LA: LA State Library in Baton Rouge, in ME: ME State Library in Augusta, in MD: MD State Library in Annapolis, MD Historical Society in Baltimore, in MA: Boston Public Library, New England Historic Genealogical Society in Boston, in MI: Detroit Public Library, in MN: Minneapolis Public Library, in MS: MS Department of Archives and History in Jackson, in MO: Kansas City Public Library, St. Louis Public Library,

___In NE: NE State Historical Society in Lincoln, Omaha Public Library, in NV: Washoe County Library in Reno, in NY: NY City Public Library, NY Genealogical and Biographical Society in NY City, in NC: NC State Library in Raleigh, in OH: Cincinnati Public Library, OH State Library in Columbus, Western Reserve Historical Society in Cleveland, in OK: OK State Historical Society in Oklahoma City, in OR: Genealogical Forum of Portland, Portland Library Association, in SC: South Caroliniana Library in Columbia,

___In SD: State Historical Society in Pierre, in TN: TN State Library and Archives in Nashville, in TX: Dallas Public Library, Fort Worth Public Library, in UT: Brigham Young University Library in Provo, in VA: VA State Library and VA Historical Society Library in Richmond, in WA: Seattle Public Library, in WV: WV Department of Archives and History in Charleston, in WI: Milwaukee Public Library, State Historical Society in Madison.

Chapter 4

RESEARCH PROCEDURE & COUNTY LISTINGS

■■■■■■■■■■■■■■■
1. Finding the county
■■■■■■■■■■■■■■■

Now that you have read Chapters 1-3, you should have a good idea of PA history, its genealogical records, and the locations and availability of these records. Your situation is that now you can begin to use these resources. The single most important thing to discover about a PA ancestor is the county in which he or she lived. This is because the majority of records pertaining to individuals and their activities were generally produced at the county level. The most efficient method for locating the county depends on the time period in which your ancestor lived. We will discuss county finding techniques for three basic periods in PA history: (1) after 1910, (2) 1780-1910, and (3) 1682-1780. If your ancestor lived in PA after 1910, the information as to the county of his residence is probably available to you from older members of your family. There are also the state-wide birth and death records after 1905 (sections 4 and 12, Chapter 2). However, if your ancestor lived in PA before 1910, it may be the case (as it often is) that you only know that he or she lived somewhere in the state. If you happen to have the good fortune of knowing the county, then this permits you to proceed without working through the problem of locating it. You may skip directly to section 2 of this chapter. If you don't know the county, discovery of it is your first priority.

Should your ancestor's time period be 1780-1910, the major resources for locating the county are the 1780 Stemmons STATE-WIDE TAX INDEX, the index to the 1798 US DIRECT TAX IN PA, and the indexes to the 1790, 1800/10/20/30/40/50/60/70/80, 1900/10/20 censuses (Chapter 2, section 6). If these fail to locate your forebear, then you need to look carefully into a number of other state-wide indexes which could list her or him. Among the most useful of these for the period 1780-1910 are:
___Indexes to the PPA (Chapter 2, section 10).
___Surname search of card and microform catalogs in the SLP, LHS, CLP, and FHC (Chapter 3, sections 2, 4, 5, 7).
___Surname search in books by Rider, Filby and Meyer, Hoenstine, Jordan, Jackson, and Egle, and other indexes in Chapter 2, section 17.
___Indexes to Revolutionary War, War of 1812, and Civil War Records (Chapter 2, sections 24-26).
___State-wide Land Grant Record Indexes (Chapter 2, section 20).
___Indexes to Naturalization Records (Chapter 2, section 28).

If your ancestor's time period is <u>1682</u>-<u>1780,</u> the first items to be consulted are the extensive indexes to the PPA (Chapter 2, section 10). Should you not succeed in finding your ancestor in these indexes, then the following sources should be looked into.

___Surname search in books by Rider, Filby and Meyer, Hoenstine, Jordan, Jackson, Egle, and other indexes of colonial records (Chapter 2, sections 10 and 17).

___Surname search in card and microform catalogs in SLP, LHS, CLP, and FHC (Chapter 3, sections 2, 4, 5, 7).

___Indexes to Colonial and Revolutionary War Records (Chapter 2, sections 23-24).

___State-wide Land Grant Record Indexes (Chapter 2, section 20).

___Indexes to Naturalization Records (Chapter 2, section 28).

As you can see from the above considerations, the key item for the period <u>after</u> <u>1910</u> is family information. The key items for the period <u>1780</u>-<u>1910</u> are the census and tax list compilation indexes. These items are available in SLP, PSA, LHS, CLP, FHL, FHC, NA, NAFB, NAPB, and in many LGL, RL, and LL. The key item for the period <u>1682</u>-<u>1780</u> is the PPA. This set of 138 volumes is in SLP, PSA, LHS, LWP, CLP, FHL, and in many LGL, RL, and LL. If these key items do not turn up your ancestor, the subsidiary finding aids mentioned above must be gone through. It is also well to recognize that in the period 1682-1780 there were three original counties in 1682 and this grew to only 11 counties in 1780. So if necessary, a county-by-county search during this period is not too forbidding.

This work of locating your ancestor's county can generally be done near where you live because the key finding items for the 1780-1910 and the 1682-1780 periods are in many LGL and RL outside of PA, as well as being available through FHC. Therefore, you should not have to travel too far to find the indexes you need. If, however, it is more convenient, you may choose to hire a searcher in Harrisburg, PA, to do the locating of the county.

2. Recommended approaches

Having identified the county of your ancestor's residence, you are in position to begin to ferret out the details. This means that you need to discover what non- governmental, federal, state, and county records are available, then to locate them, and finally to examine them in detail. The most useful non-governmental records have been discussed in Chapter 2 (sections 2-3, 5, 7-10, 15-19, 21, 27, 29-31). The federal records which are most important for your consideration also have been treated in Chapter 2 (sections 6, 14, 24-26, 28). State records of the greatest utility for genealogical research are discussed in both Chapter 2 (sections 4, 6, 11-14, 17, 20, 22, 23-28, 32-33) and in Chapter 3 (sections 2-4). The county records that you should look for in each county are discussed in Chapter 1 (section 10). And the county records which have been microfilmed and published, and are therefore available chiefly in PSA, LHS, and FHL (FHC) are listed in detail in Chapter 4 under each of the counties. You should make a thorough examination of <u>all</u> the records which apply to your ancestor's dates, since this will give you the best chance of finding the maximum amount of information.

The <u>best</u> <u>approach</u> for doing PA research is one in which (1) you examine all the holdings of libraries near you, including the closest LGL, then (2) you go to Harrisburg to use the materials in SLP and PSA, then (3) you go to the county where you look first in the local historical society library [if any], second in the local public library, third in the CH, and then (4) you inquire as to whether there are further records [particularly church records] in Philadelphia at LHS and in Pittsburgh at LWP and CLP. It is especially important that you inquire in Philadelphia if the county of interest is in eastern PA and in Pittsburgh if the county is in western PA.

The <u>second</u> <u>best</u> approach, which is applicable if you are nearer Salt Lake City, UT, than you are to Harrisburg, PA, is one in which (1) you examine all the holdings of libraries near you, including the closest LGL, then (2) you go to Salt Lake City and use the materials in FHL, then (3) you hire researchers in PA to carry out the investigations indicated in items (2, 3, 4) in the previous paragraph. Be sure and inform the researchers exactly what records you have seen so that you will not have to pay for duplication of your work.

The <u>third</u> <u>best</u> approach, which is applicable if you deem yourself to be too far away from both Salt Lake City and Harrisburg is one in which (1) you examine all the holdings of libraries near you, including the clos-est LGL, then (2) you go to the nearest FHC and have them borrow for you microfilms of the records you need, then (3) you hire researchers in PA to carry out the investigations indicated in items (2, 3, 4) in the second paragraph above. Carefully indicate to the researchers what records you have already used so that they will not redo what you have done.

In selecting an approach, whether it be one of the above or one at which you arrive by consideration of Chapter 3, you need to think about three items carefully. The first is expense. In visiting Harrisburg (for SLP and PSA) or Salt Lake city (for FHL), 3 or 4 full working days should be planned for if the county listings in Chapter 4 indicate a sizable number of microfilmed records to be available. If few microfilmed records are available, then 2 full working days should suffice. To visit a county seat (CH, local historical society library, LL) will require 2 to 4 days depending on how many records you have been able to explore in microfilm form at SLP and PSA. To explore the materials in Philadelphia (LHS) or Pittsburgh (LWP and CLP) after examining the holdings in SLP and PSA and CH will generally require only about a day. In using the facilities of a FHC, your initial visit for index checking and micro-film-ordering will require about a day, but your return visits will take more time depending on how many microfilms you order and whether they come together or piecemeal. For all the above visits, travel, meal, and lodging costs will be involved, and in addition, costs for borrowing microfilms from FHC must be included. The total of all these expenses must be weighed over against the cost of hiring a researcher to go to SLP, PSA, CH, LL and either LHS or LWP and CLP. Of course, your desire to look at the records yourself may be an important consideration.

The second item is a reminder about interlibrary loans. With the exception of the microfilms of FHC and the census and military National Archives microfilms available through your LL, and the AGLL, very few libraries and even fewer archives will lend out their genealogical holdings on interlibrary loan. This is practically always the case for original records and manuscripts. This means that the amount of information you may obtain through interlibrary loan is quite limited.

The third item is also a reminder, this being a restatement of what was said in Chapter 3. You will have noticed that correspondence with librarians and archivists of SLP, PSA, LHS, LWP, CLP, FHL, FHC, LGL, RL, and county employees in CH has not been mentioned in the above paragraphs. This is because these helpful and hard-working state, local, and private employees do not have time to do detailed work for you because of the demanding duties of their offices. In some cases, these people have time to look up one specific item for you (a land grant date, a deed record, a will, a plat book entry, a military pension) if an overall index is available. But please don't ask them for detailed data. If you do write them, enclose a long SASE, a check for $4 with the payee line left blank, a brief (no more than one-third page) request for one specific item, and a request that if they do not have the time, that they hand the check and your letter to a researcher who can do the task.

3. State-wide records

In this section, a summary of the most important readily-available state-wide records of genealogical significance for PA is given. This listing is to remind you of the sorts of things you should look for at the state level. These state-wide records have been discussed in some detail in Chapter 2, and essentially all of them are available at PSA. Of course, the most concentrated collection of state-wide records is the Published PA Archives (PPA), which were discussed in detail in section 10 of Chapter 2.

First, we will remind you of important original or microfilm records in PSA. Details on these records will be found in the books by Dructor, Fortna & Suran, Baumann & Wallace, Suran, and Whipkey which were listed in section 3 of Chapter 3. Auditor General Records (RG2): letter books (1809-66, 1894-7), Revolutionary War pensions (1809-93), War of 1812 soldier index, War of 1812 pensions (1866-96), militia records (1809-64), military pensions (1790-1883), Mexican War records (1846-80), Civil War records (1861-73), military claims (1862-1905). Comptroller General Records (RG4): county tax (1781-1808), militia (1777-91, 1801-9), Revolutionary War pay accounts (1784-93), donation lands, Revolutionary War militia, navy, and service (1775-1809), Revolutionary War pensions (1785-1809), tax & exoneration lists (1762-94), warrants (1782-1808). General Assembly (RG7): tax census (1779-1863). General Loan Office & State Treasurer (RG8): mortgages (1773-93). Internal Affairs Records (RG14): marriages (1885-9), medical practitioners (1881-9). Department of Justice (RG15): prison records. Bureau of Land Records (RG17): quit rents (1741-2, 1757-76), rent rolls (1683-1776), unpatented land (1820-37), survey (1701-1874), warrants (1684-1864). Department of Military Affairs Records (RG19): Mexican War service (1846-8), militia (1841-4), Civil War veterans (1861-6), Civil War sick & wounded (1861-5), Civil War rolls (1861-6), Civil War draft & deserter lists (1862-5), PA Civil War volunteers (1861-5), Civil War substitutes (1862-5), Spanish-American service (1898), Civil War surgeons records (1861-6). Proprietary Government Records (RG21): naturalizations (1740-73), governor's court of chancery (1720-36), marriage & tavern & peddler licenses (1742-52, 1759-63). Register General Records (RG24):

militia (1789-93), tavern license (1790-1809), warrants (1789-1802). Department of State Records (RG26): militia (1792-4), births & deaths & marriages (1852-4), German ship passengers (1727-1808), military commissions (1790-1944), soldiers' votes (1861-5), state & county officer bonds (1790-1808). PA Revolutionary Government Records (RG27): pass applications (1778-83), forfeited estates (1777-90), marriage bonds 1784-6), oaths of allegiance (1777-8). Treasury Department Records (RG28): warrant & patent receipts (1809-85), Continental certificates (1777-92), tavern licenses (1794-1801), Revolutionary War pensions (1834-7). Eastern District Supreme Court Records (RG33): divorces (1786-1815), judgment index (1756-1896), coroners inquisitions (1751, 1768-96), declarations of intent (1832-1906), naturalizations (1794-1868), Revolutionary War claims (1786-9). Supreme Court Records (RG33): Southern District naturalizations (1815-29), Western District naturalizations (1812-67). PA Land Office Records: applications, warrants, surveys, patents.

Second, we will list important non-governmental types of records which often have state-wide applicability. Details were given in Chapter 2, so this is simply a summarized reminder (with the section in Chapter 2 given in parentheses). Other records: Bible(2), biography(3), cemetery(5), church(7), city directory(8), colonial(10), genealogical indexes(17), genealogical periodicals(18), manuscripts(21), mortuary(27), newspaper(29), published genealogies(30), regional(31), state histories.

Finally, we will jog your memory with reference to the major federal records: censuses(6), immigration(14), and military [Revolutionary War, War of 1812, Civil War, other wars](24-26).

---

4. The format of the listings

In the numerous sections to follow, summaries of basic information on the PA counties along with the records available outside the counties are given. There are seven major sources of PA county governmental records: (1) original records in the CH, (2) original records in the local historical society library and LL, (3) microfilm copies of the records in PSA, (4) microfilm copies of the records in LHS, (5) microfilm copies of the records in FHL which are available through FHC, (6) published copies of the records in the local historical society and LL, (7) published copies of the records in SLP, LHS, LWP, CLP, FHL (available through FHC), and many LGL and RL. There are seven major sources of county non-governmental records: (1)

local historical society library and LL, (2) SLP, (3) LHS, (4) LWP and CLP, (5) FHL with availability through FHC, (6) many LGL and RL, (7) many church and some manuscript archives.

In section 1 of Chapter 3, we gave a fairly detailed list of the types of county governmental records that you might look for in the CH, LL, and local historical society library of your ancestor's county. Please turn back and take a careful look at that list before you read on. This list is not the records that you will find, but a schedule of items that you should search for when you go to the county. In addition, you should go through the county non-governmental records in the LL and the local historical society library. The types of records you should search for are listed in the headings of many of the sections of Chapter 2 (2-3, 5, 7-10, 15-18, 21, 27, 29). We will now turn our attention to the many county records available outside those counties.

Take a look at the Adams County materials (the next section) which we will use to illustrate the format for the county record summaries. In the first paragraph, the name of the county is given, then the approximate date in which the area was originally settled. This is followed by the date in which the county was formed along with the county or counties from which it came. Lastly, the county seat and the zip code of the CH are given.

The next paragraph lists county records which are available in various forms outside the county. The first section deals with microfilms of CH records which start before 1900. Along with the types of available microfilms, the approximate dates for which they are available are provided in parentheses. These dates indicate the span of years in which you may expect to find sizable records, even though every year may not necessarily be represented. Most of the listed microfilms will be found in PSA, LHS, and FHL, those in FHL being available through FHC. The next section lists other microfilms & publications, including microfilmed non-governmental county records, census microfilms, and published county records of both the governmental and non-governmental types. Most of the listed items are available in Harrisburg (at SLP and PSA), many at LHS, and many at FHL. Those at FHL are also obtainable through FHC. For counties in western PA, many of the items are also available in Pittsburgh (at LWP and CLP). The section which comes next, the PPA section, gives the records which have been printed in the Published PA Archives along with references to their location. The letter C or the number before the parentheses indicates the series [C for Colonial], the numbers in the parentheses indicate the volume(s), and the numbers after the parentheses indicate the pages. You should pay attention to the indexes to the PPA as described in section 10 of Chapter 2, since this will assist you in using the PPA. Sets of the PPA are available in SLP, PSA, LHS, LWP, CLP, FHL, and in many LGL, RL, and LL. The last section entitled other materials indicates whether genealogical periodicals, maps, manuscripts, and/or newspapers are available for the county. These items are located mainly in Harrisburg (at SLP and PSA) with some also possibly being available at LHS, LWP, CLP, FHL (FHC), LGL, RL, and LL.

The third paragraph under each county lists the county record repositories, that is, the places within the county where records are kept, both governmental and non-governmental records. Addresses are provided in parentheses. It is always wise to contact these agencies before visiting them to inform them of your coming and to obtain information on their hours. Finally, societies, both historical and genealogical, which are located in the county are listed along with their addresses.

5. Adams County

Area first settled in 1730, formed in 1800 from York County, county seat Gettysburg (17325).
Microfilm CH records:birth (1852-5, 1893-9), census-tax (1800), death (1852-5, 1874-81, 1893-1905), deed (1800-1937), estate (1800-64), marriage (1852-5, 1885-1950), orphans court (1800-1936), tax (1799-1842), will (1800-64). Other microfilms & publications: atlas (1858), biography, birth & death & marriage (1852-4), Brethren, Catholic, cemetery, census (1800R, 1810R, 1820RI, 1830R, 1840RP, 1850RAIM, 1860RAIM, 1870RAIM, 1880RAIM, 1890C, 1900R, 1910R, 1920R), Congregational, Covenantor, DAR, Dutch Reformed, Episcopal, Evangelical, Evangelical Lutheran, family history, genealogical collection, history (1846, 1886), inhabitants (1779), Irish, Lutheran, military, newspaper excerpts, Presbyterian, Quaker, Reformed, tax census (1800). PPA: War of 1812 6(7) 311-68. Other materials: genealogical periodical, landowner map (1852, 1858), manuscript, map, newspaper.
County record repositories: CH, Adams County Historical Society Library (PO Box 4325, Gettysburg 17325), Lutheran Theological Seminary (Gettysburg 17325), Adams County Public Library (59 East High St., Gettysburg 17325). Society: Adams County Historical Society (address above).

6. Allegheny County

Area first settled in 1760, formed in 1786 from Westmoreland and Washington Counties, county seat Pittsburgh (15219).

Microfilm CH records: death (1874-1903), delayed birth registration, estate (1788-1971), marriage (1885-1925), orphans court (1789-1905), proceedings of register of wills (1788-1971), tax (1784-5, 1791, 1793, 1800), will (1789-1906). Other microfilms & publications: atlas (1876), biography (1889, 1897, 1913, 1939), birth & death & marriage (1852-4), Brethren, Catholic, cemetery, census (1790R, 1800R, 1810R, 1820RI, 1830R, 1840RP, 1850RAIM, 1860RAIM, 1870RAIM, 1880RAIM, 1890C, 1900R, 1910R, 1920R), city directory (1813-), Congregational, court of quarter sessions, DAR, deed (1787-92), Episcopal, Evangelical, Evangelical Lutheran, family history, genealogical collection, histories (1876, 1888, 1889, 1904, 1922, 1976), Jewish, Lutheran, Methodist, military, naturalization (1798-1891), newspaper excerpts, Presbyterian, Quaker, Reformed, tax census (1800), will (1789-1869). PPA: election returns (1789) 6(11) 5, militia (1790-1800) 6(5) 5-100, military officer returns (1790-1817) 6(4), state officers 2(3), tax (1791) 3(22) 645-97, War of 1812 6(7) 775-93. Other materials: genealogical periodical, landowner map (1817, 1851, 1855, 1862, 1883, 1890, 1898), manuscript, map, newspaper.

County record repositories: CH (the CH itself, the City-County Building & the County Office Building, all at or near Grant and Forbes Sts.,) CLP, LWP, Hillman Library of the University of Pittsburgh (see Chapter 3 for addresses and details. Societies: Western PA Genealogical Society (4338 Bigelow Blvd., Pittsburgh 15213-2695), Historical Society of Western PA (same address).

7. Armstrong County

Area first settled in 1780, formed in 1800 from Allegheny, Westmoreland, and Lycoming Counties, county seat Kittanning (1620-21).

Microfilm CH records: commissioner (1873-1959), death (1852-5), deed (1805-1941), estate (1832-68), mortgage (1805-1943), orphans court (1805-1931), probate (1805-1935), register of wills docket (1805-1935), survey (1801-1906) , will (1800-1961). Other microfilms & publications: atlas (1876), biography (1891), census (1800R, 1810R, 1820RI, 1830R, 1840RP, 1850RAIM, 1860RAIM, 1870RAIM, 1880RAIM, 1890C, 1900R, 1910R, 1920R), directory, Episcopal, Evangelical, Evangelical Lutheran, family history, genealogical collection, history (1883, 1891, 1914, 1939), land warrant (1801-84), Lutheran, Methodist, newspaper excerpts, Presbyterian, Reformed, tax census (1800), will

(1807-27). PPA: land warrantee (1801-84) 3(26) 645-60, War of 1812 6(7) 775-93. Other materials: genealogical periodical, landowner map (1861), manuscript, map, newspaper.

County record repositories: CH, Armstrong County Historical Society Library (300 North McKean St., Kittanning 16201), Kittanning Free Library (280 N. Jefferson St., Kittanning 16201). Society: Armstrong County Historical Society (address above).

8. Beaver County — Area first settled in 1760, formed in 1800 from Allegheny and Washington Counties, county seat Beaver (15009).

Microfilm CH records: deed (1800-1918), land office (1800-1919), mortgage (1800-1918), tax (1784-5, 1793). Other microfilms & publications: atlas (1876), biography (1899), census (1800R, 1810R, 1820RI, 1830R, 1840RP, 1850RAIM, 1860RAIM, 1870RAIM, 1880RAIM, 1890C, 1900R, 1910R, 1920R), DAR, Episcopal, Evangelical Lutheran, family history, genealogical collection, history (1888, 1904, 1914), Lutheran, Methodist, newspaper excerpts, Presbyterian, warrantee map, will (1800-1900). PPA: War of 1812 6(7) 797-835. Other materials: genealogical periodical, landowner map (1860), manuscript, map, newspaper.

County record repositories: CH, Carnegie Library (1301 Seventh Ave., Beaver Falls 15010). Society: Beaver County Genealogical Society, 1301 Seventh Ave. (Beaver 15010), Beaver County Historical Society (County CH, Beaver 15009).

9. Bedford County — Area first settled in 1750, formed in 1771 from Cumberland County, county seat Bedford (15522).

Microfilm CH records: birth (1852-4, 1893-1905), death (1852-4, 1890-1906), deed (1771-1950), delayed birth registration, estate (1771-1906), guardian (1772-1900), marriage (1855-1963), mortgage (1771-1963), orphans court (1772-1900), probate (1772-1814), tax (1772, 1856, 1859-67), will (1771-1963). Other microfilms & publications: atlas (1877), biography (1899), Brethren, Catholic, cemetery, census (1790R, 1800R, 1810R, 1820RI, 1830R, 1840RP, 1850RAIM, 1860RAIM, 1870RAIM, 1880RAIM, 1890C, 1900R, 1910R, 1920R), Christian, death (1893-1906), directory, Evangelical, Evangelical Lutheran, family history, genealogical collection, history (1846, 1856, 1884, 1906, 1971), inhabitants (1790), land (1771, 1782), landowner map (1818, 1861), land warrant (1771-1893), Lutheran, Methodist, military, naturalization, newspaper excerpts, orphans court (1779-1813), Presbyterian, probate (1771-1819), Quaker, Reformed, tax (1772-6, 1779, 1783-4), tax census (1779/86, 1800), will (1770-1819 and 1771- 1900). PPA: militia (1775-87) 2(14) and 3(23) 456-7 and 5(5) 49-121, election returns (1777-89) 6(11) 9-50, land warrantees (1771-1893) 3(25) 449-673, lieutenants accounts (1777-83) 3(7) 23-35, militia (1790-1800) 6(5) 103-117, militia officer returns (1790-1817) 6(4), militia (1783-90) 6(3) 5-51, provincial officers (1729-76) 2(9) 796-7, proprietary rights 3(3), state officers 2(3), tax (1773-6, 1779, 1783-4) 3(22) 3-323, War of 1812 6(7) 671-706. Other materials: genealogical periodical, manuscript, map, newspaper.

County record repositories: CH, Bedford County Library (240 South Wood St., Bedford 15522). Society: Bedford County Historical Commission (231 South Juliana St., Bedford 15522), Pioneer Historical Society of Bedford County (PO Box 421, Bedford 15522).

10. Berks County

Area first settled in 1690, formed in 1752 from Bucks, Chester, Lancaster, and Philadelphia Counties, county seat Reading (19601).

Microfilm CH records: birth (1894-1906), court (1752-1936), death (1852-5, 1894-1906), deed (1752-1936), directors of the poor (1824-1975), estate (1752-1915), marriage (1885-1906), mortgage (1752-1926), naturalization (1798-1914), oaths of allegiance (1777-8), orphans court (1752-1947), probate (1752-92, 1815-51), tax (1752-1889), will (1752-1915. Other microfilms & publications: atlas (1862, 1876), Bible, biography (1898, 1909, 1967), Brethren, Catholic, cemetery, census (1790R, 1800R, 1810R, 1820RI, 1830R, 1840RP, 1850RAIM, 1860RAIM, 1870RAIM, 1880RAIM, 1890C, 1900R, 1910R, 1920R), Civil War, Congregational, Covenantor, deed (1752-66), directory, Episcopal, estate (1752-1850), Evangelical, Evangelical Lutheran, family history, genealogical collection, history (1844, 1886, 1909, 1925), indentured servant (1749-1913), land warrant (1730-1868), Lutheran, Mennonite, Methodist, military, Moravian, newspaper excerpts, Presbyterian, Quaker, Reformed, residents (1682-9), tax (1753-69, 1779-81, 1784-5), tax census (1779/86/93, 1800), warrantee maps, will (1752-1850). PPA: militia (1774-82) 2(14) and 5(5) 125-295, election returns (1756-89) 6(11) 53-84, land warrantees (1752-1890) 3(26) 241-335, lieutenants accounts (1777-80) 3(6) 271-322, militia (1790-1800) 6(5) 121-9, militia (1783-90) 6(3) 55-96, provincial officers (1729-76) 2(9) 784-7, proprietary rights 3(3), state officers 2(3), tax (1767-8, 1779-81, 1784-5), War of 1812 6(7) 371-419. Other materials: genealogical periodical, landowner map (1812, 1820, 1854, 1860), manuscript, map, newspaper.

County record repositories: CH, Historical Society of Berks County Library (940 Centre Ave., Reading 19605), Reading Public Library (100 S. 5th St., Reading 19602). Societies: Berks County Genealogical Society (PO Box 14774, Reading 19612), Historical Society of Berks County (address above).

11. Blair County

Area first settled in 1760, formed in 1846 from Huntingdon and Bedford Counties, county seat Hollidaysburg (16648).

Microfilm CH records: none. Microfilms & published records: atlas (1873), biography (1892), birth in Altoona (1886-1905), Catholic, cemetery, census (1850RAIM, 1860RAIM, 1870RAIM, 1880RAIM, 1890C, 1900R, 1910R, 1920R), directory, Evangelical, Evangelical Lutheran, family history, genealogical collection, history (1865, 1880, 1883, 1892, 1911, 1931, 1945), Lutheran, marriage, military, newspaper excerpts, Presbyterian, Reformed, tax (1846), undertaker (1883-1910). PPA: land warrantees (1846-90) 3(26) 19-23. Other materials: genealogical periodical, landowner map (1859), manuscript, map, newspaper.

County record repositories: CH, CH Annex, Martinsburg Community Library (201 South Walnut St., Martinsburg 16662), Hoenstine Rental Library (Hollidaysburg 16648), Blair County Historical Society Library (PO Box 1083, Altoona 16603), Altoona Area Public Library (1600 Fifth Ave., Altoona 16602). Societies: Blair County Genealogical Society (PO Box 855, Altoona 16603), Blair County Historical Society (address above).

12. Bradford County

Area first settled in 1770, formed in 1810 from Luzerne and Lycoming Counties, called Ontario County 1810-2, county seat Towanda (18848).

Microfilm CH records: birth (1852-4), death (1852-4). Other microfilms & publications: atlas (1869), Baptist, biography (1910, 1915), Catholic, cemetery, census (1820RI, 1830R, 1840RP, 1850RAIM, 1860RAIM, 1870RAIM, 1880RAIM, 1890C, 1900R, 1910R, 1920R), Congregational, DAR, Episcopal, Evangelical Lutheran, family history, French, genealogical collection, history (1878, 1885, 1891, 1913-5, 1926), land (1810-30), Lutheran, Methodist, military (1800-40), newspaper excerpts, Presbyterian, Quaker. PPA: land warrantees (1812-96) 3(24) 307-12. Other materials: genealogical periodical, landowner map (1858), manuscript, map, newspaper.

County record repositories: CH, Bradford County Historical Society Library (21 Main St., Towanda 18848), Troy Free Public Library (200

East Main St., Troy 16947). Society: Bradford County Genealogical Society (address above), Bradford County Historical Society (address above).

13. Bucks County

Area first settled in 1680, established in 1682 as one of the original counties, county seat Doylestown (18901).

Microfilm CH records: apprentice (1809-93), birth (1852-4, 1893-1907), commissioners (1778-1946), court of common pleas & quarter sessions (1684-1805), coroner (1710-1946), death (1852-5, 1893-1907), deed (1684-1919), delayed birth registration, estate (1684-1939), guardian (1683-1958), indentured servants (1809-93), marriage (1852-4, 1885-1946), military (1776-1802), mortgage (1684-1919), oaths of allegiance (1777-86), orphans court (1683-1958), poor records (1809-95), residents (1677-89), register of wills docket (1839-1913), slave (1783-1830), survey (1675-9, 1682-1761), tax (1693, 1721-64, 1776, 1782-1860, also 1786, 1800), treasurer (1747-96), warrants (1734-53). Other microfilms & publications: atlas (1850, 1876), Bible, biography (1899), Catholic, cemetery, census (1790R, 1800R, 1810R, 1820RI, 1830R, 1840RP, 1850RAIM, 1860RAIM, 1870RAIM, 1880RAIM, 1890C, 1900R, 1910R, 1920R), Congregational, DAR, court of common pleas & quarter sessions (1684-1700), directory, Dutch Reformed, Episcopal, estate (1684-1850), Evangelical, Evangelical Lutheran, family history, funeral, gazetteer, genealogical collection, history (1876, 1887, 1905, 1972), Lutheran, newspaper extracts, naturalizations (1802-1906), oaths of allegiance (1776-86), Presbyterian, Quaker, Reformed, tax (1693-1779), tax census (1786, 1800), will (1684-1850). PPA: militia (1775-83) 2(14) and 5(5) 299-448, census (1784) 3(13) iii, committee of safety minutes (1774-6) 2(15) 341-69, election returns (1756-89) 6(11) 87-119, land warrantees (1733-1889) 3(24) 109-77, lieutenants accounts (1777-83) 3(5) 765-84 and 3(6) 1-149, marriages before 1810 2(9), militia (1783-90) 6(3) 99-119, provincial officers (1682-1776) 2(9) 742-66, proprietary and old rights 3(3), state officers 2(3), tax (1779, 1781-7), War of 1812 6(7) 105-214. Other materials: genealogical periodical, landowner map (1817, 1850), manuscript, map, newspaper.

County record repositories: CH, Historical Society of Bucks County, Spruance Library (84 South Pine St., Doylestown 18901), Bucks County Free Library (150 South Pine St., Doylestown 18901). Societies: Historical Society of Bucks County (address above), Bucks County Genealogical Society (PO Box 1092, Doylestown 18901).

14. Butler County

Area first settled in 1780, formed in 1800 from Allegheny County, county seat Butler (16001).

Microfilm CH records: birth (1852-4, 1893-1905), death (1852-4, 1893-1905), deed (1800-1925), delayed birth registration, guardian (1800-1970), marriage (1885-1913), mortgage (1800-1928), orphans court (1800-1971), probate (1800-1910), will (1800-1971). Other microfilms & publications: atlas (1874), Baptist, cemetery, census (1800R, 1810R, 1820RI, 1830R, 1840RP, 1850RAIM, 1860RAIM, 1870RAIM, 1880RAIM, 1890C, 1900R, 1910R, 1920R), DAR, directory, Episcopal, estate (1800-1900), Evangelical, Evangelical Lutheran, history (1883, 1887, 1895, 1905, 1909, 1927, 1950), land (1800-3), Lutheran, Methodist, military, newspaper excerpts, Presbyterian, probate (1800-1900), Reformed. PPA: War of 1812 6(7) 797-835. Other materials: genealogical periodical, landowner map (1817, 1868), manuscript, map, newspaper.

County record repositories: CH, Butler Area Public Library (218 North McKean St., Butler 16001). Society: Butler County Historical Society (PO Box 414, Butler 16001).

15. Cambria County

Area first settled in 1770, formed in 1804 from Somerset, Bedford, and Huntingdon Counties, county seat Ebensburg (15931).

Microfilm CH records: birth (1852-5, 1893-9), commissioner (1807-1975), death (1852-5), marriage (1852-5). Other microfilms & publications: atlas (1890), biography (1896, 1910), birth & death & marriage (1850-5), cemetery, census (1810R, 1820RI, 1830R, 1840RP, 1850RAIM, 1860RAIM, 1870RAIM, 1880RAIM, 1890C, 1900R, 1910R, 1920R), directory, Episcopal, estate (1804-1900), Evangelical Lutheran, history (1846, 1896, 1907, 1926, 1954), Lutheran, newspaper excerpts, Presbyterian, probate (1804-1900), will (1804-1900). PPA: War of 1812 6(7) 671-706. Other materials: genealogical periodical, landowner map (1817, 1867), manuscript, map, newspaper.

County record repositories: CH, Cambria County Historical Society Library (521 West High St., Ebensburg 15931), Cambria County Library System (248 Main St., Johnstown 15901). Societies: Cambria County Historical Society (615 North Center, Ebensburg 15931), Windber-Johnstown Genealogical Society (409 19th St., Apt. A,Windber 15963).

16. Cameron County

Area first settled in 1810, formed in 1860 from Clinton, Elk, McKean, and Potter Counties, county seat Emporium (15834).

Microfilm CH records: birth (1893-1906), death (1893-1906), deed (1860-1902), delayed birth registration, guardian (1859-1972), marriage (1885-1910), orphans court (1854-1972), will (1862-1972). Other microfilm & publications: Bible, Catholic, cemetery, census (1870RAIM, 1880RAIM, 1890C, 1900R, 1910R, 1920R), Congregational, Episcopal, Evangelical, genealogical collection, history (1890, 1905, 1943), Methodist, newspaper excerpts, Presbyterian, warrantee maps. PPA: War of 1812 6(7) 311-68. Other materials: landowner map (1856-7), manuscript, map, newspaper.

County record repositories: CH, Cameron County Historical Society Library (Rt. 2, Box 54, Emporium 15834), Cameron County Public Library (One East Fourth St., Emporium 15834). Society: Cameron County Historical Society (address above).

17. Carbon County

Area first settled in 1740, formed in 1843 from Northampton and Monroe Counties, county seat Jim Thorpe (18229).

Microfilm CH records: vital records (1852-4), court of oyer & terminer (1872, 1876-8). Other microfilms & publications: atlas (1875), biography (1894, 1913), cemetery, census (1850RAIM, 1860RAIM, 1870RAIM, 1880RAIM, 1890C, 1900R, 1910R, 1920R), Episcopal, Evangelical, Evangelical Lutheran, family history, genealogical collection, history (1845, 1884, 1913), Lutheran, Methodist, military (1861, 1867), newspaper excerpts, Presbyterian, Reformed. PPA: none. Other materials: landowner map (1860), manuscript, map, newspaper.

County record repositories: CH, Dimmick Memorial Library (54 Broadway, Jim Thorpe 18229).

18. Centre County

Area first settled in 1760, formed in 1800 from Lycoming, Mifflin, Northumberland, and Huntingdon Counties, county seat Bellefonte (16823).

Microfilm CH records: vital records (1852-4). Other microfilms & publications: atlas (1874), biography (1898, 1941), cemetery, census (1800R, 1810R, 1820RI, 1830R, 1840RP, 1850RAIM, 1860RAIM, 1870RAIM, 1880RAIM, 1890C, 1900R, 1910R, 1920R), DAR, Evangelical, Evangelical Lutheran, history (1847, 1877, 1883, 1925), Lutheran, Methodist, newspaper excerpts, Presbyterian, Quaker, Reformed, tax census (1800), will (1800-53). PPA: land warrantees (1801-91) 3(25) 785-809, War of 1812 6(7) 647-67. Other materials: genealogical periodical, landowner map (1815, 1861), manuscript, map, newspaper.

County record repositories: CH, Centre County Library (203 North Allegheny St., Bellefonte 16823). Society: Centre County Historical Society (1001 East College Ave., State College 16801), Centre County Genealogical Society (PO Box 1135, State College 16801).

19. Chester County

Area first settled in 1640, formed in 1682 as one of the original counties, county seat West Chester (19380).

Microfilm CH records: birth (1852-5, 1893-1905), commissioners (1740-1918), court (1682-1783), court of common pleas (1882-1905), court of oyer & terminer (1802-1935), court of quarter sessions (1714-1906), death (1852-5, 1878-1905), deed (1688-1922), estate (1713-1937), marriage (18-52-5, 1885-1967), mortgage (1688-1929), orphans court (1716-1968), pauper (1859-1910), petition (1717-50), provincial tax (1756-78), sheriff (1773-1905), survey & warrant (1672-1775), tax (1693-1900), will (1712-1924). Other microfilms & publications: atlas (1783), Baptist, biography (1893, 1904), cemetery, census (1790R, 1800R, 1810R, 1820RI, 1830R, 1840RP, 1850RAIM, 1860RAIM, 1870RAIM, 1880RAIM, 1890C, 1900R, 1910R, 1920R), court (1681-1710), Covenantor, DAR, directory, Episcopal, estate (1713-1850), Evangelical, Evangelical Lutheran, family history, gazetteer (1961), genealogical collection, history (1877, 1881, 1898, 1932), Lutheran, marriages in deeds (1705-1882), Mennonite, Methodist, newspaper excerpts, oaths of allegiance (1777-85), orphans court (1716-47), Presbyterian, Quaker, Reformed, tax census (1779/86, 1800), undertaker, will (1713-1850). PPA: assessment of tax (1785) 3(12) 665-823, militia (1774-82) 2(14) 63-139 and 3(23) 402-23, 5(5) 451-888, election returns (1756-89) 6(11) 123-49, land warrantees 3(24) 61-106, lieutenants accounts (1777-83) 3(6) 151-268, marriages before 1810 2(8) 591-8, militia (1783-90) 6(3) 123-345, provincial officers (1682-1776) 2(9) 673-97, old & proprietary rights 3(3), state officers 2(3), tax (1765-9, 1771, 1774, 1779-81) 3(11) 3-783 and 3(12) 3-823, War of 1812 6(7) 217-57. Other materials: genealogical periodical, landowner map (1820, 1847, 1856, 1860), manuscript, map, newspaper.

County record repositories: CH, Chester County Historical Society Library (225 North High St., West Chester 19380), Chester County Archives & Records Service (117 West Gay St., West Chester, 19380). Society: Chester County Historical Society (address above).

20. Clarion County

Area first settled in 1800, formed in 1839 from Venango and Armstrong Counties, county seat Clarion (16214).

Microfilm CH records: none. Other Microfilms & publications: atlas (1877), biography (1898), cemetery, census (1850RAIM, 1860RAIM, 1870RAIM, 1880RAIM, 1890C, 1900R, 1910R, 1920R), DAR, directory, genealogical collection, history (1887), Lutheran, Methodist, newspaper excerpts, Reformed. PPA: land warrantees (1841-79) 3(26) 383-6. Other materials: landowner map (1865), manuscript, map, newspaper.

County record repositories: CH, Clarion County Historical Society Library (18 Grant St., Clarion 16214), Clarion Free Library (640 Main St., Clarion 16214). Society: Clarion County Historical Society (address above).

21. Clearfield County

Area first settled in 1800, formed in 1804 from Huntingdon and Lycoming Counties, county seat Clearfield (16830).

Microfilm CH records: estate (1823-60), vital records (1852-4), will (1823-60). Other microfilms & publications: atlas (1878), Baptist, biography (1898), Brethren, Catholic, cemetery, census (1810R, 1820RI, 1830R, 1840RP, 1850RAIM, 1860RAIM, 1870RAIM, 1880RAIM, 1890C, 1900R, 1910R, 1920R), DAR, directory, Evangelical, Evangelical Lutheran, family history, genealogical collection, history (1887, 1911, 1925), Lutheran, Methodist, newspaper excerpts, Presbyterian, Quaker. PPA: land warrantee (1806-96) 3(25) 411-7. Other materials: genealogical periodical, landowner map (1818, 1866), manuscript, map, newspaper.

County record repositories: CH, Clearfield County Historical Society Library (104 East Pine St., Clearfield 16830), Shaw Public Library (6 South Front St., Clearfield 16830). Society: Clearfield County Historical Society (address above).

22. Clinton County

Area first settled in 1760, formed in 1839 from Lycoming and Centre Counties, county seat Lock Haven (17745).

Microfilm CH records: birth (1852-5), death (1852-5, 1893-1905), delayed birth register, marriage (1852-5, 1885-1906), orphans court (1839-1974), will (1839-1907). Other microfilms & publications: Baptist, biography (1892, 1893, 1898), Brethren, cemetery, census (1840RP,1850RAIM, 1860RAIM, 1870RAIM, 1880RAIM, 1890C, 1900R, 1910R, 1920R), family history,

history (1847, 1875, 1883, 1892), Lutheran, Methodist, will (1839-72). PPA: land warrantees (1839-93) 3(26) 3-15. Other materials: genealogical periodical, landowner map (1862), manuscript, map, newspaper.

County record repositories: CH, Clinton County Historical Society Library (362 East Water St., Lock Haven 17745), Ross Library (232 West Main St., Lock Haven 17745), Centre County Library (203 North Allegheny St., Bellefonte 16823). Society: Clinton County Historical Society (address above).

---

23. Columbia County

Area first settled in 1770, formed in 1813 from Northumberland County, county seat Bloomsburg (17815).

Microfilm CH records: birth (1852-6, 1893-1942), court of common pleas (1814-61), death (1852-5, 1853-73, 1893-1905), deed (1813-1973), delayed birth registration, marriage (1885-1907), mortgage (1813-1973), naturalization (1814-61), orphans court (1814-69), probate (1813-1974), will (1813-1974). Other microfilms & publications: atlas (1876), biography (1899, 1915), Brethren, cemetery, census (1820RI, 1830R, 1840RP, 1850RAIM, 1860RAIM, 1870RAIM, 1880RAIM, 1890C, 1900R, 1910R, 1920R), Evangelical, Evangelical Lutheran, family history, history (1847, 1876, 1883, 1887, 1915, 1958), Lutheran, Methodist, newspaper excerpts, Presbyterian, Quaker, Reformed, tax census (1821). PPA: none. Other materials: genealogical periodical, landowner map (1860), manuscript, map, newspaper.

County record repositories: CH, Columbia County Historical Society Library (Bloomsburg State College, Bloomsburg 17815), Bloomsburg Public Library (225 Market St., Bloomsburg 17815). Society: Columbia County Historical Society (PO Box 197, Orangeville 17859), Columbia County Genealogy Club (PO Box 197, Orangeville 17859).

---

24. Crawford County

Area first settled in 1780, formed in 1800 from Allegheny County, county seat Meadville (16335).

Microfilm CH records: birth (1893-1906), death (1852-4, 1893-1905), deed (1800-1925), delayed birth register, marriage (1852-4, 1885-1951), mortgage (1800-1925), orphans court (1800-1921), register of wills docket (1800-1970), will (1805-1907). Other microfilms & publications: atlas (1865), biography, cemetery, census (1800R, 1810R, 1820RI, 1830R, 1840RP, 1850RAIM, 1860RAIM, 1870RAIM, 1880RAIM, 1890C, 1900R, 1910R, 1920R), Evangelical & Reformed, family history, history (1885,

1891), Lutheran, Methodist, newspaper excerpts, Presbyterian, will (1805-41). PPA: War of 1812 6(7) 797-385. Other materials: genealogical periodical, landowner map (1818, 1839, 1865), manuscript, map, newspaper.

County record repositories: CH, Crawford County Historical Society Library (848 North Main St., Meadville 16335). Societies: Crawford County Historical Society (address above), Genealogical Society of Crawford County (same address).

25. Cumberland County

Area first settled in 1720, formed in 1750 from Lancaster County, county seat Carlisle (17013).

Microfilm CH records: almshouse (1830-76), birth (1852-5, 1894-1905), commissioners (1790-1820, 1828-1979), coroner (1862-1912), court of common pleas (1750-1905), court of oyer & terminer (1798-1895), court of quarter sessions (1750-1909), death (1852-5, 1894-1905), deed (1750-1950), delayed birth register, divorce (1810-1905), Episcopal, estate (1750-1937), lunacy (1890-1912), marriage (1852-5, 1885-1930), mortgage (1777-1956), naturalization (1798-1905), orphans court (1751-1929), register of wills docket (1750-1906), slave (1780-1, 1788-1826, 1833), survey (1738-1890), tavern (1750-1855), tax (1750-1850), will (1750-1937). Other microfilms & publications: atlas (1872), biography (1876, 1905), Brethren, cemetery, census (1790R, 1800R, 1810R, 1820RI, 1830R, 1840RP, 1850RAIM, 1860RAIM, 1870RAIM, 1880RAIM, 1890C, 1900R, 1910R, 1920R), Covenantor, DAR, directory, Episcopal, Evangelical, Evangelical Lutheran, family history, genealogical collection, history (1846, 1879, 1886, 1951), land (1755-1868), Lutheran, Methodist, oaths of allegiance (1761, 1777-8), Presbyterian, Quaker, Reformed, Seventh Day Adventist, tax census (1793, 1800). PPA: militia (1774-83) 2(14) 369-472 and 2(15) 563-624 and 3(23) 444-454 and 5(6) 3-658, election returns (1756-87) 6(11) 153-177, land warrantees (1750-1874) 3(24) 627-792, lieutenants accounts (1777-83) 3(6) 653-717, marriages prior to 1810 2(8) 563-90, militia (1790-1800) 6(5) 165-227, militia officer returns (1790-1817) 6(4), militia (1783-90) 6(3) 349-51, militia (1777-822) 3(23) 611-809, provincial officers (1729-76) 2(9) 788-92, proprietary rights 3(3), state officers 2(3), tax (1778-82, 1785) 3(20) 3-781, War of 1812 6(7) 423-540. Other materials: genealogical periodical, landowner map (1858), manuscript, map, newspaper.

County record repositories: CH, Hamilton Library and Cumberland County Historical Society (21 North Pitt St., Carlisle 17013), Bosler Free Library (158 West High St., Carlisle 17013). Societies: Cumberland

County Historical Society (address above), Capital Area Genealogical Society (PO Box 4502, Harrisburg 17111).

---

26. Dauphin County

Area first settled in 1720, formed in 1785 from Lancaster County, county seat Harrisburg (17101).

Microfilm CH records: birth (1852-4, 1893-1906), births in Harrisburg (1875-86, 1906-15), death (1852-5, 1893-1906), deaths in Harrisburg (1883-6, 1892), deed (1785-1917), delayed birth register, estate (1785-1917), marriage (1852-5, 1885-1950), medical & health (1887-1923), orphans court (1785--1850), physician (1881-1915), poor children (1832-41), tax (1785-1850), will (1785-1875). Other microfilms & publications: atlas (1875), biography (1896), cemetery, census (1790R, 1800R, 1810R, 1820RI, 1830R, 1840RP, 1850RAIM, 1860RAIM, 1870RAIM, 1880RAIM, 1890C, 1900R, 1910R, 1920R), city directory, Covenantor, directory, Episcopal, Evangelical, Evangelical Lutheran, family history, genealogical collection, history (1846, 1877, 1883, 1886, 1907), Lutheran, marriage (1793-1810), Methodist, military, newspaper excerpts, Presbyterian, Quaker, Reformed, tax census (1786, 1800/7), warrantee maps, will (1785-1850). PPA: election returns (1785-9) 6(11) 181-5, land warrantees (1785-1895) 3(24) 571-615, lieutenants accounts (1785-8) 3(7) 147-59, marriages before 1810 2(8) 779-90, militia (1790-1800) 6(5) 231-99, militia officer returns (1790-1817) 6(4), militia (1783-90) 6(3) 355-409, state officers 2(3), War of 1812 6(7) 371-419. Other materials: genealogical periodical, landowner map (1819, 1858, 1862), manuscript, map, newspaper.

County record repositories: CH, Dauphin County Historical Society Library (219 South Front St., Harrisburg 17104), Dauphin County Library (101 Walnut St., Harrisburg 17101), SLP, PSA. Societies: Historical Society of Dauphin County (address above), Capitol Area Genealogical Society (PO Box 4502, Harrisburg 17111).

---

27. Delaware County

Area first settled in 1640, formed in 1789 from Chester County, county seat Media (19063).

Microfilm CH records: birth (1852-4, 1893-1907), births in Chester (1889-1906), death (1852-4, 1893-1907), delayed birth register, deed (1789-1914), estate (1790-1917), marriage (1852-4, 1885-1907), mortgage (1789-1925), orphans court (1789-1973), petitions for roads (1785-1815), recognizance (1835-88), tax (1715, 1781-9), will (1789-1973). Other microfilms & publications: atlas (1870, 1875, 1880), Baptist, biography (1894), census

(1790R, 1800R, 1810R, 1820RI, 1830R, 1840RP, 1850RAIM, 1860RAIM, 1870RAIM, 1880RAIM, 1890C, 1900R, 1910R, 1920R), directory, Episcopal, estate (1789-1850), Evangelical Lutheran, family history, genealogical collection, history (1862, 1877, 1884, 1894, 1914, 1932), inhabitants (1772), Methodist, Presbyterian, Quaker, Reformed, tax census (1793, 1800), undertaker, will (1789-1850). PPA: election returns (1789) 6(11) 189-90, militia (1790-1800) 6(5) 303-6, militia officer returns (1790-1817) 6(4), state officers 2(3), War of 1812 6(7) 217-57. Other materials: genealogical periodical, landowner map (1818, 1848, 1862, 1876), manuscript, map, newspaper.

County record repositories: CH, Delaware County Historical Society Library (15th and Walnut Sts., Chester 19013), Crozer Library (620 Engle St., Chester 19063), Media-Upper Providence Free Library (Front and Jackson Sts., Media 19063). Society: Delaware County Historical Society (85 N. MalinRd., Broomall 19008).

28. Elk County

Area first settled in 1810, formed in 1843 from Jefferson, McKean, and Clearfield Counties, county seat Ridgway (15853).

Microfilm CH records: deed (1844-1910), estate (1844-1971), orphans court (1857-86), register of wills docket (1844-1971), vital records (1852-4), will (1845-97). Other microfilms & publications: atlas (1860), biography, census (1850RAIM, 1860RAIM, 1870RAIM, 1880RAIM, 1890C, 1900R, 1910R, 1920R), Evangelical, history (1890), Lutheran, Methodist. PPA: land warrantees (1848-93) 3(26) 681-2. Other materials: genealogical periodical, landowner map (1855, 1856, 1878), manuscript, map, newspaper, warrantee maps.

County record repositories: CH, Elk County Historical Society Library (109 Center St., Ridgway 15853), Ridgway Free Public Library (329 Center St., Ridgway 15853), Saint Marys Public Library (127 Center St., Saint Marys 15857). Society: Elk County Genealogical Society (PO Box 142, Johnsonburg 15845), Elk County Historical Society (PO Box 361, Ridgeway 15853).

29. Erie County

Area first settled in 1790, formed in 1800 from Allegheny County, functioned under Crawford County 1800-3, fully organized in 1803, county seat Erie (16501), fire in 1823 destroyed many records.

Microfilm CH records: birth (1892-1906), death (1892-1906), deed (1823-1946), delayed birth register, estate (1823-1971), marriage

(1885-1919), mortgage (1823-1919), orphans court (1823-68), register of wills proceedings (1823-1958), register of wills docket (1839-64), tax (1816-70), town lots (1796-1919), will (1823-1906). Other microfilms & publications: atlas (1865, 1876), biography (1896), Catholic, cemetery, census (1800R, 1810R, 1820RI, 1830R, 1840RP, 1850RAIM, 1860RAIM, 1870RAIM, 1880RAIM, 1890C, 1900R, 1910R, 1920R), directory, family history, history (1884, 1894, 1909, 1925), Jewish, Latter Day Saints, naturalization (1825-1906), newspaper excerpts, Presbyterian. PPA: War of 1812 6(7) 797-835. Other materials: genealogical periodical, landowner map (1818, 1855), manuscript, map, newspaper, warrantee maps.

County record repositories: CH, Erie County Library (3 South Perry Square, Erie 16501). Societies: Erie County Society for Genealogical Research (PO Box 1403, Erie 16512), Erie County Historical Society (417 State St., Erie 16501).

---

30. Fayette County

Area first settled in 1750, formed in 1783 from Westmoreland County, county seat Uniontown (15401).

Microfilm CH records: black births (1788-1826), commissioners (1812-24, 1834-41, 1848-63, 1869-73), court of quarter sessions (1783-1808), death (1852-5), deed (1784-1950), estate (1850-71), marriage (1852-5), mortgage (1784-1950), orphans court (1784-1950), probate (1784-1950), prothonotary dockets (1784-1818), sheriff (1785-1875), survey (1784-1900), tax (1785-1860), warrants (1784-1900), will (1784-1950). Other microfilms & publications: atlas (1872, 1896), Baptist, biography (1889, 1900, 1912), cemetery, census (1790R, 1800R, 1810R, 1820RI, 1830R, 1840RP, 1850RAIM, 1860RAIM, 1870RAIM, 1880RAIM, 1890C, 1900R, 1910R, 1920R), Dutch Reformed, Episcopal, family history, genealogical collection, history (1882, 1912), inhabitants (1785), Lutheran, Methodist, newspaper excerpts, Presbyterian, Quaker, Reformed, tax census (1786, 1800), will (1783-1900). PPA: election returns (1784-9) 6(11) 193-6, militia (1790-1800) 6(5) 309-220, militia officer returns (1790-1817) 6(4), state officers 2(3), tax (1785-6) 3(22) 543-641, treasurer (1785-90) 3(7) 459-561, War of 1812 6(7) 709-59. Other materials: genealogical periodical, landowner map (1817, 1858, 1865, 1872), manuscript, map, newspaper.

County record repositories: CH, Uniontown Public Library (24 Jefferson St., Uniontown 15401). Society: Fayette County, PA, Genealogical Research Asso. (3690 Peacock Ct., Apt. 2, Santa Clara, CA 95051).

31. Forest County

Area first settled in 1800, formed in 1848 from Jefferson, then territory added in 1866 from Venango, county seat Marienville until 1866, then Tionesta (16353).

Microfilm CH records: deed (1857-1933), orphans court (1855-88), road (1850-90), sheriff (1852-1903), will (1857-1911). Other microfilms & publications: biography (1899), census (1860RAIM, 1870RAIM, 1880RAIM, 1890C, 1900R, 1910R, 1920R), Evangelical Lutheran, genealogical collection, history (1890), Presbyterian. PPA: land warrantees (1858-91) 3(26) 689-90. Other materials: landowner map (1864, 1876, 1881-2, 1895), map, newspaper.

County record repositories: CH, Forest County Library (156 Elm St., Tionesta 16353).

32. Franklin County

Area first settled in 1730, formed in 1784 from Cumberland County, county seat Chambersburg (17201).

Microfilm CH records: birth (1894-1906), death (1893-1906), deed (1785-1963), delayed birth register, estate (1784-1963), guardian (1850-1908), marriage (1885-1963), medical (1881-1959), mortgage (1811-68), orphans court (1785-1963), plat (1785-1963), tax (1791-1847), vital records (1852-4), will (1784-1963). Other microfilms & publications: atlas (1868), biography (1876, 1905), Brethren, cemetery, census (1790R, 1800R, 1810R, 1820RI, 1830R, 1840RP, 1850RAIM, 1860RAIM, 1870RAIM, 1880RAIM, 1890C, 1900R, 1910R, 1920R), directory, Episcopal, Evangelical Lutheran, family history, genealogical collection, history (1846, 1878, 1884, 1887), LDS, Lutheran, Methodist, military, newspaper excerpts, Presbyterian, Quaker, Reformed, tax census (1786, 1800/7/14/21/28/25/42). PPA: election returns (1784-9) 6(11) 205-8, land warrantees (1784-1895) 3(25) 3-51, lieutenants accounts (1785-89 3(7) 163-72, militia officer returns (1790-1817) 6(4), militia (1783-90) 6(3) 413-35, state officers 2(3), War of 1812 6(7) 423-540. Other materials: genealogical periodical, landowner map (1858), manuscript, map, newspaper.

County record repositories: CH, Kittochtinny Historical Society Library (158 Lincoln Way East, Chambersburg 17201), Coyle Free Library (102 North Main St., Chambersburg 17201). Societies: Kittochtinny Historical Society (PO Box 732, Chambersburg 17201), Franklin County Heritage Association (East King at North Second St., Chambersburg 17201).

33. Fulton County

Area first settled in 1750, formed in 1850 from Bedford County, county seat McConnellsburg (17233).

Microfilm <u>CH</u> records: birth (1894-1905), death (1852-4, 1874-81, 1895-1905), deed (1850-1937), delayed birth register, estate (1851-1963), guardian (1851-1909), marriage (1852-4, 1885-1963), mortgage (1851-99), orphans court (1851-1936), probate (1851-1963), will (1851-1908). Other <u>microfilms</u> & <u>publications</u>: Baptist, cemetery, census (1850RAIM, 1860RAIM, 1870RAIM, 1880RAIM, 1890C, 1900R, 1910R, 1920R), Covenantor, DAR, Evangelical, Evangelical Lutheran, family history, history (1884), LDS, Lutheran, Mennonite, Methodist, military, naturalization, Presbyterian, Reformed. <u>PPA</u>: land warrantees (1850-96) 3(24) 335-41. Other <u>materials</u>: genealogical periodical, landowner map (1873), manuscript, map, newspaper, warrantee maps.

<u>County record repositories</u>: CH, Fulton County Historical Society Library (PO Box 115, McConnellsburg 17233). <u>Society</u>: Fulton County Historical Society (PO Box 115, McConnellsburg 17233).

34. Greene County

Area first settled in 1750, formed in 1796 from Washington County, county seat Waynesburg (15370).

Microfilm <u>CH</u> records: court of quarter sessions (1797-1803), deed (1796-1941), estate (1850-69), mortgage (1796-1941), orphans court (1799-1949), road (1839-1969), vital records (1852-4), will (1796-1961). Other <u>microfilms</u> & <u>publications</u>: atlas (1876), biography (1888, 1912), cemetery, census (1800R, 1810R, 1820RI, 1830R, 1840RP, 1850RAIM, 1860RAIM, 1870RAIM, 1880RAIM, 1890C, 1900R, 1910R, 1920R), DAR, family history, genealogical collection, history (1882, 1888, 1969, 1975), Presbyterian, tax (1784-5, 1793), tax census (1800), will (1796-1900). <u>PPA</u>: land warrantees (1795-1894) 3(26) 627-41, War of 1812 6(7) 763-71. Other <u>materials</u>: genealogical periodical, landowner map (1865, 1897), manuscript, map, newspaper, warrantee maps.

<u>County record repositories</u>: CH, Greene County Historical Society Library (519 Fourth St., Waynesburg 15370). <u>Societies</u>: Cornerstone Genealogical Society (PO Box 547, Waynesburg 15370), Greene County Historical Society (R. D. 2, Waynesburg 15370).

35. Huntingdon County

Area first settled in 1750, formed in 1787 from Bedford County, county seat Huntingdon (16652).

Microfilm CH records: birth (1852-3, 1893-1905), death (1852-4), deed (1786-1972), delayed birth register, estate (1787- 1918), marriage (1852-4, 1885-1907), mortgage (1786-1891), orphans court (1788-1972), will (1787-1918). Other microfilms & publications: Amish, atlas (1873), Baptist, biography (1897, 1936), Catholic, cemetery, census (1790R, 1800R, 1810R, 1820RI, 1830R, 1840RP, 1850RAIM, 1860RAIM, 1870RAIM, 1880RAIM, 1890C, 1900R, 1910R, 1920R), DAR, directory, Episcopal, Evangelical Lutheran, family history, genealogical collection, history (1847, 1856, 1876, 1883, 1936), Lutheran, Mennonite, Methodist, Presbyterian, Quaker, Reformed, tax census (1800/21), undertaker, will (1787-1807). PPA: election returns (1787-9) 6(11) 199-201, land warrantees (1787-1889) 3(25) 677-781, militia (1790-1800) 6(5) 323-9, militia officer returns (1790-1817), militia (1783-90) 6(3) 439-51, state officers 2(3), tax (1788) 3(22) 327-66, War of 1812 6(7) 647-67. Other materials: genealogical periodical, landowner map (1856), manuscript, map, newspaper, warrantee maps.

County record repositories: CH, Huntingdon County Historical Society Library (106 Fourth St., Huntingdon 16652), Huntingdon County Library (330 Penn St., Huntingdon 16652), Juniata College Library (18th and Moore Sts., Huntingdon 16652). Society: Huntingdon County Historical Society (PO Box 305, Huntingdon 16652).

36. Indiana County

Area first settled in 1770, formed in 1803 from Westmoreland County, county seat Indiana (15701).

Microfilm CH records: birth (1852-6), deed (1803-1928), mortgage (1803-1969), orphans court (1803-1970), tax (1820-2, 1852-61), vital records (1852-4), will (1805-72). Other microfilms & publications: atlas (1871), biography (1891, 1978), cemetery, census (1810R, 1820RI, 1830R, 1840RP, 1850RAIM, 1860RAIM, 1870RAIM, 1880RAIM, 1890C, 1900R, 1910R, 1920R), DAR, directory, Episcopal, Evangelical Lutheran, family history, genealogical collection, history (1846, 1880, 1913, 1953, 1974, 1978-85), inhabitants (1807), LDS, Lutheran, Methodist, military, Presbyterian, Reformed, will (1803-1900). PPA: land warrantees (1805-94) 3(26) 663-77, War of 1812 6(7) 775-93. Other materials: genealogical periodical, landowner map (1856), manuscript, map, newspaper.

County record repositories: CH, Historical and Genealogical Society of Indiana County Library (200 South Sixth St., Indiana 15701). Society: Historical and Genealogical Society of Indiana County (address above).

37. Jefferson County

Area first settled in 1800, formed in 1804 from Lycoming County, county seat Brookville (15825).

Microfilm CH records: birth (1893-1906), death (1853-4, 1893-1906), deed (1810-1910), delayed birth register, marriage (1852-5, 1885-1950), naturalization (1809-56), orphans court (1832-1944), register of will dockets (1832-1906), will (1852-1906). Other microfilms & publications: atlas (1878), biography (1898, 1917), cemetery, census (1810R, 1820RI, 1830R, 1840RP, 1850RAIM, 1860RAIM, 1870RAIM, 1880RAIM, 1890C, 1900R, 1910R, 1920R), Episcopal, family history, genealogical collection, history (1888, 1898, 1917, 1982), Lutheran, Methodist, Presbyterian, Reformed, tax census (1800). PPA: none. Other materials: landowner map (1857), manuscript, map, newspaper.

County record repositories: CH, Historical and Genealogical Society of Jefferson County Library (PO Box 51, Brookville 15825). Societies: Historical and Genealogical Society of Jefferson County (address above), Troy Genealogical Associates (10 Cherry St., Brookville 15825), Punxsu tawney Area Historical & Genealogical Society (PO Box 286, Punxsutawney, 15767).

38. Juniata County

Area first settled in 1750, formed in 1831 from Mifflin County, county seat Mifflintown (17059).

Microfilm CH records: birth (1893-1907), death (1852-72, 1893-1907), deed (1831-1967), delayed birth register, estate (1852-1937), marriage (1852-3, 1885-1911), orphans court (1831-81), recorders dockets (1831-1967), vital records (1852-4), will (1831-1973). Other microfilms & publications: atlas (two in 1877), Baptist, Bible, biography (1897), Catholic, cemetery, census (1840RP, 1850RAIM, 1860RAIM, 1870RAIM, 1880RAIM, 1890C, 1900R, 1910R, 1920R), DAR, Evangelical Lutheran, family history, genealogical collection, history (1847, 1856, 1886, 1889, 1913), heads of families (1790), Lutheran, newspaper excerpts, Presbyterian, Reformed, undertaker. PPA: land warrantees (1833-91) 3(24) 321-8. Other materi als: genealogical periodical, manuscript, map, newspaper.

County record repositories: CH, Juniata County Historical Society Li brary (498 Jefferson St., Mifflintown 17059). Society: Juniata County Historical Society (address above).

39. Lackawanna County

Area first settled in 1760, formed in 1870 from Luzerne County, county seat Scranton (18503).

Microfilm CH records: none. Other microfilms & publications: atlas (1894), biography (1897, 1906), cemetery, census (1880RAIM, 1890C, 1900R, 1910R, 1920R), Congregational, Episcopal, Evangelical Lutheran, family history, genealogical collection, Greek Catholic, history (1880, 1928), LDS, Lutheran, Methodist, newspaper excerpts, Presbyterian. PPA: land warrantees (1886-96) 3(24) 345. Other materials: genealogical periodical, landowner map (1865, 1897), manuscript, map, newspaper, warrantee maps.

County record repositories: CH, Lackawanna County Historical Society Library (232 Monroe St., Scranton 18510), Scranton Public Library (500 Vine St., Scranton 18503), Carbondale Public Library (24 Sixth Ave., Carbondale 18407). Society: Lackawanna County Historical Society (address above).

40. Lancaster County

Area first settled in 1700, formed in 1729 from Chester County, county seat Lancaster (17602).

Microfilm CH records: birth (1852-4, 1875-1907), commissioners (1729-1944), court (1735-1810), death (1852-5, 1865-1950), deed (1729-1894), delayed birth register, marriage (1852-5, 1885-1936), mortgage (1729-1940), orphans court (1742-1891), register of wills books (1742-1867), tax (1729-1855), warrant (1713-42), will (1729-1947). Other microfilms & publications: atlas (1864, 1875, 1899), Bible, biography (1872, 1889, 1894, 1903, 1974), Brethren, Catholic, cemetery, census (1790R, 1800R, 1810R, 1820RI, 1830R, 1840RP, 1850RAIM, 1860RAIM, 1870RAIM, 1880RAIM, 1890C, 1900R, 1910R, 1920R), DAR, deed (1729-70), directory, Dunkard, Episcopal, estate (1729-1850), Evangelical, Evangelical Lutheran, family history, genealogical collection, history (1844, 1869, 1883, 1892, 1894, 1924), Jewish, Lutheran, Mennonite, military, Moravian, newspaper excerpts, oaths of allegiance (1729-70), orphans court (1742-58), Presbyterian, Quaker, Reformed, tax census (1779/86/93, 1800), will (1729-1850). PPA: militia (1774-83) 2(13) 269-552 and 3(23) 423-43 and 5(7) 3-1150, baptism & marriage (1752-86) 6(6) 149-282, commissioners & treasurer (1782-92) 3(7) 387-447, election returns (1756-88) 6(11) 211-27, land warrantees (1733-1896) 3(24) 349-568, lieutenants accounts (1777-85) 3(6) 325-650, marriages prior to 1810 2(9), militia (1790-1800) 6(5) 333-88, militia officer returns

(1790-1817) 6(4), militia (1783-90) 6(3) 455-634, provincial officers (1729-76) 2(9) 769-79, proprietary rights 3(3), state officers 2(3), tax (1771-82) 3(17) iii-viii and 3-898, War of 1812 6(7) 261-307. Other materials: genealogical periodical, landowner map (1819, 1921, 1824, 1842, 1851, 1858), manuscript, map, newspaper, warrantee maps.

County record repositories: CH (Archives Division), Lancaster County Historical Society Library (905 N. Duke St., Lancaster 17602), Mennonite Historical Society Library (2215 Millstream Rd., Lancaster 17602), Reformed Church Seminary, Fackenthall Library (Franklin & Marshall College, James and College Ave., Lancaster 17602). Societies: Lancaster County Historical Society (address above), Mennonite Historical Society (address above), Historical Society of the Cocalico Valley (249 Main St., Ephrata 17522).

41. Lawrence County

Area first settled in 1790, formed in 1849 from Beaver and Mercer Counties, county seat New Castle (16101).

Microfilm CH records: coroner (1852-1910), vital records (1852-4). Other microfilms & publications: atlas (1872), biography (1897), cemetery, census (1850RAIM, 1860RAIM, 1870RAIM, 1880RAIM, 1890C, 1900R, 1910R, 1920R), family history, history (1877, 1908, 1968), LDS, Lutheran, Presbyterian. PPA: land warrantees (1850-83) 3(24) 331. Other materials: landowner map (1860), manuscript, map, newspaper.

County record repositories: CH, Lawrence County Historical Society Library (in New Castle Public Library, 207 East North St., New Castle 16101). Society: Lawrence County Historical Society (address above).

42. Lebanon County

Area first settled in 1700, formed in 1813 from Dauphin and Lancaster Counties, county seat Lebanon (17042).

Microfilm CH records: birth (1852-5, 1893-1906), commissioners (1840-1906), death (1893-1906), deed (1813-1932), delayed birth register, marriage (1852-5, 1885-1949), orphans court (1813-55), tax (1842-6, 1849), will (1813-1935). Other microfilms & publications: atlas (1875), Bible, biography (1904), Brethren, Catholic, cemetery, census (1820RI, 1830R, 1840RP, 1850RAIM, 1860RAIM, 1870RAIM, 1880RAIM, 1890C, 1900R, 1910R, 1920R), directory, Episcopal, Evangelical, Evangelical Lutheran, family history, genealogical collection, history (1844, 1883), Lutheran, military, Moravian, newspaper excerpts, Presbyterian, Quaker, Reformed. PPA: land warrantees (1813-89) 3(24) 619-23. Other materials:

genealogical periodical, landowner map (1819, 1860), manuscript, map, newspaper.

County record repositories: CH, Lebanon County Historical Society Library (924 Cumberland St., Lebanon 17042), Lebanon Community Library (125 N. Seventh St., Lebanon 17042). Society: Lebanon County Historical Society (address above).

43. Lehigh County

Area first settled in 1720, formed in 1812 from Northampton County, county seat Allentown (18105).

Microfilm CH records: vital records (1852-4), warrant and survey (1743-1830), will (1812-50). Other microfilms & publications: atlas (1876, 1888), biography (1894, 1905), Brethren, cemetery, census (1820RI, 1830R, 1840RP, 1850RAIM, 1860RAIM, 1870RAIM, 1880RAIM, 1890C, 1900R, 1910R, 1920R), directory, Episcopal, estate (1812-50), Evangelical, Evangelical Lutheran, family history, genealogical collection, history (1845, 1860, 1884, 1905, 1914), Lutheran, Mennonite, Methodist, Moravian, newspaper excerpts, Presbyterian, Reformed, will (1812-50). PPA: Reformed baptisms (1734-1834) 6(6) 3-146, land warrantees (1814-92) 3(26) 215-23, marriages before 1810 2(9). Other materials: genealogical periodical, landowner map (1816, 1862, 1865), manuscript, map, newspaper.

County record repositories: CH, Lehigh County Historical Society Library (Old Court House, Fifth & Hamilton Sts., Allentown 18105), Allentown Public Library (1210 Hamilton St., Allentown 18102). Society: Lehigh County Historical Society (address above).

44. Luzerne County

Area first settled in 1760, formed in 1786 from Northumberland County, county seat Wilkes-Barre (18702).

Microfilm CH records: birth (1895), death (1893-1905), deed (1787-1907), marriage (1885-1906), mortgage (1788-1924), orphans court (1787-1909), register of wills (1788-1875), vital records (1852-4), will (1786-1918). Other microfilms & publications: atlas (1873, 1894), biography (1890, 1910), cemetery, census (1790R, 1800R, 1810R, 1820RI, 1830R, 1840RP, 1850RAIM, 1860RAIM, 1870RAIM, 1880RAIM, 1890C, 1900R, 1910R, 1920R), directory, Episcopal, Evangelical, Evangelical Lutheran, family history, genealogical collection, history (1830, 1845, 1858, 1866, 1880, 1892, 1893), LDS, Lutheran, Methodist, newspaper excerpts, Presbyterian, Quaker, Reformed, Russian Orthodox, tax census (1800). PPA: commissioners of land titles (1810) 2(18) 573-609, election returns

(1787-9) 6(11) 231-3, land warrantees (1787-1896) 3(24) 181-297, militia (1790-1800) 6(5) 391-6, militia officer returns (1790-1817) 6(4), militia (1783-90) 6(3) 637-8, state officers 2(3), War of 1812 6(7) 569-641. Other materials: genealogical periodical, landowner map (1864), manuscript, map, newspaper, warrantee maps.

County record repositories: CH, Wyoming Historical and Geological Society Library (49 South Franklin St., Wilkes-Barre 18701), Osterhout Free Library (71 South Franklin St., Wilkes-Barre 18701). Society: Wyoming Historical and Geological Society (address above).

---

45. Lycoming County

Area first settled in 1760, formed in 1795 from Northumberland County, county seat Williamsport (17701).

Microfilm CH records: vital records (1852-4). Other microfilms & publications: atlas (1873, 1888), Baptist, biography (1906), births in Williamsport (1869-1917), Brethren, Catholic, cemetery, census (1800R, 1810R, 1820RI, 1830R, 1840RP, 1850RAIM, 1860RAIM, 1870RAIM, 1880RAIM, 1890C, 1900R, 1910R, 1920R), DAR, directory, Episcopal, Evangelical, Evangelical Lutheran, genealogical collection, history (1876, 1892, 1895, 1929), Lutheran, Methodist, newspaper excerpts, Presbyterian, probate (1795-1850), Quaker, tax census (1800), will (1795-1845). PPA: commissioners of land titles (1810) 2(18) 573-609, land warrantees (1795-1896) 3(25) 377-407. Other materials: genealogical periodical, landowner map (1861), manuscript, map, newspaper.

County record repositories: CH, Lycoming County Historical Society Library (858 West Fourth St., Williamsport 17701), Muncy Historical Society Library (44 North Main St., Muncy 17756), Brown Library of Williamsport and Lycoming County (19 East Fourth St., Williamsport 17701). Societies: Lycoming County Historical Society (address above), Muncy Historical Society (address above), Lycoming County Genealogical Society (Rt. 1, Box 347, Jersey Shore 17740), Montgomery Area Genealogical Society (Montgomery Public Library, 1 S. Main St., Montgomery 17756).

---

46. McKean County

Area first settled in 1800, formed in 1804 from Lycoming County, county seat Smethport (16749).

Microfilm CH records: birth (1893-1906), death (1893-1906), deed (1806-1967), marriage (1885-1908), medical & health (1880-1920), mortgage (1811-1972), orphans court (1827-1908), probate (1826-64), Quaker, register of wills

(1826-1960), veterans burial (1778-1973), vital records (1852-4), will (1826-48). Other microfilms & publications: biography (1913), birth (1852), cemetery, census (1810R, 1820RI, 1830R, 1840RP, 1850RAIM, 1860RAIM, 1870RAIM, 1880RAIM, 1890C, 1900R, 1910R, 1920R), death (1852), Evangelical, family history, history (1877, 1890, 1925), Lutheran, marriage (1852), military (1861-5), Quaker, will (1827-52). PPA: land warrantees (1818-92) 3(25) 421-2. Other materials: genealogical periodical, landowner map (1856-7, 1878-9), manuscript, map, newspaper, warrantee maps.

County record repositories: CH, McKean County Historical Society Library (Courthouse, Smethport 16749), Hamlin Memorial Library (123 S. Mechanic St., Smethport 16749). Societies: McKean County Historical Society (address above), McKean County Genealogical Society (PO Box 207A, Derrick City 16727).

47. Mercer County

Area first settled in 1790, formed in 1800 from Allegheny County, operated out of Crawford County 1800-3, fully organized in 1803, county seat Mercer (16137).

Microfilm CH records: birth (1893-1905), death (1893-1905), deed (1803-1971), delayed birth register, estate (1800-1971), marriage (1885-1908), mortgage (1804-1971), orphans court (1804-67), register of wills dockets (1805-1907), tax (1804-13), vital records (1852-4), will (1800-1971). Other microfilms & publications: atlas (1873), Bible, biography (1888), cemetery, census (1800R, 1810R, 1820RI, 1830R, 1840RP, 1850RAIM, 1860RAIM, 1870RAIM, 1880RAIM, 1890C, 1900R, 1910R, 1920R), directory, Disciples, Evangelical Lutheran, family history, history (1877, 1880, 1888, 1909), Lutheran, Methodist, newspaper excerpts, Presbyterian, Reformed, will (1820-32). PPA: none. Other materials: genealogical periodical, landowner map (1860), manuscript, map, newspaper, warrantee maps.

County record repositories: CH, Mercer County Historical Society Library (119 South Pitt St., Mercer 16137), Mercer Public Library (143 North Pitt St., Mercer 16137). Societies: Mercer County Genealogical Society (PO Box 812, Sharon 16146), Mercer County Historical Society (address above).

48. Mifflin County

Area first settled in 1760, formed in 1789 from Cumberland and Northumberland Counties, county seat Lewistown (17044).

Microfilm CH records: birth (1893-1906), tax (1823-7), vital records (1852-4), will

(1789-1903). Other microfilms & publications: Amish, atlas (1877), biography (1897, 1942), Brethren, cemetery, census (1790R, 1800R, 1810R, 1820RI, 1830R, 1840RP, 1850RAIM, 1860RAIM, 1870RAIM, 1880RAIM, 1890C, 1900R, 1910R, 1920R), Episcopal, family history, genealogical collection, history (1847, 1879, 1886, 1939), Mennonite, Methodist, naturalization (1803-1906), newspaper excerpts, Presbyterian, tax census (1800/21), will (1789-1860). PPA: militia (1790-1800) 6(5) 399-405, militia officer returns (1790-1817) 6(4), state officers 2(3), War of 1812 6(7) 647-67. Other materials: genealogical periodical, landowner map (1820, 1863), manuscript, map, newspaper.

County record repositories: CH, Mifflin County Historical Society Library (17 North Main St., Lewistown 17044), Mifflin County Library (123 North Wayne St., Lewistown 17044). Society: Mifflin County Historical Society (address above).

49. Monroe County

Area first settled in 1720, formed in 1836 from Northampton and Pike Counties, county seat Stroudsburg (18360).

Microfilm CH records: commissioners (1840-1960), vital records (1852-4). Other microfilms & publications: atlas (1875), Baptist, biography (1898, 1900), cemetery, census (1840RP, 1850RAIM, 1860RAIM, 1870RAIM, 1880RAIM, 1890C, 1900R, 1910R, 1920R), DAR, Dutch Reformed, Evangelical Lutheran, family history, genealogical collection, history (1845, 1870, 1866, 1927), Lutheran, Methodist, newspaper excerpts, Presbyterian, Quaker, Reformed. PPA: none. Other materials: landowner map (1860), manuscript, map, newspaper.

County record repositories: CH, Monroe County Historical Society Library (537 Ann St., Stroudsburg 18360), Monroe County Public Library (913 Main St., Stroudsburg 18360). Society: Monroe County Historical Society (PO Box 488, Stroudsburg 18630).

50. Montgomery County

Area first settled in 1680, formed in 1784 from Philadelphia County, county seat Norristown (19404).

Microfilm CH records: birth (1852-5, 1893-1908), commissioners (1790-1890), death (1852-5, 1894-5), deed (1784-1877), delayed birth register, estate (1794-1941), marriage (1852-5, 1885-1973), mortgage (1784-1946), orphans court (1784-1866), poor records (1808-41), probate (1784-1973), tax (1785-1846), will (1784-1942). Other microfilms & publications: atlas (1871, 1877, 1893), Baptist, biography (1879, 1895, 1904), Brethren, business, cemetery, census (1790R, 1800R, 1810R, 1820RI, 1830R, 1840RP, 1850RAIM, 1860RAIM, 1870RAIM, 1880RAIM, 190C, 1900R, 1910R, 1920R), directory, Dunkard, Episcopal, Evangelical, Evangelical Lutheran, family history, genealogical collection, history (1859, 1884, 1923, 1931, 1951), Lutheran, Mennonite, Methodist, military, newspaper excerpts, Presbyterian, Quaker, Reformed, tax census (1786/93, 1800/7), will (1784-1850). PPA: election returns (1780-9) 6(11) 237-42, marriages before 1810 2(8-9), militia (1790-1800) 6(5) 409-17, militia officer returns (1790-1817) 6(4), militia (1783-90) 6(3) 641-743, state officers 2(3), War of 1812 6(7) 105-214. Other materials: genealogical periodical, landowner map (1849, 1893), manuscript, map, newspaper.

County record repositories: CH, Montgomery County Historical Society Library (1654 DeKalb St., Norristown 19401), Hicksite Quaker Library (Haverford College, Haverford 19401), Montgomery County-Norristown Public Library (1001 Powell St., Norristown 19401). Society: Montgomery County Historical Society (address above).

51. Montour County

Area first settled in 1770, formed in 1850 from Columbia County, county seat Danville (17821).

Microfilm CH records: birth (1892-1905), court of common pleas (1850-1907), death (1893-1905), deed (1850-1958), delayed birth register, estate (1850-1912), marriage (1852-4, 1885-1909), naturalization (1850-1907), orphans court (1851-65), vital records (1852-4), will (1850-1912). Other microfilms & publications: atlas (1876), biography (1899, 1915), cemetery, census (1850RAIM, 1860RAIM, 1870RAIM, 1880RAIM, 1890C, 1900R, 1910R, 1920R), Evangelical, Evangelical Lutheran, family history, history (1874, 1887, 1915), Lutheran, Methodist, Moravian, Presbyterian, Reformed. PPA: land warrantees (1850-77) 3(26) 685. Other materials: landowner map (1860), manuscript, map, newspaper.

County record repositories: CH, Montour County Historical Society Library (1 Bloom St., Danville 17821), Beaver Free Library (25 East Market St., Danville 17821). Society: Montour County Historical Society (address above).

52. Northampton County

Area first settled in 1720, formed in 1752 from Bucks County, county seat Easton (18042).

Microfilm CH records: birth (1893-1908), births in Easton (1888-1907), births in South Easton (1893-8), Brethren, burials in Easton

(1888-1905), burials in South Easton (1893-5), commissioners (1755-83), death (1893-1913), deaths in Easton (1888-1907), deaths in South Easton (1893-8), deed (1752-1926), delayed birth register, marriage (1852-4, 1885-1907), mortgage (1752-1922), orphans court (1752-1882), survey & warrant (1734-1879), tax (1761-93, 1808-15), vital records (1852-49), will (1752-1966). Other microfilms & publications: atlas (1874), Bible, biography (1894, 1920), Brethren, cemetery, census (1790R, 1800R, 1810R, 1820RI, 1830R, 1840RP, 1850RAIM, 1860RAIM, 1870RAIM, 1880RAIM, 1890C, 1900R, 1910R, 1920R), DAR, directory, Evangelical Lutheran, family history, history (1845, 1877, 1879, 1920, 1926, 1953), Lutheran, Methodist, military, Moravian, newspaper excerpts, Presbyterian, Reformed, tax (1772-87), tax census (1786-1800), will (1752-1850). PPA: militia (1774-86) 2(14) 547-633 and 3(23) 455-6 and 5(8) 3-626, election returns (1756-89) 6(11) 245-74, land warrantees (1752-1886) 3(26) 27-211, lieutenants accounts (1777-83) 3(6) 721-78, marriages before 1810 2(9), militia (1790-1800), 6(5) 421-32, militia officer returns (1790-1817) 6(3) 747-901, provincial officers (1729-76) 2(9) 792-6, proprietary rights 3(3), state officers 2(3), tax lists (1772, 1785-6) 3(19) 5-400, War of 1812 6(7) 543-66. Other materials: genealogical periodical, landowner map (1815, 1860), manuscript, map, newspaper.

County record repositories: CH, Northampton County Historical Society Library (107 South Fourth St., Easton 18042), Easton Area Public Library (6th and Church Sts., Easton 18042), Moravian Archives Library (41 West Locust St., Bethlehem 18018), Bethlehem Public Library (11 West Church St., Bethlehem 18018). Society: Northampton County Historical and Genealogical Society (address above).

53. Northumberland County

Area first settled in 1760, formed in 1772 from Lancaster, Berks, Cumberland, Northampton, and Bedford Counties, county seat Sunbury (17801).

Microfilm CH records: birth (1852-5, 1893-1905), commissioners (1786-1879), death (1852-5, 1893-1905), deed (1772-1914), delayed birth register, estate(1792-1907), marriage (1852-5), mortgage (1772-1974), naturalization (1802-1906), orphans court (1772-1930), will (1772-1930). Other microfilms & publications: Baptist, biography (1889, 1899, 1911), cemetery, census (1790R, 1800R, 1810R, 1820RI, 1830R, 1840RP, 1850RAIM, 1860RAIM, 1870RAIM, 1880RAIM, 1890C, 1900R, 1910R, 1920R), directory, Evangelical Lutheran, family history, genealogical collection, history (1847, 1876, 1877, 1891), land (1784-5), Lutheran, Methodist, military, newspaper excerpts, Presbyterian, Quaker, Reformed, tax census (1800), will and probate (1772-1849). <u>PPA</u>: militia (1776-89) 2(14) 313-67, election returns (1776-89) 6(11) 277-312, land warrantees (1772-1892) 3(25) 55-358, lieutenants accounts (1777-84) 3(7) 1-19, lottery warrants (1785) 3(25) 361-74, militia (1790-1800) 6(5) 435-41, militia officer returns (1790-1817) 6(4), militia (1783-90) 6(3) 905-39, provincial officers (1729-76) 2(9) 798-9, proprietary rights 3(3), state officers (1776) 2(3), tax lists (1778-87) 3(19) 405-805, War of 1812 6(7) 569-641. <u>Other materials</u>: genealogical periodical, landowner map (1858, 1874), manuscript, map, newspaper.

    <u>County record repositories</u>: CH, Historical Society of Northumberland County Library (1150 North Front St., Sunbury 17801), Kaufman Public Library (228 Arch St., Sunbury 17801). <u>Society</u>: Historical Society of Northumberland County (address above).

---

54. Perry County

Area first settled in 1750, formed in 1820 from Cumberland County, county seat New Bloomfield (17068).

    <u>Microfilm CH records</u>: birth (1852-5, 1893-1919), death (1852-5, 1893-1919), deed (1820-1950), delayed birth register, marriage (1852-5, 1885-1950), orphans court (1820-1950), tax (1820-49), will (1820-1911). <u>Other microfilms & publications</u>: atlas (1877), biography (1897), Brethren, cemetery, census (1820RI, 1830R, 1840RP, 1850RAIM, 1860RAIM, 1870RAIM, 1880RAIM, 1890C, 1900R, 1910R, 1920R), Evangelical Lutheran, family history, history (1846, 1873, 1886, 1922), Lutheran, Methodist, military, Presbyterian, Reformed. <u>PPA</u>: land warrantees (1812-92) 3(25) 425-40. <u>Other materials</u>: genealogical periodical, landowner map (1863), manuscript, map, newspaper.

    <u>County record repositories</u>: CH, Historical Society of Perry County Library (129 North Second St., Newport 17074), Perry Historians Library (Rt. 34, PO Box 73, Newport 17074). <u>Society</u>: Historical Society of Perry County (PO Box 81, Newport 17074), Perry Historians Genealogical Society (PO Box 73, Newport 17074).

---

55. Philadelphia County

Area first settled in 1650, formed in 1682 as one of the three original counties, county seat Philadelphia (19107). Do not fail to consult J. Daly, DESCRIPTIVE INVENTORY OF THE ARCHIVES OF THE CITY AND COUNTY OF PHILADELPHIA, City of Philadelphia, Philadelphia, PA, 1970.

Microfilm CH records: briefs of title (1682-1900), burial (1807-40), city census (1793, 1850, 1863), coroner (1854-7, 1877-80, 1885-6, 1906), county prison (1790-1916), court of common pleas (1736-1905), court of quarter sessions (1713-1914), death (1803-60), deed (1683-1851), estate (1682-1900), immigrants (1727-1808), indentures (1751-1888), lunacy (1781-1824), marriage (1784-6, 1814-55 incomplete, and 1885-1968), mayors court (1789-1822), naturalization (1800-1906), orphans court (1716-1852), passenger lists (1800-1921), poor records (1751-1904), road (1685-1870), tax (1693, 1754, 1756, 1765, 1767, 1772, 1779-1842, 1844), will (1682-1901). Other microfilms & publications: atlas, Baptist, biography (1859, 1864, 1911, 1933), Catholic, cemetery, census (1790R, 1800R, 1810R, 1820RI, 1830R, 1840RP, 1850RAIM, 1860RAIM, 1870RAIM, 1880RAIM, 1890C, 1900R, 1910R, 1920R), Congregational, directory (1785-1901), Episcopal, Evangelical Lutheran, family history, genealogical collection, history (1839, 1884, 1887, 1895-8, 1912), immigrants (1641-1819), LDS, Lutheran, Methodist, military, Moravian, naturalization (1789-1880), newspaper excerpts, passenger lists (1800-1921), port records (1783-1880), Presbyterian, Quaker, Quaker arrivals (1682-1750), Reformed, tax census (1793, 1800, 1863), warrants and surveys (up to 1759), will (1682-1850). PPA: militia (1775-83) 2(13) 553-794 and 2(14) 1-61 and 3(23) 401-2 and 6(1) 3-987, confiscated estates (1780) 6(13) 312, election returns (1756-89) 6(11) 315-89, land warrantees (1733-1866) 3(24) 3-58, lieutenants accounts (1777-80) 3(5) 375-763, militia (1790-1800) 6(5) 445-560, militia officer returns (1790-1817) 6(4), militia (1783-90) 6(3) 945-1360, provincial officers (1682-1776) 2(9) 697-741, old & proprietary rights 3(2-3), tax (1769-83), War of 1812 6(7) 15-102. Other materials: genealogical periodical, landowner map (1819, 1843), manuscript, map, newspaper.

County record repositories: CH and the associated City and County Archives, LHS, Free Library of Philadelphia (Logan Square, 19th & Fine Sts., Philadelphia 19103), Van Pelt Library (University of PA, 3420 Walnut St., Philadelphia 19104). Society: PA Genealogical Society (1301 Locust St., Philadelphia 19107), Historical Society of PA (1300 Locust St., Philadelphia 19107).

56. Pike County

Area first settled in 1680, formed in 1814 from Wayne County, county seat Milford (18337).

Microfilm CH records: birth (1892-1906), death (1892-1906), deed (1814-66), marriage (1885-1906), tax (1776, 1790, 1798, 1803-4). Other microfilms & publications: biography (1898, 1900), cemetery, census (1820RI, 1830R, 1840RP, 1850RAIM, 1860RAIM, 1870RAIM,

1880RAIM, 1890C, 1900R, 1910R, 1920R), Evangelical Lutheran, family history, genealogical collection, history (1880, 1886, 1900), Methodist. PPA: land warrantees (1815-83) 3(26) 233-8. Other materials: landowner map (1814, 1856, 1872), manuscript, map, newspaper, warrantee maps.

County record repositories: CH, Pike County Public Library (217 Broad St., Milford 18337). Society: Pike County Historical Society (PO Box 915, Milford 18337).

57. Potter County — Area first settled in 1800, formed in 1804 from Lycoming County, county seat Coudersport (16915).

Microfilm CH records: birth (1892-1906), death (1892-1906), deed (1806-1972), delayed birth register, marriage (1885-1906), mortgage (1804-1931), orphans court (1836-85), register of wills dockets (1836-1972). Other microfilms & publications: Baptist, biography (1890),cemetery, church, census (1810R, 1820RI, 1830R, 1840RP, 1850RAIM, 1860RAIM, 1870RAIM, 1880RAIM, 1890C, 1900R, 1910R, 1920R), DAR, directory, family history, genealogical collection, history (1875, 1890, 1905, 1925, 1934, 1962), Methodist. PPA: none. Other materials: landowner map (1856, 1893), manuscript, map, newspaper, warrantee maps.

County record repositories: CH, Potter County Historical Society Library (308 North Main St., Coudersport 16915), Coudersport Public Library (502 Park Ave., Coudersport 16915). Society: Potter County Historical Society (address above).

58. Schuylkill County — Area first settled in 1740, formed in 1811 from Berks and Northampton Counties, county seat Pottsville (17901).

Microfilm CH records: birth (1893-1905), death (1893-1905), deaths in Pottsville (1897-1907), vital records (1852-4). Other microfilms & publications: atlas (1875), biography (1893, 1906), cemetery, census (1820RI, 1830R, 1840RP, 1850RAIM, 1860RAIM, 1870RAIM, 1880RAIM, 1890C, 1900R, 1910R, 1920R), church, DAR, directory, Evangelical, Evangelical Lutheran, family history, genealogical collection, history (1845, 1881, 1907, 1911, 1916, 1950), LDS, Lutheran, Presbyterian, Reformed, school, will (1812-44). PPA: land warrantees (1811-90) 3(26) 339-80. Other materials: genealogical periodical, landowner map (1817, 1830, 1855, 1863-4), manuscript, map, newspaper, warrantee maps.

County record repositories: CH, Schuylkill County Historical Society Library (16 North Third St., Pottsville 17901), Pottsville Free Public

Library (16 North Third St., Pottsville 17901). <u>Society</u>: Schuylkill County Historical Society (address above).

59. Snyder County

Area first settled in 1750, formed in 1855 from Union County, county seat Middleburg (17842).

<u>Microfilm CH records</u>: none. <u>Microfilms & publications</u>: atlas (1868), biography (1898, 1938), cemetery, census (1860RAIM, 1870RAIM, 1880RAIM, 1890C, 1900R, 1910R, 1920R), church, Congregational, family history, genealogical collection, history (1855, 1886, 1919, 1948), Lutheran, marriage (1855-99), Presbyterian, tax (1855-85). <u>PPA</u>: land warrantees (1855-92) 3(26) 697-8. <u>Other materials</u>: manuscript, map, newspaper.

<u>County record repositories</u>: CH, Snyder County Historical Society Library (30 East Market St., Middleburg 17842). <u>Society</u>: Snyder County Historical Society (PO Box 276, Middleburg 17842).

60. Somerset County

Area first settled in 1760, formed in 1795 from Bedford County, county seat Somerset (15501).

<u>Microfilm CH records</u>: auditors dockets (1839-1907), birth (1852-4, 1893-1908), coroner (1853-1922), court of oyer and terminer (1855-99), court of quarter sessions (1795-1920), deed (1795-1921), delayed birth register, estate (1795-1921), marriage (1885-1968), medical (1881-1934), military (1862-1968), mortgage (1795-1964), sheriff (1803-1922), survey (1795-1899), tax (1795-1879), vital records (1852-4), will (1795-1922). <u>Other microfilms & publications</u>: atlas (1876), Bible, biography (1899, 1980), Brethren, cemetery, census (1800R, 1810R, 1820RI, 1830R, 1840RP, 1850RAIM, 1860RAIM, 1870RAIM, 1880RAIM, 1890C, 1900R, 1910R, 1920R), church, Evangelical, Evangelical Lutheran, family history, genealogical collection, history (1884, 1906, 1932, 1945), Lutheran, naturalization (1802-52), Reformed, tax census (1800), will (1795-1900). <u>PPA</u>: militia officer returns (1790-1817) 6(4), War of 1812 6(7) 671-706. <u>Other materials</u>: genealogical periodical, landowner map (1818, 1830, 1855, 1860), manuscript, map, newspaper.

<u>County record repositories</u>: CH, Somerset County Historical and Genealogical Society (PO Box 533, Somerset 15501), Somerset County Library (230 South Rosina Ave., Somerset 15501). <u>Society</u>: Somerset County Historical and Genealogical Society (address above), Somerset Historical Society (Rt. 2, Box 238, Somerset 15501).

61. Sullivan County

Area first settled in 1790, formed in 1847 from Lycoming County, county seat Laporte (18626).

Microfilm CH records: birth (1893-1905), death (1893-1905), deed (1847-76), delayed birth register, marriage (1852-5, 1885-1913), naturalization (1848-1906), orphans court (1848-1931), will (1847-1931). Other microfilms & publications: biography, cemetery, census (1850RAIM, 1860RAIM, 1870RAIM, 1880RAIM, 1890C, 1900R, 1910R, 1920R), church, family history, genealogical collection, history (1899, 1903, 1921). PPA: land warrantees (1854-71) 3(26) 693. Other materials: landowner map (1872), manuscript, map, newspaper, warrantee maps.

County record repositories: CH, Sullivan County Historical Society Library (Court House Square, Laporte 18626), Sullivan County Library (311 Main St., Dushore 18614). Society: Sullivan County Historical Society (Meylert St., LaPorte 18626).

62. Susquehanna County

Area first settled in 1780, formed in 1810 from Luzerne County, county seat Montrose (18801).

Microfilm CH records: vital records (1852-4). Other microfilm & publications: atlas (1872), biography (1900), cemetery, census (1820RI, 1830R, 1840RP, 1850RAIM, 1860RAIM, 1870RAIM, 1880RAIM, 1890C, 1900R, 1910R, 1920R), church, directory, family history, genealogical collection, history (1873, 1887), Methodist, Presbyterian. PPA: land warrantees (1814-85) 3(24) 301-3. Other materials: genealogical periodical, landowner map (1858), manuscript, map, newspaper, warrantee maps.

County record repositories: CH, Susquehanna County Historical Society and Free Library (Monument Square, Montrose 18801). Society: Susquehanna County Historical Society (address above), Susquehanna Depot Historical Society (PO Box 161, Susquehanna 18847).

63. Tioga County

Area first settled in 1790, formed in 1804 from Luzerne County, county seat Wellsboro (16901).

Microfilm CH records: vital records (1852-4). Other microfilms & publications: atlas (1875), cemetery, census (1810R, 1820RI, 1830R, 1840RP, 1850RAIM, 1860RAIM, 1870RAIM, 1880RAIM, 1890C, 1900R, 1910R, 1920R), church, DAR, deed, directory, family history, history (1883, 1885, 1897, 1908, 1916), land titles (1799-1830), Lutheran, mortgage (1806-12), orphans court (1812-61), Presbyterian, will (1812-61).

PPA: land warrantees (1807-78) 3(24) 315-8. Other materials: genealogical periodical, landowner map (1862), manuscript, map, newspaper, warrantee maps.

County record repositories: CH, Green Free Library (134 Main St., Wellsboro 16901). Society: Tioga County Historical Society (PO Box 724 Wellsboro 16901).

64. Union County

Area first settled in 1760, formed in 1813 from Northumberland County county seat Lewisburg (17837).

Microfilm CH records: commissioners (1813-31, 1843-94), license (1822-56), military (1886-1915), survey (1813-8), tavern (1814-87), tax (1814-82), vital records (1852-4). Other microfilms & publications: atlas (1868), Bible, biography (1898), cemetery, census (1820RI, 1830R, 1840RP, 1850RAIM, 1860RAIM, 1870RAIM, 1880RAIM, 1890C, 1900R, 1910R, 1920R), church, DAR, Evangelical Lutheran, family history, genealogical collection, history (1847, 1855, 1877, 1886, 1963), Lutheran, orphans court, Presbyterian, probate (1814-55), Reformed, will (1813- 38). PPA: none. Other materials: genealogical periodical, landowner map (1815, 1856), manuscript, map, newspaper.

County record repositories: CH, Union County Historical Society Library (2nd & St. Louis Sts., Lewisburg 17837), Himmelreich Memorial Library (18 Market St., Lewisburg 17837). Society: Union County Historical Society (103 S. Second St., Lewisburg 17837).

65. Venango County

Area first settled in 1790, formed in 1800 from Allegheny and Lycoming Counties, functioned under Crawford County 1800-5, fully organized in 1805, county seat Franklin (16323).

Microfilm CH records: birth (1893-1905), births in Oil City (1882-1909), death (1893-1906), deed (1800-1925), delayed birth register, marriage (1852, 1885-1906), marriages in Oil City (1882-97), mortgage (1800-1926), orphans court (1806-1970), vital records (1852-4), will (1800-1968). Other microfilms & publications: atlas (1865), biography (1911, 1919), census (1800R, 1810R, 1820RI, 1830R, 1840RP, 1850RAIM, 1860RAIM, 1870RAIM, 1880RAIM, 1890C, 1900R, 1910R, 1920R), church, directory, family history, genealogical collection, history (1879, 1890, 1919, 1983), Presbyterian, wills (book 1). PPA: War of 1812 6(7) 797-835. Other materials: genealogical periodical, landowner map (1815, 1857, 1865), manuscript, map, newspaper, warrantee maps.

County record repositories: CH, Venango County Historical Society Collection (Franklin Public Library, 421 Twelfth St., Franklin 16323), Drake Well Museum Library (RD #3, Box 7, Titusville 16354). Societies: Venango County Genealogical Society (PO Box 811, Oil City 16301), Venango County Historical Society (PO Box 101, Franklin 16323).

66. Warren County

Area first settled in 1790, formed in 1800 from Allegheny and Lycoming Counties, was attached for judicial purposes to Crawford County 1800-5, then to Venango County 1805-19, organized to operate separately in 1819, county seat Warren (16365).

Microfilm CH records: birth (1893- 1905), deed (1819-97), delayed birth register, marriage (1852-3, 1885- 1909), orphans court (1844-1947), register of wills dockets (1820-1971), vital records (1852-4). Other microfilms & publications: atlas (1865, 1878), biography (1899), cemetery, census (1800R, 1810R, 1820RI, 1830R, 1840RP, 1850RAIM, 1860RAIM, 1870RAIM, 1880RAIM, 1890C, 1900R, 1910R, 1920R), directory, family history, genealogical collection, history (1887, 1905, 1932), military, newspaper excerpts, Presbyterian, Quaker. PPA: War of 1812 6(7) 797-835. Other materials: genealogical periodical, landowner map (1815, 1838, 1865, 1881-2, 1889, 1900), manuscript, map, newspaper, warrantee maps.

County record repositories: CH, Warren Library Association (205 Market St., Warren 16365), Warren County Historical Society Library (Warren 16365). Society: Warren County Historical Society (PO Box 427, Warren 16365), Warren County Genealogical Society (51 Fourth St., Youngsville 16371).

67. Washington County

Area first settled in 1760, formed in 1781 from Westmoreland County, county seat Washington (15301).

Microfilm CH records: deed (1781-1924), mortgage (1781-1952), orphans court (1781-1952), slave (1782-1952), vital records (1852-4), will (1781-1939). Other microfilms & publications: atlas (1876), Baptist, biography (1882, 1893, 1902, 1950), cemetery, census (1790R, 1800R, 1810R, 1820RI, 1830R, 1840RP, 1850RAIM, 1860RAIM, 1870RAIM, 1880RAIM, 1890C, 1900R, 1910R, 1920R), church, Covenantor, DAR, deed (1782-5), directory, estate (1781-96), Evangelical Lutheran, family history, genealogical collection, history (1871, 1882, 1910, 1926), inhabitants (1776-1800), Lutheran, Methodist, Presbyterian, Quaker,

Reformed, tax (1784-5, 1793), tax census (1786, 1800), will (1781-1900), Yohogania County estate (1776-81), Yohogania County deed (1786-91). PPA: militia (1775-81) 2(14) 729-52 and 6(2) 3-258, election returns (1781-9) 6(11) 393-400, land warrantees (1784-1892) 3(26) 531-624, lieutenants accounts (1781-3) 3(7) 139-44, militia (1790-1800) 6(5) 563-643, militia officer returns (1790-1817) 6(4), militia (1783-90) 6(3) 1363-76, state officers 2(3), tax lists (1781) 3(22) 701-82, War of 1812 6(7) 763-71. Other materials: genealogical periodical, landowner map (1817, 1856, 1861), manuscript, map, newspaper, warrantee maps.

County record repositories: CH, Citizens Library (55 South College St., Washington 15301), Washington County Historical Society Library (49 East Maiden St., Washington 15301), Washington and Jefferson College Library (E. Wheeling & Lincoln Sts., Washington 15301), Southwest PA Genealogical Society Library (PO Box 894, Washington 15301). Society: Southwest PA Genealogical Society (address above).

68. Wayne County

Area first settled in 1750, formed in 1798 from Northampton County, county seat Honesdale (18431).

Microfilm CH records: birth (1893-1906), court of common pleas (1824-1912), death (1893-1906), deed (1798-1941), delayed birth register, marriage (1885-1906), mortgage (1798-1941), orphans court (1803-69), vital records (1852-4), will (1798-1925). Other microfilms & publications: atlas (1872), biography (1892), cemetery, census (1800R, 1810R, 1820RI, 1830R, 1840RP, 1850RAIM, 1860RAIM, 1870RAIM, 1880RAIM, 1890C, 1900R, 1910R, 1920R), church, directory, family history, history (1870, 1880, 1886, 1900, 1902), Lutheran, Presbyterian, tax census (1800). PPA: land warrantees (1803-90) 3(26) 227-9, militia officer returns (1790-1817) 6(4), War of 1812 6(7) 543-66. Other materials: landowner map (1814, 1860), manuscript, map, newspaper, warrantee maps.

County record repositories: CH, Wayne County Historical Society Library (810 Main St., Honesdale 18431), Wayne County Public Library (1406 North Main St., Honesdale 18431). Society: Wayne County Historical Society (PO Box 446, Honesdale 18431).

69. Westmoreland County

Area first settled in 1760, formed in 1773 from Bedford County, county seat Greensburg (15601).

Microfilm CH records: vital records (1852-4). Other microfilms & publications: atlas (1867, 1876), Baptist, biography (1882, 1890, 1898), birth

(1852-5), Catholic, cemetery, census (1790R, 1800R, 1810R, 1820RI, 1830R, 1840RP, 1850RAIM, 1860RAIM, 1870RAIM, 1880RAIM, 1890C, 1900R, 1910R, 1920R), church, DAR, death (1852-5), deed (1773-1825), directory, estate (1773-1830), Evangelical Lutheran, family history, genealogical collection, history (1882, 1906, 1918, 1941), Lutheran, marriage (1852-5), Methodist, naturalization (1802-52), newspaper excerpts, original landowners, Presbyterian, Reformed, survey (1769-1905), tax (1786-1827), tax census (1786, 1800), will (1773-1896). PPA: militia (1776-82) 2(14) 671-81 and 3(23) 457-8 and 6(2) 261-410, election returns (1776-89) 6(11) 403-11, land warrantees (1773-1892) 3(26) 389-528, lieutenants accounts (1777-84) 3(7) 117-36, militia (1790-1800) 6(5) 647-826, militia officer returns (1790-1817) 6(4), militia (1783-90) 6(3) 1379-1409, provincial officers (1729-76) 2(9) 799-800, proprietary rights 3(3), state officers 2(3), tax lists (1783/6) 3(22) 369-540, treasurers ac counts (1783-8) 3(7) 451-6, War of 1812 6(7) 709-59. Other materials: genealogical periodical, landowner map (1818, 1857), manuscript, map, newspaper.

County record repositories: CH, Greensburg Library (237 South Pennsylvania Ave., Greensburg 15601). Society: Historical Society of Westmoreland County (981 Old Salem Rd., Greensburg 15601).

70. Wyoming County

Area first settled in 1770, formed in 1842 from Luzerne County, county seat Tunkhannock (18657). Microfilm CH records: birth (1893-1906), death (1853-4, 1874-1906), deed (1842-1916), delayed birth register, marriage (1885-1906), naturalization (1843-1916), orphans court (1843-66), register of wills dockets (1842-1938), will (1843-1938). Other microfilms & publications: biography (1897), cemetery, census (1850RAIM, 1860RAIM, 1870RAIM, 1880RAIM, 1890C, 1900R, 1910R, 1920R), church, directory, family history, genealogical collection, history (1872, 1880), newspaper excerpts, Presbyterian, Quaker, tax census (1849). PPA: land warrantees (1847-95) 3(25) 443-6. Other materials: genealogical periodical, landowner map (1869), manuscript, map, newspaper.

County record repositories: CH, Tunkhannock Public Library (9 Marion St., Tunkhannock 18657), Wyoming Historical and Genealogical Society Library (49 South Franklin, Wilkes-Barre 18701). Society: Wyoming Historical and Genealogical Society (PO Box 309, Tunkhannock 18657).

71. York County

Area first settled in 1720, formed in 1749 from Lancaster County, county seat York (17401).

Microfilm CH records: apprentice (1860-1911), birth (1893-1907), commissioners (1749-1831), death (1877-1907), deed (1749-1940), marriage (1885-1901), mortgage (1885-1901), orphans court (1749-1887), records of poor (1845-1918), tax (1758-1849), vital records (1852-4), will (1749-1940). Other microfilms & publications: atlas (1876, 1903), Baptist, biography (1886, 1930, 1944), cemetery, census (1790R, 1800R, 1810R, 1820RI, 1830R, 1840RP, 1850RAIM, 1860RAIM, 1-870RAIM, 1880RAIM, 1890C, 1900R, 1910R, 1920R), church, Congregational, court of quarter sessions (1749-54), deed (1749-63), directory, Episcopal, Evangelical, Evangelical Lutheran, family history, genealogical collection, history (1834, 1845, 1886, 1888, 1907), inhabitants (1779), Lutheran, Methodist, military, newspaper excerpts, Presbyterian, Quaker, Reformed, tax census (1786/93, 1800/7), vital records (1852-5), will (1749-1940). PPA: militia (1774-80) 2(14) 473-546 and 6(2) 413-817, election returns (1756-89) 6(11) 415-63, lieutenants accounts (1777-86) 3(7) 39-114, militia (1790-1800) 6(5) 829-35, militia officer returns (1790-1817) 6(4), militia (1783-90) 6(3) 1413-83, provincial officers (1729-76) 2(9) 779-84, proprietary rights 3(3), state officers 2(3), tax lists (1779-83) 3(21) 3-820, War of 1812 6(7) 311-68. Other materials: genealogical periodical, landowner map (1815, 1821, 1860), manuscript, map, newspaper.

County record repositories: CH, York County Historical Society Library (250 East Market St., York 17403), Martin Memorial Library (159 East Market St., York 17401). Society: York County Historical Society (address above), South Central PA Genealogical Society (PO Box 1824, York 17405).

Books by George K. Schweitzer

CIVIL WAR GENEALOGY. A 93-paged book of 316 sources for tracing your Civil War ancestor. Chapters include I: The Civil War, II: The Archives, III: National Publications, IV: State Publications, V: Local Sources, VI: Military Unit Histories, VII: Civil War Events.

GEORGIA GENEALOGICAL RESEARCH. A 238-paged book containing 1303 sources for tracing your GA ancestor along with detailed instructions. Chapters include I: GA Background, II: Types of Records, III: Record Locations, IV: Research Procedure and County Listings (detailed listing of records available for each of the 159 GA counties).

HANDBOOK OF GENEALOGICAL SOURCES. A 252-paged book describing all major and many minor sources of genealogical information with precise and detailed instructions for obtaining data from them.

ILLINOIS GENEALOGICAL RESEARCH. A 197-paged book containing 1121 sources for tracing your IL ancestor along with detailed instructions. Chapters include I: IL Background, II: Types of Records, III: Record Locations, IV: Research Procedure and Chicago/Cook County Records (detailed listings of records available for Chicago and Cook County), V: Records for Other Counties (detailed listings of records available for each of the other IL counties.

INDIANA GENEALOGICAL RESEARCH. A 189-paged book containing 1044 sources for tracing your IN ancestor along with detailed instructions. Chapters include I: IN Background, II: Types of Records, III: Record Locations, IV: Research Procedure and County Listings (detailed listing of records available for each of the 92 IN counties).

KENTUCKY GENEALOGICAL RESEARCH. A 167-paged book containing 1191 sources for tracing your KY ancestor along with detailed instructions. Chapters include I: KY Background, II: Types of Records, III: Record Locations, IV: Research Procedure and County Listings (detailed listing of records available for each of the 120 KY counties).

MARYLAND GENEALOGICAL RESEARCH. A 208-paged book containing 1176 sources for tracing your MD ancestor along with detailed instructions. Chapters include I: MD Background, II: Types of Records, III: Record Locations, IV: Research Procedure and County Listings (detailed listing of records available for each of the 23 MD counties and for Baltimore City).

MASSACHUSETTS GENEALOGICAL RESEARCH. A 279-paged book containing 1709 sources for tracing your MA ancestor along with detailed instructions. Chapters include I: MA Background, II: Types of Records, III: Record Locations, IV: Research Procedure and County-Town-City Listings (detailed listing of records available for each of the 14 MA counties and the 351 cities-towns).

NEW YORK GENEALOGICAL RESEARCH. A 252-paged book containing 1426 sources for tracing your NY ancestor along with detailed instructions. Chapters include I: NY Background, II: Types of Records, III: Record Locations, IV: Research Procedure and NY City Record Listings (detailed listing of records available for the 5 counties of NY City), V: Record Listings for Other Counties (detailed listing of records available for each of the other 57 NY counties).

NORTH CAROLINA GENEALOGICAL RESEARCH. A 169-paged book containing 1233 sources for tracing your NC ancestor along with detailed instructions. Chapters include I: NC Background, II: Types of Records, III: Record Locations, IV: Research Procedure and County Listings (detailed listing of records available for each of the 100 NC counties).

OHIO GENEALOGICAL RESEARCH. A 212-paged book containing 1241 sources for tracing your OH ancestor along with detailed instructions. Chapters include I: OH Background, II: Types of Records, III: Record Locations, IV: Research Procedure and County Listings (detailed listing of records available for each of the 100 OH counties).

PENNSYLVANIA GENEALOGICAL RESEARCH. A 201-paged book containing 1309 sources for tracing your PA ancestor along with detailed instructions. Chapters include I: PA Background, II: Types of Records, III: Record Locations, IV: Research Procedure and County Listings (detailed listing of records available for each of the 67 PA counties).

REVOLUTIONARY WAR GENEALOGY. A 110-paged book containing 407 sources for tracing your Revolutionary War ancestor. Chapters include I: Revolutionary War History, II: The Archives, III: National Publications, IV: State Publications, V: Local Sources, VI: Military Unit Histories, VII: Sites and Museums.

SOUTH CAROLINA GENEALOGICAL RESEARCH. A 170-paged book containing 1107 sources for tracing your SC ancestor along with detailed instructions. Chapters include I: SC Background, II: Types of Records, III: Record Locations, IV: Research Procedure and County Listings (detailed listing of records available for each of the 47 SC counties and districts).

TENNESSEE GENEALOGIARCH. A 132-paged book containing 1073 sources for tracing your TN ancestor along with detailed instructions. Chapters include I: TN Background, II: Types of Records, III: Record Locations, IV: Research Procedure and County Listings (detailed listing of records available for each of the 96 TN counties).

VIRGINIA GENEALOGICAL RESEARCH. A 216-paged book containing 1273 sources for tracing your VA ancestor along with detailed instructions. Chapters include I: VA Background, II: Types of Records, III: Record Locations, IV: Research Procedure and County Listings (detailed listing of records available for each of the 100 VA counties and 41 major cities).

WAR OF 1812 GENEALOGY. A 75-paged book of 289 sources for tracing your War of 1812 ancestor. Chapters include I: History of the War, II: Service Records, III: Bounty Land and Pension Records, IV: National and State Publications, V: Local Sources, VI: Military Unit Histories, VII: Sites and Events.

All of the above books may be ordered from Dr. George K. Schweitzer at the address given on the title page. Or send a long SASE for a FREE descriptive leaflet on any or all of the books.